Chicken Soup
for the Soul.

D0032976

Mom
Knows Best

Mar 19

Chicken Soup for the Soul: Mom Knows Best
101 Stories of Love, Gratitude & Wisdom
Amy Newmark

Published by Chicken Soup for the Soul, LLC www.chickensoup.com
Copyright ©2019 by Chicken Soup for the Soul, LLC. All Rights Reserved.

The publisher gratefully acknowledges the many publishers and individuals who granted Chicken Soup for the Soul permission to reprint the cited material.

Front cover photo of family courtesy of iStockphoto.com/Neustockimages (©Neustockimages)
Front cover photo wooden frame background courtesy of iStockphoto.com/Merinka (©Merinka)
Front cover photo of flowers courtesy of iStockphoto.com/alubalish (©alubalish)
Back cover and interior image of picture frame courtesy of iStockphoto.com/glegorly (©glegorly)
Back cover and interior image of cross-stitched ornaments courtesy of iStockphoto.com/ Yuliya Perederiy (©Yuliya Perederiy)
Photo of Amy Newmark courtesy of Susan Morrow at SwickPix

Cover and Interior by Daniel Zaccari

Distributed to the booktrade by Simon & Schuster. SAN: 200-2442

Publisher's Cataloging-In-Publication Data
(Prepared by The Donohue Group, Inc.)

Names: Newmark, Amy, compiler.
Title: Chicken soup for the soul : Mom knows best : 101 stories of love, gratitude & wisdom / [compiled by] Amy Newmark.
Other Titles: Mom knows best : 101 stories of love, gratitude & wisdom
Description: [Cos Cob, Connecticut] : Chicken Soup for the Soul, LLC, [2019]
Identifiers: ISBN 9781611599879 | ISBN 9781611592870 (ebook)
Subjects: LCSH: Mothers--Literary collections. | Mothers--Anecdotes. | Mother and child--Literary collections. | Mother and child--Anecdotes. | Grandmothers--Literary collections. | Grandmothers--Anecdotes. | LCGFT: Anecdotes.
Classification: LCC HQ759 .C455 2019 (print) | LCC HQ759 (ebook) | DDC 306.874/3--dc23

Library of Congress Control Number: 2018965073

PRINTED IN THE UNITED STATES OF AMERICA
on acid∞free paper

25 24 23 22 21 20 19   01 02 03 04 05 06 07 08 09 10 11

Chicken Soup for the Soul.

MOM KNOWS BEST

101 Stories of Love, Gratitude & Wisdom

Amy Newmark

Chicken Soup for the Soul, LLC
Cos Cob, CT

Changing the world one story at a time®
www.chickensoup.com

Table of Contents

❶
~The Best Advice~

❷
~Lessons for Life~

❸
~Gratitude~

❹
~Role Models~

❺
~Like Mother, Like Daughter~

❻

~Wise Words~

❼

~Embracing Change~

8

~Always There for Us~

9

~Special Fun~

10

~A Mother's Strength~

Chapter 1

The Best Advice

Pink Pyrex

Mother's love grows by giving.
~Charles Lamb

I can think of thousands of things my mom has taught me over the years and still teaches me every day. We have argued and disagreed, but then we laugh and understand each other even better than we did before. Last week was no exception.

My mom and I joined my oldest son on his yearly trip to Columbia, Missouri, for his scholarship conference. Looking forward to a mini-vacation, we planned ahead. We have recently discovered that we loved antique shopping, and Columbia provided a host of shops to explore. One day, we found an antique shopper's paradise, with 72,000 feet of treasures to explore.

Within the first few aisles, we found a booth with an exquisite set of pink Pyrex casserole dishes. They were in perfect condition, and I fell in love. I had been looking for pink Pyrex for a while, so I was pretty excited — until I saw the price tag.

My mom asked why I was not getting the set, and I explained that I could not justify the expense for something I did not need but just wanted. She reminded me how perfect they were, and how I would never find them again. But I did not change my mind and left them on the shelf.

We decided to split up since we were looking for different items. When we met at the checkout I noticed she had the pink Pyrex dishes in her cart. I wouldn't let her buy them for me, though, so I handed them to the clerk to be put back on the shelf. My mom gave me a frustrated look, and then we checked out and went back to our hotel.

The next morning, we went back to the antique mall to see more of the booths. We split up and agreed to meet in a couple hours. And once again, I found my mother at the checkout with the pink Pyrex dishes in her cart.

I hurried up to her and reminded her that I did not need those dishes. They were far too expensive and frivolous.

My mom turned to me and said, "Sometimes, you just have to buy the pink Pyrex."

I felt guilty she had spent so much, but she didn't seem to mind. When we got home from our trip, I looked carefully around my house, trying to find the perfect spot for my treasure. I decided to make a spot on my baker's rack since it was central to the home, and I could view the dishes while working in the kitchen.

I had such a happy day arranging the dishes just so, and although it sounds silly, they really did bring a smile to my face. I realized what my mom meant when she said, "Sometimes, you just have to buy the pink Pyrex." We get so busy taking care of everyone and everything else in our lives that we forget to treat ourselves. Taking care of our own happiness makes us project that happiness forward.

I am a very blessed woman to have such a wise mom, and I plan to tell my own daughters to buy their own version of the pink Pyrex!

— Michelle Bruce —

No

*If you want to do something, go for it —
you've got nothing to lose.*
~Louis Tomlinson

My palms were sweating. I was sure I could hear my heart pounding. This was the worst. Why did I even think I could do this? Here was proof that I was completely out of my mind. I hated feeling this way, but I had to do what I was about to do. I sought out a small bit of my inner strength and opened my mouth.

"Excuse me. I was just wondering. Would it be possible to maybe get that table over there by the window instead?" I asked. My voice sounded hollow and strange to me, as if a stranger from a distance had asked the question instead of me. I waited.

"No, I'm sorry, but that table is reserved," the hostess replied kindly as she led me into the dining area.

As I followed her to my table, I realized that the earth had not opened up and swallowed me. I had not passed out or died of humiliation. The entire population of the restaurant was not laughing at my audaciousness for asking for a table by the window. I had asked and been told "no." That was all. Nothing more.

For someone like me, who is chronically shy and insecure, asking for a different table was a huge challenge. But I've started doing it on a regular basis because of a simple piece of advice my mother told me: "The worst they can say is 'no.'"

And so, I have learned to actually ask for what I want. I've learned to reach for my dreams and pursue my goals. I've auditioned for plays. I've asked men out on dates. I got a job that I wanted. I've even gotten prices reduced on a huge variety of items. Because I asked. Because my mom was right.

Sure, I have been turned down. I can't say I have never been embarrassed. I have been, but I keep trying. I will continue to ask for what I want out of life and from other people. What could happen? The worst they can say is "no."

— Traci E. Langston —

Full of Memories

Nobody can do for little children what grandparents do.
Grandparents sort of sprinkle stardust
over the lives of little children.
~Alex Haley

Thanksgiving was in full swing. My parents' home was filled with family, the house smelled of roasting turkey and warm bread, and the sounds of football.

Cooking with my family is one of my favorite Thanksgiving traditions. Mom was making stuffing. Dad was chopping, dicing and slicing the fruit salad. All the sisters were making pies, sweet-potato casserole, and cranberry dressing. We were sharing stories and laughing.

My two-year-old son, Jackson, was curious and underfoot, as always. He needed to taste the fruit. He wanted to see what was baking in the ovens.

"Jackson, where is your ball?" I asked, trying to redirect him.

Jackson ran to the other room for a few minutes. Shortly, he returned. He pulled on my shirt, saying, "Choo, choo. All aboard!"

"Not now, sweetie. We can play after dinner. Mommy needs to cook for our yummy Thanksgiving dinner."

"Come on, Momma," he persisted.

"Jackson, go find Daddy. He will play," I said.

Jackson sighed dejectedly and walked over to Mammaw.

"Mammaw," Jackson said, batting his sweet, blue eyes. "Choo, choo. All aboard."

"Okay, sweet guy. Let's go see." Mammaw washed her hands and then held her hand down for Jackson to grasp. He led her proudly to the dining room.

"Wow," Mammaw said, looking at the dining-room chairs lined up in a neat row.

Jackson patted the chair in which Mammaw should sit. Mammaw sat obediently in her assigned chair. Grinning from ear to ear, Jackson and Mammaw yelled, "Choo, choo. All aboard!" several times.

"I get Papaw," Jackson said, smiling.

"Yes, he will love your train," Mammaw encouraged.

Jackson walked over to Papaw. Papaw washed his hands and allowed Jackson to lead him to the train. Papaw happily found his seat on Jackson's train.

Jackson, Mammaw, and Papaw yelled gleefully, "Choo, choo. All aboard!"

Jackson's baby brother crawled over to join the train. Jackson decided he needed Daddy and Great-Grandma on his train. Mammaw helped Great-Grandma to her chair, and Jackson pulled Daddy away from his computer.

Jackson once again came to me. "Choo, choo. All aboard?"

"Thank you!" I said. Jackson led me to his train and showed me my seat.

All our Thanksgiving cooking stopped. The pies were not watched. The potatoes were not mashed.

However, we did have a four-generation train in our dining room.

Mammaw and Baby Brother stomped their feet, yelling, "Chugga, chugga, chugga, chugga." Papaw yelled, "Choo, choo." Daddy and Great-Grandmother told Jackson that he had a wonderful train. I gasped, "Oh, Jackson, I see a cow outside my train window. Look, everyone, at that tall tree!" Jackson sat in the conductor's seat, smiling broadly.

Finally, Jackson yelled, "We are hewe!"

Everyone disembarked the train, thanking Jackson for the wonderful train ride. Jackson shook each rider's hand. He had thoroughly enjoyed every second of his four-generation Thanksgiving Day train ride.

The dining-room chairs were returned to order. Dinner was late, the pies were a bit too brown, and the homemade cranberry dressing was omitted from the menu.

After dinner was eaten and cleaned up, my mom and I sat rocking my sweet boys to sleep.

"Momma, our train ride in the dining room was so much fun. I feel a bit bad that dinner was late, though," I said.

"Oh, sweetheart. I have learned something very important since becoming a grandmother. Stuffing can always wait so that great memories can be made."

Ten years from now, no one is going to remember that dinner was a half-hour late or that the pecan pie was a bit overcooked. No one will even recall exactly which foods made it to the table. What everyone will remember is that we had a four-generation Thanksgiving Day train ride with two-year-old Jackson as our conductor.

— Marie Loper Maxwell —

4

Give It a Year

Knowledge speaks, but wisdom listens.
~Jimi Hendrix

My mother gave me the best advice when I was pondering a big decision: "Give it a year. A lot of things change in a year. Don't make a rash decision. If, in a year, you haven't worked things out, then it's time for a change." These wise words worked for almost every situation: job changes, friendship struggles, and even marriage.

When I was having issues with my teenage son and my marriage I confided in my mom. "I really thought we had it together, and suddenly everything is falling apart. His moods are just too much to take," I admitted.

"I know things are stressful with Gavin, but he will grow out of it. Teenagers go through this. You and your sister really put us through it. But look how that worked out." Mom patted my hand kindly. "We love your husband, but we saw the change in him. You need to really think about things now. Give it a year, but during that time prepare yourself. You know what you have to do." She hugged me, and when I returned home that night I felt more composed. I was ready to make my stand. I put the kids to bed and prepared for "the talk."

I was honest with him. His depression was not only affecting him, but it was crushing the kids and me. The mood swings were too much to handle.

I wanted my own room, for space and comfort. His erratic sleep schedule and late-night gaming sessions were keeping me from sleeping. Over the past few months, he'd spent less time with us and more time burying himself in his games.

"I'm giving us a year." I looked him dead in the face. "You need to get help, and I'll give you that time. I'll make my decision in a year."

"I will do it for you and the kids. I love my family, and you're worth fighting for." He kept my gaze, not looking down as he had so often before.

If I had gone with how I felt at that moment, I would have taken the kids and left him, changing all our lives.

That year started as the year from hell. I prepared, tucking away money and making plans. I watched him carefully.

He began therapy. It was obvious to everyone he wanted change, and there he found direction. He had a few slip-ups, but they happened less often and, eventually, not at all.

Mid-year, my mother invited us over for dinner. I knew family dinners made him anxious. "I'll make an excuse for you," I offered, not wanting to send him into a nosedive.

"No, I want to go. I should go," he offered.

I was stunned, but happy.

My mother made prime rib. At the end of the meal, she picked up the dishes and returned to the kitchen, coming back out with a heart-shaped cake on a platter. It was iced in white and framed with maraschino cherries.

"Happy birthday!" she and my father sang, with my husband and children joining in.

Regardless of being two weeks early, the sentiment was there. When I was a girl, my mother would always make me a heart cake for my birthday since it was so close to Valentine's Day. It had been years since she'd made me one. She must have known how much I loved those cakes. Tears welled up as I thanked her.

I saw the love not only in my parents' eyes, but my children's and my husband's.

He even reached under the table and squeezed my hand. I thought I'd been on a solo journey, struggling alone. That cake reminded me that I was loved and worthy of being loved. I thought about all the birthdays that had come and gone, and how different each year had been. Every 365 days had their own set of triumphs and struggles.

That evening marked a changing point. From that day on, I was willing to trust the legitimacy of my husband's change and allow the year to work itself out naturally.

When my children are adults, when they struggle as we all do, I will pass on the wisdom my mother shared, reminding them to "give it a year." So much can change in 365 days.

— Nicole Ann Rook McAlister —

5

Chicken Soup
for the Soul.

Shopping with Mom

We're so busy watching out for what's just ahead of us
that we don't take time to enjoy where we are.
~Bill Watterson

I raced through the grocery aisles. Three-year-old Ben grabbed at items on the shelves as we went by. Several bags of bread slid from their display and hit the floor. I scooped them up and shoved them back in place.

"No," I said. "Stop touching things." Seated in the grocery cart, Ben squirmed like a restrained animal. He kicked his shoes against the metal basket, making a racket.

"Stop that."

Ben stretched out his arms, trying to reach even more items on the shelves. I tossed a bag of carrots into the cart and trotted toward the front of the store. Shopping was over.

While we waited to check out, I occupied Ben with my key ring. An older woman, who stood in the line next to ours, smiled at me. Then she stepped over and gave Ben a soft squeeze on his cheek. "My, aren't you the cutie."

Ben narrowed his eyes and screwed up his face. I could see his mind grind away with a comeback. "You... You... cabbage you."

"Benjamin!"

Heat flared in my cheeks. I turned to the woman. "I'm so sorry."

The smile disappeared from her face. She jerked upright, shot a stare of disapproval my way, and returned to her place in line.

I wanted to melt into the magazine rack beside us.

"You're going to take a nap when we get home."

Suddenly, as if my mother stood next to me, I heard her voice whisper, "When a child acts the most unlovable, that's when he needs the most love."

I looked at my watch: 1:30. Not only had we missed lunch, but we'd skated right past Ben's naptime. I put my arms around him and gave my little man a hug. "We'll be home soon."

In the parking lot, I buckled Ben into his car seat and loaded the groceries into the trunk. Several minutes later, I glanced in the review mirror. Ben was sound asleep.

Mom's old adage echoed in my head all the way home. Maybe Ben's behavior in the store had more to do with me than with him.

As our family expanded and grew, Mom's advice proved true. I learned to recognize the signs when one of our children teetered on the edge of a colossal meltdown. Sometimes, when they misbehaved, it was because I had crammed too many activities into one day. Though they didn't always escape discipline, when the unlovable behavior emerged, I kept Mom's saying in mind and sandwiched the necessary consequence with love.

However, I did my best to avoid these traumatic events. I planned our daily routines around naptimes and tried not to overload our schedule. I carried snacks and water in the car with us. As the parent, it was my job to resist our culture's drive to fill every minute with activity, and instead create a calm environment that nurtured my children.

Sometimes, we simply turned off the phone, cuddled on the couch and read books. Other times, we played board games or took walks and listened to the birds. Though at times we still struggled with attitudes, my strategy eliminated much of the unwanted drama. Our slower lifestyle made for calm days and a more peace-filled home.

We raised three children on Mom's wisdom. Her sage advice continues to influence our kids' lives, as they now parent our seven grandchildren.

— Kathleen Kohler —

What I Never Knew I Knew

Advice is like snow — the softer it falls, the longer it
dwells upon, and the deeper it sinks into the mind.
~Samuel Taylor Coleridge

Everyone else was celebrating the end of high school, but I was stuck at my computer, trying to write a speech. It was a week before graduation, and I still had nothing. Not that I hadn't tried. For days, I had searched the web for examples of great graduation speeches, scanned my diaries for anything insightful, and combed my memory for any high-school event worth recalling.

It seemed that I had no insights to offer my classmates. After all, I was eighteen. What did I know about life? What inspiring wisdom could I offer? What could I say that didn't sound trite? I gave up and put away the computer as I had the previous two days.

The next day at school, various people pitched in to help me with my writer's block. One classmate suggested that I should just whisper, "Freedom," drop the mike, and walk off. A teacher suggested the words, "It's been real. It's been fun. But it hasn't been real fun. Have a nice life." But their input wasn't helpful. No one suggested anything that resonated with me or that I deeply felt to be true. No one suggested anything that I could say with conviction in front of a thousand people. In despair, I went to the library after the bell rang, sat at a computer, and thought.

That's when it came to me. Suddenly, I found myself typing,

slapping the keys in a frenzy, spewing forth sage advice that I never knew I knew. Here are some of the things I wrote:

1. Never worry about what other people think of you because no one cares enough about you to pay that much attention to you anyway.
2. Do listen to what your friends and family think because they do care about you and are more likely to tell you when you're doing something completely crazy.
3. Never be afraid of hard work because hard work usually doesn't kill anyone… usually.
4. Always remember that your honesty is more important than your reputation.

Several minutes after school let out, I finished and hit "Print." I thought that I just might have a speech! Nonetheless, for the next few days, I kept trying to perfect it. Finally, I had to get a second opinion. I took some drafts to my mom and asked for her input. As soon as she finished reading the first draft, her lip wobbled, and she said that it made her want to cry. I couldn't figure out why, as none of my cheeky wisdom was meant to be emotional. But at least my words had elicited some sort of reaction, which was more than I had expected. I decided the speech was finished.

Only after the commencement ceremony did I discover the reason for the tears. The speech was a success, and it kept the audience in stitches for a full five minutes. Even I laughed while giving it. Afterward, one of my mom's friends addressed her in confusion.

"You told me the speech made you cry," she said. "I was expecting something sappy, but it was hilarious!"

My mom said that the four bits of wisdom had done it.

"Those were things I used to say," she explained. "And she was listening!"

— Angelique Morvant —

Evening Things Up

*A mother is a woman who shows you the light
when you just see the dark.*
~Grimaldos Robin

Every once in a while, my husband graciously offers me time off from our five kids. Actually, I think he allows this time because he realizes I'm seeking answers that he can't provide in this thick, overgrown parenting forest we're trying to navigate. Mom is my tree of knowledge in this forest.

Today was no exception. I rushed into my mother's apartment, and said, "It doesn't matter what it is. The kids argue with each other about everything. They even argue with me."

Mom wore that all-knowing smile on her face as she watched me pace her living-room floor. I stopped pacing and faced her. "Michelle and William always fight over the Legos and building blocks. And we have hundreds of them!"

Mom must have known I wasn't finished yet. She didn't say anything, so I continued.

"The twins tell me I give one girl or the other the bigger hunk of ice-cream sandwich." I pointed my finger at her. "It's not true, Mom." I resumed pacing. "And Marie and Michelle always seem to want the wagon at the same time." I threw my hands up in defeat and collapsed onto her couch. "We certainly don't need more than one wagon. Didn't I teach them how to share?"

I sighed and waited for the knowledge tree to speak. Mom took a deep breath.

"Vicki, because my sister and I also argued all the time about chores, toys, or the division of food, my mother finally came up with a system to settle all arguments. She had one of us write up the chore list, numbering each chore. Then she had the other girl choose odds or evens. The writing of the chore list would switch, and each girl had the opportunity to write the list — but the other sister always chose first."

My eyes widened.

"My mother had one of us cut the piece of cake or ice-cream sandwich," she continued. "And the other girl chose first."

The sun was beginning to shine through the dense parenting forest.

"You can be sure," my mother said, "that those pieces of cake were cut as evenly as anyone could get them, with the same amount of frosting on each piece. The list of chores had the ones we didn't like to do in both the odd and the even numbers."

"Brilliant!" I exclaimed.

"Yes," my mother said. "And it takes you out of the mix. One kid divides up the building blocks, and the other child chooses a pile first. One daughter uses the wagon, and the other daughter sets a timer for how long. But then that daughter has the same amount of time with it."

I clapped my hands and rose to put on the kettle for a pot of tea. This was going to change everything.

— Victoria Marie Lees —

The Mom Gene

Accept good advice gracefully as long as it doesn't
interfere with what you intended
to do in the first place.
~Gene Brown

My mother-in-law called to tell me something I already knew. "Now, remember, tomorrow is Labor Day, and that means we won't be getting any mail."

"Thank you for the reminder," I said. But what I wanted to say was, "Yes, Mom, I've lived through forty-three Labor Days now, so I knew that already."

"Now, you need to turn here," she told me when I was driving her to the doctor's office — the same doctor's office I drove her to last month and the month before. "Thanks, Mom," I said, instead of, "Yeah, I know how to get there because I've been to your doctor's office a few dozen times already."

"Do you have a cold?" she said when she heard me sniffle. "Because there's medicine you can take for that. They sell it at Walgreens."

"I'm fine, Mom," I said, instead of, "Yep, I've taken cold medicine before, and they sell it at CVS, Target, and Walmart, too."

My mother-in-law really likes to give me advice, whether I need it or not. And my own mom is not much better.

"Make sure you put jackets on the kids tomorrow," she told me. "It's supposed to be cold."

"Thank you, Mom," I said, instead of, "It's November, and I live in the Midwest. I could've figured out all on my own that my kids would need jackets."

Nearly every day, one of my moms calls me to tell me something that I already know. But I was handling it with aplomb. Until we went on vacation. With both of them. At the same time.

"Can the kids swim? If not, you'll need to put life jackets on them," one mom said.

"And if we're going to be outside, they'll need sunscreen. You know, so they don't get sunburned," my other mom said.

I looked at my husband. "Thank you, Captain Obvious," I whispered.

"Hang in there, love," he said. "They mean well."

My husband was right. They did mean well, and I reminded myself of that fact repeatedly during that vacation — until I'd had enough, and I snapped.

We were eating dinner on the last night of the trip. I'd ordered my meal, as well as a kid's meal for my youngest son. He'd requested fruit as his side dish.

"Does that fruit include grapes?" my mom asked the waitress. "If it does, my daughter will need to cut them in half."

"Oh, yes," my mother-in-law continued. "Grapes are a choking hazard, you know."

"Yes, I do know that," I snapped. I pointed at my oldest son. "He has survived under my care all these years. He is a teenager now, and I never let him choke on a grape or drown in a pool or get stung by a jellyfish or anything. Why can't you guys just trust me to be a good mom?"

My moms' mouths dropped open. "Do you think we don't know you're a good mom?" my mother-in-law said with tears in her eyes.

"You're a great mom," my mom said. "We both know that."

"Then why do you constantly tell me what to do? You both act like I don't know anything."

My moms looked at one another. "We're just trying to help you," one said. "We remember that being a mom is hard, and everyone needs help."

"I'm happy to have your help," I said. "But the unsolicited advice gets to be a little much."

"Oh, we're just reminding you of things you may have forgotten," my mom said. "We're not telling you what to do or anything."

"It makes me feel like you think I can't handle things on my own," I said.

"We're sorry," they said. "You're a wonderful mom. We didn't mean to upset you."

I nodded, feeling sheepish that I'd lost my temper. "It's okay. I appreciate your help."

We hugged it out, and I thanked them both for caring about my family so much.

The next morning, we were getting ready to leave the hotel and make the long drive from the Sunshine State back to the Midwest.

"Did you use the potty?" I asked my younger son. When he nodded, I looked at my older son. "Did you?"

He shook his head. "I don't need to go."

"Are you sure? It's a long drive. We won't be stopping for a few hours, and you'll have to hold it. Maybe you should try. You know, just in case."

My son burst out laughing. He looked at my husband. "It's like a genetic thing. They can't help themselves. I don't think they even know they're doing it."

My husband nodded. "It's the Mom Gene. It's the genetic predisposition to over-parent their children, no matter how old they get." He smiled at me. "And, apparently, it's hereditary."

I started laughing, too. I couldn't help it. Just twelve hours before, I'd gotten mad at our moms for giving unsolicited advice, and now I'd done it to my teenage son.

"I'm sorry, bud," I said. "I shouldn't have said anything. You are old enough to make your own bathroom decisions."

"That's okay, Mom." He looked down and shrugged. "Last night, when you got mad at the grandmas, I understood how you felt."

I nodded. "It's hard to let your kids grow up." And then I realized that my moms probably felt the same way. Just as I loved my kids and wanted to protect them, my moms loved me and wanted only the best for me.

I'd love to tell you that my moms have gotten out of the unsolicited-advice business, but they haven't. They both still call me daily with warnings about the weather, pollen counts, and other concerns, both real and imagined. Mostly imagined.

But oddly, it doesn't bother me as much as it used to. When I start to get irked, I remember the time that I encouraged a teenager who was old enough to drive to use the potty before we traveled. Turns out, I was more like my moms than I want to admit.

We moms love our kids and want the best for them. And sometimes that means we offer unwanted advice.

We can't help it. It's the Mom Gene.

It might be annoying to our children — even our adult children — but we always, always mean well.

—Sarah Williams—

Worth Passing On

We are made wise not by the recollection of our past,
but by the responsibility for our future.
~George Bernard Shaw

All women experience that moment — the moment when they open their mouths and their mother comes out.

"Shut the door! Were you raised in a barn?"

"Clean up after yourself. I'm your mother, not your maid."

And my personal favorite, "Eat your dinner. There are kids starving in Africa who would love to have this food."

I can't get away from it. For better or worse, my mother is the voice in my head, part of who I am and how I handle my day-to-day life. I almost feel as though the years of advice she poured into me have acquired a sentient life of their own and are helping me make good decisions for the tiny humans now in my charge.

"A full load of laundry dries faster than a partial one."

"Make it/grow it yourself. It'll taste better and be healthier."

"Don't give your body to a boy who doesn't respect you as a person."

And, finally, the mantra I live by: "If you're not sure you should, you shouldn't."

I can't remember when my mom first laid that one on me — probably right about the time I started making my own decisions and then second-guessing them.

It's been a good rule of thumb my whole life. Generally, I know what I should do — the big stuff anyway. So, if I'm not sure I should, chances are, I shouldn't. I wasn't sure I should go away to college, so I didn't. I stayed home and married my husband.

My mom was trying to make a decision a while back and called to talk it over with me. I couldn't resist. "Well… my mom used to say," I teased, "'if you're not sure you should…'" We laughed together. Mom is always tickled when I quote her. Maybe because it's proof I was paying attention.

Last week, when a friend sat in my kitchen trying to decide whether or not to take a job, I opened my mouth and passed it on again. "Well," I began, "if you're not sure you should, you shouldn't."

She smiled. "That's good advice."

"I know," I replied. "My mom gave it to me."

I inherited a lot of things from my mother — antique furniture, recipes, her nose — but what I treasure most is her voice in my head, proof that wherever I go and whatever I do, a part of her will always be with me. And every now and then, the voice comes up with something extraordinary. Something worth passing on.

— Shannon Pannell —

Chapter
2

Lessons
for Life

The Girls of Troop 32

God could not be everywhere,
and therefore he made mothers.
~Rudyard Kipling

My mother never intended to make a political statement. She never carried protest signs or marched in a civil-rights parade. But in her practical, down-to-earth way, with no fanfare or credit, she modeled her commitment to equality and integrity.

Thanks to my mother, I was in an integrated Brownie troop. This was surprisingly radical in Virginia in the late 1950s. Three years after the Supreme Court ruled in Brown vs. Board of Education that segregated schools were illegal, African-Americans in our town still had separate public schools, swimming pools, and neighborhoods. Changing that reality was more than a decade in the future.

In 1957, the Catholic Diocese opened a new elementary school in our town. Sacred Heart Academy was open to all children regardless of race. I was in the first first-grade of this brand-new school; twenty-eight of us were in that class, including several black girls. This commitment to integration was quite unusual in Virginia. The public schools in our town were segregated, and the nearby town of Front Royal had closed its entire public-school system rather than allow blacks to attend, setting up whites-only private schools. Catholic parents from Front Royal hired a bus to send their children to the integrated parochial school in our town, twenty-five miles away.

When I was in second grade, my mother, a white Polish-American, and Delaney Byrd's mother, an African-American, met while serving as lunchroom volunteers. They decided to form a Brownie troop for the girls in my class, even though neither had been a Girl Scout in her youth. We met in the somewhat musty basement of the Catholic church, proudly wearing our brown uniform dresses and Brownie beanies, and we did all the things Brownies were doing everywhere. At school, at Brownies, and at church, the African-American girls were not black friends; they were just our friends.

In the summer, Mom and Mrs. Byrd ran a day camp for our troop at a nearby seminary. What a magical place and time! The seminarians hung sparkly and colorful decorations in the trees and scattered large, wooden cartoon characters along the paths for us to discover on our walks in the woods, and our leaders gave us plenty of time to wander on the grounds. We played together in the swimming pool under the watchful eyes of the moms and complained about the rotten-egg smell of the water. We made jewelry out of macaroni, and sculptures out of clay. We drew pictures and put on short plays. We learned about nature and a few rudimentary camping skills. And we sang songs—my mother has a remarkable trove of silly songs and ditties. We had our own favorite anthem:

> Hi-yike-e-yike-us, nobody like us
> We are the girls of Troop 32
> Always a winning, always a grinning
> Always a feeling fine!

Many years later, I took a class on women in the civil-rights movement. I had been a child in the 1960s and, for the most part, I was pretty sheltered. When I told my mother what I had learned, she explained why she and Mrs. Byrd had taken vacations from their jobs to run a day camp.

At that time, black girls were not permitted to attend the Brownie camps sponsored by the local Girl Scout council. In fact, the nearby Girl Scout camp and the national Girl Scout camp in Washington, D.C.

only allowed African-American girls during designated blacks-only weeks. Integrated troops were not welcome or, to put it bluntly, were completely excluded from the sponsored camp sessions.

We could not stay together as a troop using official scouting facilities and, since there were relatively few African-American Girl Scouts in our town, some of our friends would not be able to attend camp at all. Mom and Mrs. Byrd agreed that they had to operate their own program. Neither of them had ever run a day camp before, but they figured they could learn by doing. And they did.

Our mothers probably had very little impact on overall race relations in our town or even in changing the culture of the Girl Scouts organization. That was not their goal. In their quiet, unassuming ways, these two wonderful mothers created a brief oasis of hope and promise for the young girls — white and black — of Brownie Troop 32 in Winchester, Virginia.

— Nancy Learned Haines —

11

Lessons from a Six-Carat Diamond

Through darkness diamonds spread their richest light.
~John Webster

My mom was not a vain person, but a natural beauty who spent very little time on her physical appearance — especially in terms of fancy clothes, manicures or hairstyles. She declared herself a tomboy and didn't care about stuff like that. She kept beautiful her way: rest, water, exercise, vegetables, and laughter.

Some say it was a generational thing, being raised in and around the Great Depression. From a young age, my mom had her mind conditioned about money. She would tell me that her father was tight-fisted and miserly with a touch of lazy, and he had her run his little corner store from the age of ten. She saw the poor people of her neighborhood come in, heads hung low, scrounging for food and making hard choices, like meat or cheese, powdered milk or juice. She took their coins with an eye on the bottom line. It was up to her, though just in elementary school, to make sure the register balanced at the end of the day. That experience taught her early that life is all about making choices — the seemingly small salami or bologna choices that direct a person's long-term security.

For all of her thriftiness, my mom had one weakness: diamonds. In 1958, my teenage dad gave her a diamond chip as an engagement ring, which she proudly wore until she had squirreled away enough for an "upgrade." By then, she was in her late thirties, and had worked hard and done without in order to acquire a beautiful Tiffany two-carat solitaire ring. I witnessed the small sacrifices and hard choices she made to get that diamond. Over the years, with patience and perseverance, my mom also acquired other gorgeous diamond pieces like earrings, pendants, and bracelets. Mom wore those diamonds proudly, whether she was pulling weeds, going to Walmart, or at the bridge table. She simply loved the way her diamonds sparkled. Sure, her clothes may have looked like floral draperies, and her hair may have been a mess, but she didn't care — as long as she was garnished with her precious diamonds.

Years passed, and it came time for my parents' 50th wedding anniversary. My only brother and I did it up big for our parents, whisking them away to Atlanta to treat them to dinner at our mother's favorite restaurant. It made her happy, but Mom had her eye on a very big diamond to mark the occasion. "The bigger the better," she said. And she had earned it, after all. Her wholesale (naturally) diamond guy found her a six-carat, round-cut one. Mom cooed over that rock, exclaiming that each carat represented a decade that she loved my dad, plus one to grow on. Mom had that gorgeous stone mounted with baguettes showcasing it on both sides. For the next six years, she never took it off her finger. She loved it and what it represented.

One summer day, out of the blue, things changed on a dime. There we were six years later, hearing the word "incurable." What a powerful word when it is directed at someone you love.

My mom proudly wore her diamonds to all of her chemotherapy appointments. Occasionally, as I sat with her, I would catch her glancing sadly at the six-carat ring on her IV-bruised hand. Many nurses would remark on its beauty, as my mom would proudly announce that she had earned every last carat. Indeed, she had.

Knowing how my mom loved that diamond made it all the more special when she left it to me. After wearing it on my hand for a year or so, I decided to set it into a necklace where it would be closer to my heart. It reminds me of my mom every day, no matter what I am doing, and it speaks to me in weird ways.

There was the time when I was tempted to buy asparagus at $5.99 per pound. Just as I was putting a bundle into my cart, I inadvertently touched the necklace. A wave of practicality washed over me as I headed over to the green beans instead. It wasn't about what I could afford, by any means. It was as if I was genetically programmed to suddenly be practical. Another time, I thought I should buy a new car because my old one needed a tune-up and a good mechanic. "Hold on a sec. Think about what you really want and then go get it," I could almost hear her whisper in my ear. It made me pause and think about how happiness isn't derived that way. What did I want? What would make me happy?

My mom's example of practical frugality taught me a lot about how making little sacrifices along the way can bring far more satisfaction in the end. That six-carat diamond, especially, brought my mom joy without fail. For Mom, diamonds made her feel empowered even though she may have eaten canned beans for years to afford the luxury. Diamonds were her kryptonite. One thing is for certain, though: Not even my mom could have known that her beloved six-carat diamond represented both a carat for each decade that she loved my dad and a carat for each year she had left to enjoy the pleasure that diamond gave her.

In some ways, it makes me *carpe diem* the hell out of life. What does "stuff" matter, anyhow? Other days, it makes me say and do whatever I want. Again, what does it matter anyway? Life is tricky that way.

My mom was far from perfect, and we fought sometimes. I was so obtuse, though. I never realized how much I dug her until it was time to dig her grave. All the diamonds in the world don't sparkle as much as she did.

— Kim Kelly Johnson —

The Cycles of Life

Don't judge each day by the harvest you reap but by
the seeds that you plant.
~Robert Louis Stevenson

Tiny leaves, shaped like babies' tears, cascade over the sides of the container. From twelve small clippings given to me several years ago, I now nurture a beautiful plant.

Originally, I thought I had killed it. Withered, brown leaves hung down the sides of the pot in such profusion there was no doubt it was time to end our mutual misery. I carried the remains to my mother and asked if she could revive what appeared to be a lost cause. She smiled at me and took the container from my hands.

My mother Rose tenderly pruned and pared back the stems, watered and fed the few remaining stragglers I hadn't completely killed, and gently urged the stems and leaves hiding under the soil into sunlight. For several months each year, the plant thrived and grew, but in the winter months it would shrivel and turn brown. For several years, Mom cared for the plant through the winter, rewarded with a revival of greenery each year in the early days of spring.

My mother's health grew worse over the decade of the plant's life, mirroring in many ways the seasons of wellness and concern for her survival. During a visit from Aunt Marion in late spring, when both the plant and my mom faced a particularly difficult recovery, the plant changed hands again. Mom asked her sister if she could rejuvenate the remains. Leaving Mom's house with a pot of soil and the sickly dried stems of winter, Aunt Marion carried the patient home, determined to save it.

During that summer, the leaves broke through the soil, and the once-barren plant grew again on a kitchen windowsill. As before, each winter it withered, to be renewed again in spring, starting with tiny shoots pushing through, developing tear-shaped leaves, which would cascade down the sides of the planter until the dormancy of winter.

The plant cycled as it had done under my short care and my mother's term as caretaker until one spring many years later when Aunt Marion deemed it unsalvageable and put it out with the trash. On a visit, my cousin Carole, seeing the shriveled remains on the trash heap, decided to give the determined plant one further chance for revival. Carole took the container to her sunroom in the hope she could do something with it.

In the years since I first brought the plant home, four women from the family have cared and nurtured it, each in her own time. During those years, I also cycled through times when life was lush and green and times when I felt there would be no restoration of my heart's remains following difficult barren periods. A decade after my mother died, I moved over 500 miles from home, hoping for new beginnings. During the long winter months after the move, everything familiar was distant, and I longed for the connections left behind even as I tentatively discovered new horizons.

The first June after the move, I returned for a visit and stayed with my cousin Carole. I was eager to see the family and friends I had sorely missed.

One morning, as we shared coffee and conversation at Carole's kitchen table, I commented on the beauty of the plant hanging in her kitchen window. It shimmered in the sunlight, and tiny, dark green leaves spilled over the sides of the flowerpot.

"That was your mother's plant," Carole told me. "I'll send a few cuttings back with you."

Gone nearly twelve years, my mom returned to me in spirit that soft spring morning. It seemed impossible that something as delicate as a plant could have survived the intervening years, but the memory of it returned clearly as I gazed at it hanging in the window.

"They'll never endure the car ride or my gardening skills," I protested, but she felt certain the clippings would make it.

"I've given clippings to so many people. It seems the more you cut it back, the fuller and stronger it becomes."

She then told me the story of how she had gotten the plant from her mother, who had gotten it from mine.

My eyes filled as I examined it more closely, recognizing the tiny leaves. I recalled my mother rescuing it from my inexperienced care. When I packed my bags into the car, a wet paper towel containing about a dozen strings of stems with tiny, green, teardrop-shaped leaves rested in the console between the front seats. They did indeed travel well.

I carefully placed the clippings in a small pot and watched them take root and grow. Eventually, they filled two large pots in my kitchen window. The plant passed through the hands of my mother, my aunt and my cousin until it returned to me twenty years after my first failure as its caregiver. It became a sweet reminder of the blessings we shared, and how together we were rooted and grew through each other's love and nurturing.

This plant, once merely another of my gardening failures, led me to a deeper and richer appreciation of the circle of life, guiding us to our own seed of understanding. My mother's love remained long beyond her time on earth. Sometimes, I question fighting for lost causes or the purpose in maintaining faith, especially when there seems to be nothing left. But when the leaves are dried and more brown than green, I now understand the need for patience. I remember to pare what is no longer viable, to nourish what remains, and to never underestimate the potential of life to rejuvenate, grow and flourish.

— Kathleen Healy-Schmieder —

13

Chicken Soup for the Soul

My Mom the Entrepreneur

Happy is the son whose faith in his mother
remains unchallenged.
~Louisa May Alcott

My name is Gavan, and I am eleven years old. I want to tell you about the inspirational story of my mom, Kelly. My mom grew up in Fergus Falls, Minnesota, with a single mom in an apartment with very little food in the fridge. She had everything she needed like clothes and a bed, but there was no extra money for things that people do every day.

My mom started babysitting, cooking and mowing lawns at the age of ten — anything to make a few dollars. She helped raise her brother Chad, who is now a successful electrical engineer, Navy veteran and husband with three kids.

My mom got through middle and high school working full-time and going to school. She managed to go to college and graduated as a dental assistant. She took out loans to get through school and she worked at the school bowling alley and a garden center, and waitressed, too, while getting top grades. She worked as a dental assistant in the Minneapolis area for fourteen years.

She married my dad, who was a forklift driver and worked his way up in the corporate world by working at least ten-hour days. My mom was twenty-one years old when they built their first house.

They had everything ready for me when I was born. My mom mostly stayed home but worked as a temporary dental assistant and a Planning and Zoning and Park Board Commissioner when my dad could take vacation or a trusted neighbor could watch me. I was given a brother before I was two years old, and my mom loves both of us very much. We moved to Fargo, North Dakota, for my dad's job. My mom did not have good luck finding a job as a dental assistant since they did not pay well enough to put my brother and me in preschool. She stayed home with us and put us in city-run events like soccer and track.

Then, my mom brainstormed and got the idea of opening a doggy daycare and grooming facility since she loves dogs, and there were not many of those businesses in the area. She looked for spaces and called a few numbers. She found one that had just opened but was failing. My mom worked hard to assume the loan and be the owner of the business. She had to pledge our house and vehicle against the loan.

My mom bought ads on a credit card to announce they were open. She got creative and did things that the other doggy daycares did not do. My mom's business has now been open for five years, and she loves her customers' dogs very much. She is able to spend time with us and work as the owner at the same time. My brother and I are able to be goalies in hockey and play in traveling lacrosse. My mom puts us in theater plays, and football and golf lessons, and we get to eat out at restaurants between events.

My mom has taken us to Disney World and Disneyland. She even bought her dream vehicle—a purple Jeep Wrangler—and loves to drive it with the top off in the summer. My mom makes sure we have plenty of healthy food at all times. I have a room full of toys, books and games, and my brother and I have our own bedrooms. My mom and dad bought an RV and rent a space to camp out most weekends in the summer. My mom just bought a boat and two jet skis for us to use as a family.

I wanted to share my mom's story because it shows that even if people grow up poor, they can change their lives if they work hard

14

Mom's Wisdom

An ounce of mother is worth a pound of clergy.
~Spanish Proverb

School mornings were always hectic. The first sentence I usually heard was, "It's time to rise and shine!" It was Mom's loudest voice, and there was no way I could ignore it or hide from it.

"Okay, Mom. I'm getting up and dressed!" I would manage to call back, although my morning voice sounded like a bullfrog.

Mom's loudest voice blared out again as she announced, "Breakfast is ready!"

By then, I could smell the heavenly aromas of breakfast, and I couldn't get to the kitchen fast enough. In fact, it was a race between my sister, my brother, and me. We usually slid into our seats at the same time, sometimes knocking each other out of our places.

"Yum! Thanks, Mom! This is my favorite," I panted, as I gobbled down the scrambled eggs, bacon, and mile-high fluffy pancakes, and guzzled down both the orange juice and hot chocolate.

"You're welcome, dear," Mom sang out. "Now, grab your lunches and books, and let's get going. The school bus will be here any minute!"

We all skedaddled out to the bus stop as we grabbed our lunch bags that contained a sandwich, fruit, and dessert — usually our favorite cookies or cupcakes.

Then, one day, much to my horror, there was no dessert in my lunch! I looked through every nook, cranny, and space of my lunch bag, and even turned it upside-down, dumping everything out. My dessert just wasn't there! What could have happened to it? Did Mom forget to make or buy it? Or was she too busy? *Oh, well,* I thought. *It's only one time, so it's no big deal.* But, for the next several days, my lunch contained no dessert! So one day, as soon as I got home from school, I bellowed out, "Hey, Mom! Why haven't you been putting a dessert in my school lunches?"

Mom stood up and responded, "Why, Eugene, I have been including a dessert in your lunch every day. In fact, this whole week I have put your favorite cookies in your lunches — chocolate chip! If you're not getting them, then who is?"

So then we reviewed my activities and schedule, and what I did with my lunch each day. As soon as I arrived at school, I always put my lunch in the classroom closet along with all of the other lunches. And that brings us to Carl — the terror of the third-grade classroom. The teacher did not like him in class and would send him to the closet, where he would spend most of each day.

Carl lived in a group foster home. He was loud, rough, and somewhat of a thief; he would take just about anything that wasn't fastened down. Mom and I concluded that with nothing else to do, and time on his hands, Carl was probably going through the lunches and eating what he liked.

My mother and I talked about ways to resolve this problem. She explained to me that Carl didn't need to be chastised; he needed, more than anything, a friend. So Mom said, "I'm going to put two packages of goodies in your lunch: one for you and one for Carl." That's what Mom did, and then I put my lunch bag in the school closet as usual.

I said nothing about the lunch goodies to Carl, but one day out on the playground, he stopped me and asked, "Why are there always two packages of goodies in your lunches?"

So I told him, "My mother put one in my lunch bag for me and one in for you."

Another day, Carl asked me if he could come to my house and meet my mother. I told him, "That will be fine, but there are certain conditions you will have to abide by."

He asked, "Such as?"

I explained, "You will be welcome at our house as long as you don't take something that doesn't belong to you, and do not fight or swear." He was agreeable.

After that, Carl would come to our house every day after school. He always obeyed our house rules, and we enjoyed our time together playing marbles and other games.

Before the school year was out, Carl was transferred to another group home and another school district. I still think of Carl and wonder what happened to him. I know what happened to me. Because of my mother's example, I learned a lifelong lesson about how to recognize need and show compassion for others.

—Eugene Mead—

15

New Shoes

*Words are not enough to express the unconditional love
that exists between a mother and a daughter.*
~Caitlin Houston

A s I was driving, eyes focused on the street, I could sense my
mother's growing impatience. "We can eat anywhere. I'm not
particular," she said, hoping I'd get the message. She was hungry. Now.

"I know. I think it's in the next block," I said, hoping that it really
was. "There it is!"

I maneuvered the car into a convenient parking spot. I exhaled a
sigh of relief at the familiar sign overhead with the script letters against
a green background: "Ernie Jr's." It didn't matter that, in my estimation,
the food was mediocre at best. My mother loved it. It was her go-to
place. Whenever she visited California from Oklahoma, she had two
destinations in mind: See's Candies and Ernie Jr's.

Maybe it was a throwback to her early days in Los Angeles. Back
then, she had a waitress job at House of Dimes, a place where the scent
of grease was as distinctive as the customers were undiscriminating. No
one would accuse it of being authentically Mexican, but the food was
filling and cheap. There, you could get a taco for two and a half dimes.

In my mother's re-telling of the story, it wasn't the money that
attracted her. She already had a day job working downtown. She just
loved tacos! She hoped to learn how this exotic food was made. I sus-
pect the worn linoleum floors, mismatched seating and working-class

clientele might have assuaged any homesickness she felt in those early years for her native Oklahoma.

This time, her return to the Golden State wasn't a family visit. She was leaving the safety of her comfortable retirement in the small town of her birth and returning permanently to Southern California where she had raised her family. Both places were home to her.

The Ernie Jr's in Pasadena had closed, so I took her to the one remaining location, in Eagle Rock. Granted, it would not have the same geriatric waiters, one in particular, who would cause her to exclaim in an incredulous whisper every single time, "Can you believe he's still here?" But the taco and enchilada combination plate provided the familiarity she craved. And this time it even tasted good to me, too.

I have no idea what we talked about, but I know it wasn't her chemo or the seriousness of her prognosis. We didn't even discuss the logistics of getting the remainder of her belongings across the country. It was just the two of us savoring an ordinary lunch, at the last remaining Ernie Jr's before it closed as well.

We'd come a long way from the time in my twenties when, in another restaurant, my mother directed me to get some beets at the salad bar. I declined politely. She insisted. I said, perhaps more emphatically than I intended, "I'm twenty-seven years old. I think I can decide whether or not I want some beets!"

Without the slightest hesitation, she looked at me and said, "And I'm paying for lunch. Get some beets." The waitress nearby could barely conceal her amusement. I have been eating and enjoying beets ever since.

As we relaxed into a pleasant state of fullness, I asked, "So you wanna go to the mall?" The question hung in the air for a moment. We both knew there was nothing we needed. And goodness knows the Eagle Rock Plaza was long past its heyday. Instead, we stopped at the nearest shoe store. As I had hoped, the carefree mood carried over from lunch. Once again, it was good to just sit and talk as I tried on shoes. We talked about the merits of this pair over that pair. It's likely she commented again on why they don't make boots large enough to accommodate her calves. And we laughed as we always did at this fundamental unfairness. My mother's curvy calves, ample hips and small waist had always been a challenge to clothe, no matter what size she was.

At 5' 4", we were exactly the same height, and I felt lucky to have inherited her tendency to maintain a small waist, but there our similarities ended. That full womanly presence she projected without effort was something I could only aspire to. I finally settled on a pair of loafers that were an unlikely combination of denim and leather. I decided on impulse to buy them. I would figure out when and where to wear them later.

"I think I'll get a pair, too," Mom said, surprising me. As much as we were alike and shared some similar tastes, I could not recall a time when we had bought an identical pair of shoes. But that was not what moved me. Over the past months, she had given away things — clothing, jewelry, household items, even her prized collection of ceramic chickens — and steadfastly refused to acquire even the smallest thing. This simple decision to buy something new signaled optimism we both desperately wanted and needed.

We paid for our purchases and walked unhurriedly to the car, our steps revealing what we knew inwardly. This sense of lightness, the feeling of being unburdened, was worth prolonging, if only for a time.

— Barbara A. Bruner —

16

My Handyman Mom

All that I am, or hope to be, I owe to my angel mother.
~Abraham Lincoln

To hear her tell it, my mother's life in Italy had been idyllic. She was the youngest of nine children and had been spoiled by her parents and her older siblings. Her life was so happy, in fact, that much to her father's chagrin, she turned down every suitor who came calling! Until my father, that is. He'd come from America in search of a wife. He took one look at my mother, and it was love at first sight.

I don't think my mother had any idea what she was getting into. My father was a chef. That meant he worked long hours and always worked holidays. Things went from bad to worse when they decided to open their own restaurant. Now it wasn't just my father working long hours, but my mother and two older brothers, too. One summer, my dad left my mom to run the restaurant while he took a job as executive chef at a popular Lake George, New York bistro. He was away three months, and my mother was livid! After that, they closed the restaurant.

Dad worked as head chef at a well-known, local eatery for a couple of years, but the best-paying jobs were at the summer resorts. After my brothers left home, the lure of high wages was too much for Dad. He agreed to oversee the kitchen of a pricey Lake George steakhouse where he worked twelve- to fourteen-hour days, seven days a week, from May through October. That meant my mother had to contend with maintaining their properties: a four-unit apartment building, a two-family house, and the restaurant space that we rented out to a pizza parlor. Not to mention that almost an acre and a half of lawn had to be cut!

Mom had helped while our house was being built and she knew how to pound nails, saw wood, paint, and tile. But that was very different from being totally responsible for building and property maintenance. Mom and Dad had struggled through the Depression, so she was frugal. She never spent money frivolously and wasn't inclined to hire someone to do the work for her. She decided to do it herself, figuring she'd learn what she didn't know how to do. Every foreman needs an assistant. Though I didn't apply for the job, I got it anyway!

I was a scrawny kid, but my mother was determined to get me in shape. The first order of business was getting the lawn cut. I now shared that duty with her. Did I mention we lived on a hill? A very steep hill! Nothing is worse than pushing a lawnmower uphill in ninety-degree heat. It was miserable work!

After a couple of weeks, I not only had muscles, but I'd gotten really good at mower maintenance: pulling and cleaning the spark plug and air filter; draining and changing the oil; and scraping out the undercarriage. My mother insisted I could do anything I set my mind to. She was also a stickler when it came to the way the property looked. She insisted that the tall grass around the trees and bushes be trimmed short. If I couldn't get close enough with the mower, she'd send me out with an assortment of clippers and lethal-looking garden tools to get the job done. If they didn't work, I used scissors.

Every time a tenant moved out, we had to scrub and repaint the apartments. Since we lived in upstate New York, tenants always waited until the warmer months to move. If we'd used water-based latex paints, I might not have minded so much. But my mother insisted on using oil-based, semi-gloss paint. Every time I rolled it out, I got flecks of paint on my hair and skin. I had to scrub it off with turpentine!

Repainting a three- or four-room apartment took us a week or more. We had to plaster cracks and nail-holes in the wall, and then wait for the spackle to dry before we could sand and paint it. While we waited, we repainted the radiators with silver metallic paint and touched up woodwork. We also replaced damaged floor tiles in the kitchen and broken ceramic ones on the bathroom walls and floors. It was drudgery! It was made worse by the fact that my mother insisted on giving everything two coats of paint, even though a year later, when the lease expired and the tenants left, we'd have to paint everything all over again!

While my friends spent their summers swimming at the lake, biking, playing ball or just hanging out, I was working up a sweat and gagging on paint fumes!

Over the years, working as Mom's assistant, I learned to unplug toilets, snake out drains, take apart sink traps, and fix screens and broken windows. She taught me how to measure and saw 2x4s, use a miter box to cut a perfect angle for a door or window frame, and put up Sheetrock like a pro. Together, we repaired and replaced concrete sidewalks, built a block retaining wall, waterproofed foundations, and even tarred and shingled a roof.

I hated doing the work then, but I'm grateful for the experience now. My mom gave me a wonderful gift. She made me self-reliant. She taught me I didn't need to depend on others to get things done. She showed me that I was smart, strong, and capable. That lesson has served me well throughout my life.

— Mary Vigliante Szydlowski —

Don't Phone It In

Happiness, not in another place but this place…
not for another hour, but this hour.
~Walt Whitman

I passed my newborn son to my mom to hold for the first time. "Is he not the sweetest thing you've ever seen?" I squealed.

"He is!" she agreed, beaming with pride. I reached for my cell phone so that I could capture this special moment. Over the next few weeks, I snapped countless pictures of Trevyn's first bath, first smile, first outing, etc. When Mom came to visit again several months later, I was still in a picture-taking frenzy.

"You know," Mom said one morning as I was scrolling through my phone to show her the latest batch of pictures, "I don't really need to see those. I'm looking at the real thing right now."

"Yeah, but he's fussy today," I said. "I want you to see this one shot of Trevyn that really shows how adorable he is."

Mom chuckled as she snuggled my son. I kept scrolling.

"Honey, seriously," Mom said, reaching for my hand to give it a squeeze. "Let's put away the phone and live in the moment instead."

I know she meant well, but I felt a little scolded. After all, I was forced to live in the moment all the time as I tended to my baby's every need.

"I'm not calling you out. It's just that I know how fleeting life is. I mean, seriously," Mom said, her voice cracking as she blinked away a stray tear, "I swear you were just a newborn yourself. Where did the time go?"

I rolled my eyes. I know, I know. I'd heard it all before. The days are long, but the years are short. Blah, blah, blah.

"I fully concede that I had it easier when I was raising you and your brother," Mom continued. "While I couldn't Google what to do with a colicky baby at 2:00 a.m., I also didn't have to deal with constant distractions and contraptions. The lack of technology really did simplify life. For one thing, my hip didn't vibrate every twenty seconds, alerting me to this, that and the other."

"Okay, Mom. I get it. Message received. Pun intended," I said with a smirk.

I felt like Mom was being overly dramatic, but I had to admit that her comment stuck with me over the next few weeks; I couldn't help noticing some rather disconcerting things about my life. For instance, when I left the house, I made sure not only to have extra diapers and wipes, but also — and perhaps most importantly — my phone! If I happened to accidentally leave my precious device at home, I felt compelled to turn around to retrieve it.

One evening after putting my son to bed, I looked around at my disaster of a house. With stuffed animals, burp rags, puzzle pieces, building blocks, and a trail of broken Cheerios littering the floor, I began the daily pick-up process. Finally, forty-five minutes later, I plopped down on the coach, eager to enjoy some chill time. The moment my butt hit the chaise lounge, panic set in.

"Where is my phone?" I freaked. My palms started sweating. Had I dropped it into one of the dozens of wicker toy baskets scattered around the house? Had it gotten kicked under a piece of furniture? Or — heaven forbid — had I accidentally tossed it into the washing machine with a pile of dirty clothes? Beads of sweat formed on my brow at the mere thought.

Suddenly, *A Charlie Brown Christmas* flashed across my mind, and I heard Lucy's voice (which sounded distinctly like my mom's) diagnosing me: "If you can't stand the thought of being separated from your mobile device, you may have nomophobia."

Gulp. As much as I hated to admit it, my phone had a hold on me.

Determined to break free of it, I vowed that when I found my phone (which was exactly where one would expect it to be — on top of the cat's litter box), I would turn it off and not look at it for an entire week. I had to admit, the notion of zero screen time made my stomach do flip-flops. But I was intent on doing it. After all, I had lived my entire childhood without a phone in my pocket.

The difference was that, in my youth, there were no handy alternatives. For instance, as a kid I did homework with paper and pencil. Now, to remotely log into my work account required access that was set up through my phone. In my youth, Mom drove me to the YMCA so I could take Jazzercise classes with her (no sign-up required). Now I needed to open the app on my phone to reserve a spot in spin class twenty-four hours prior. Growing up, I dialed phone numbers, most of which I had memorized. Now I don't know anyone's digits.

I've grown accustomed to inputting regular reminders into my phone, alerting me to meetings, deadlines, and appointments. Therefore, my device rings, dings, and pings round the clock. During my sabbatical from my cell, however, I noticed that my world remained remarkably silent. As a result, I felt less stressed, less pressed and, as Mom had suggested, more in the moment.

I found that I rather liked this new "Zen zone." To celebrate, I strapped Trevyn into the stroller and went for a walk. As we passed pedestrians on a local trail, I noticed that some were with their dogs, others were with their friends, but all were with their phones. Literally every one of them was looking down at a device — except one elderly couple. They were walking, talking, and laughing. They weren't holding their phones; they were holding hands.

That's when it hit me how spot-on my mom was about the importance of living in the here and now and appreciating those moments. While my generation may know all about staying connected, the older generation knows how to connect with what matters.

— Christy Heitger-Ewing —

18

Fueled by Love

Being a full-time mother is one of the highest salaried
jobs... since the payment is pure love.
~Mildred Vermont

The sound of my mother pressing the foot pedal of her aging Singer sewing machine reached me in my room upstairs. We were living in what I thought was a mansion, as any large house appears to a girl of six. It was a stately home, far too spacious for our needs and no doubt overwhelming for my mother to care for when combined with all her other responsibilities. And yet, late into that evening and many others, the *chug, chug, chug* of the needle lifting in and out of the fabric filled the air.

Sometimes, I would watch her as she worked. She bent over the machine, the concentration clear on her pretty face, and carefully guided the light blue fabric with tiny white polka dots through the presser foot, each small stitch giving birth to the next. I could not fathom how she would make this dress appear like the one on the pattern. The little girl on the cover looked like a princess, and I could not wait until the dress was finished so I could be that girl.

The sewing project was born of necessity. Our small hometown carved into the Appalachian foothills had a tradition in which the students at the speck of an elementary school put on a Tom Thumb Wedding. And when we returned there after living away while my father attended law school, I was in the first grade. When the parts were handed out that spring, I was named a bridesmaid.

Although my dad was by then an attorney, times were still lean. The grand home was rented and sparsely furnished. Money was tight then, as it remained throughout my childhood, but my mother always found a way. And making sure I had a beautiful bridesmaid dress to take part in the pageantry was just another instance.

My mom would work her job outside the home, take care of the housework and cooking, meet all the demands of the family, and then sit down at that machine to piece together the dress. While she had some sewing skills, it wasn't something she did often, so there were frustrations during the process. Yet I never heard her complain about having to do it. If she resented the time she spent on it, I never knew, and I felt like the luckiest girl in the world that my mom was making me this wonderful dress. If actions speak louder than words, this one shouted "I love you" to the tops of the mountains surrounding our home.

When the dress was finished, it looked just like the picture, and it was a miracle to me. I remember my happiness and pride when putting it on for the big event. No store-bought dress since has ever made me feel like I did the night of the Tom Thumb Wedding all those years ago. It was as if a piece of my mother's heart was in every stitch.

Now I am a mom. And while I never put together a pint-sized formal gown for my daughters, I have stayed up nights laboring on similar projects fueled by love, including hemming a prom dress. I do it because that is what my mother gave me: the life lesson that it isn't about the money you spend, but the love you give.

— Kim Freeman —

19

The Lovely Month of May

A kind word is like a spring day.
~Russian Proverb

Early one crisp November morning, my mother dressed me in thick corduroy slacks, wrapped me in my father's flannel shirt, and then stuffed me into her bulky sweater. "Here," she handed me my slouchy-knit, oversized beanie cap, "you'll be needing this to keep your head and ears warm."

I slipped the cap over my head and ears. "Now come outside with me." Once outside, she handed me a brown paper sack that held something that smelled like wet dirt. "We need to plant bulbs before the first hard freeze." I knelt on the ground next to her, breathing in the soft scent of the dewy morning grass and the earthy smell of freshly turned-over soil.

"I've already dug the holes," she said. "So take each bulb from the bag, drop it in the hole, and then gently push the dirt back into the hole covering the bulb — like so."

I opened the sack. "These bulbs are ugly and look dead!"

"You're right. They're not at all pretty. But they're not dead; they're just sleeping until spring."

"And all the bulbs look alike," I continued, covering the bulbs and squishing the wet dirt between my fingers. "How do we know what they'll look like come spring?"

"We won't know for sure until spring, but that's the joy of gardening. We'll just have to be patient."

Soon after planting the bulbs, the autumn winds arrived, shaking the leaves off the trees. The days shortened, and the nights closed in chilly and long. By December, the snow and harsh sleet came, and the birds disappeared from the flower garden. Often, I stood on the back porch and watched my warm breath mingle with the icy cold air, wondering if the bulbs in her garden would come alive in spring. In January and February, sunless, harsh days prevailed, and winter's dreariness settled over me.

Although my mother's garden was frozen and bare, all winter long I clung to the hope that the flowers would bloom one day. Eventually, winter's harsh sleet became rain, and sunshine drenched the earth once again. But without the gentle spring heat, nothing grew in the garden — not even the weeds. Then March arrived, as did the warmth of the sun's rays. Once more, my breaths were invisible, and the birds returned to the garden.

One day in late April, I spotted some pink poking through the ground. My mother was excited when I showed them to her. "Perfect!" she said. "They'll be ready at just the right time."

A few days later, the flowers that had been tight buds began to open and had a deeper blush of pink. I stretched out my fingers to touch the silky pink petals; they were cooler than I'd expected and much smoother, too. I laid my head on the ground and tried willing them to open faster.

"Mother Nature has its way, its timing," my mother assured me. "And she's not ready yet. But a few more days of warmth, and the flowers will bloom. Just wait. We need to be ready, though."

A few days later, she took me to the local five-and-dime store where she gathered up tissue paper, colored ribbons, notecards, and all the discounted Easter baskets she could squeeze into her shopping cart. "Okay, now we're ready."

"Ready for what?" I asked

"To make May baskets, of course."

"May baskets? What are May baskets?"

"They are small baskets filled with fresh flowers and secretly left at someone's doorstep. The giver leaves the basket on the porch, rings the doorbell, and runs away." Her blue eyes sparkled and gleamed. "So when we get home, we'll cut the flowers that are blooming in the garden to make May baskets. Then tomorrow, May first, we'll get up bright and early and deliver them to our neighbors. Doesn't that sound like fun?"

"But… but… I waited all winter for the flowers to bloom, and they're so beautiful. And… and… I thought we were keeping them forever." I bit my lower lip. "Instead, we're taking the flowers out of the garden and giving them away *and* not telling our neighbors?"

"I know you're disappointed, sweetie, but flowers — like kindness — are meant to be shared. Their beauty is not ours to keep. You understand?"

"No!" I tilted my head down and frowned. "I don't understand. I want to keep the flowers… forever."

"I know you do, sweetie. But in the end, you'll understand that every drop of kindness you give away returns to bless you in another way. Just wait and see."

So later that afternoon, we snipped most of the flowers from the garden and arranged colorful bouquets. We tied each bouquet with colored ribbon, wrapped it in tissue paper, and then placed it in the refrigerator to stay fresh overnight.

"Before you go to bed tonight, I need you to write this message on the notecards. 'A May basket is a welcome spring treat. Someone thinks you're special and so sweet.'" She handed me a stack of her tiny notecards. "Once you've written the notes, I'll tie them to the baskets. Remember to use your best handwriting."

Afterward, I headed to bed but tossed and turned all night thinking about the flowers I'd miss.

Shortly after dawn the next morning, we loaded the May baskets into my brother's wagon. We began our journey through the neighborhood. At each house, we hid behind our neighbors' shrubs. I'd run to the front door, leave the basket on the porch, and then ring the doorbell, giggling as I ran for cover. We'd hunker behind the shrubs and watch our neighbors as they looked up and down the street, wondering who'd left the May basket on the doorstep.

Chapter
3

Gratitude

Diwali with My New Family

A mother gives you a life, a mother-in-law
gives you her life.
~Amit Kalantri, Wealth of Words

My husband, a Hindu from the state of Maharashtra, and I, a Muslim from the state of Uttar Pradesh, met and fell in love in college in New Delhi. We decided to get married, but marriage between a Hindu and a Muslim in India in the year 1999 was as implausible as a marriage between a human and an ape. The chasm between the two religions and cultures was too deep to be bridged by matrimony.

My husband's and my family tried their best to dissuade us, the star-crossed lovers, from our decision to marry each other, but we believed in our promise of love. We got married, but our inter-religion marriage wasn't founded on the smiles of our families, but on their broken hearts.

Both of us worked and lived in New Delhi after our marriage, away from our parents, and strived hard to sustain our bonds with them.

The festival of Diwali came just three months into our marriage. My husband booked our tickets to Indore, his parents' hometown, to spend the holiday with them. The first Diwali for a new bride is a reason for celebration with the extended family. So, the families of my mother-in-law's sister and brother were invited, too.

As soon as I landed at my in-laws' place, the stark differences between his and my cultures shook me. They spoke Marathi; I spoke

Hindi. They were strict vegetarians; I loved to eat chicken biryani. They served food in a certain fashion: daal in the center of the plate, vegetable to the right; I had no such customs.

My mother-in-law asked me to wear my mangalsutra around my neck at all times. I, a modern, independent woman, who earned more than my husband at that time, did not want to wear the symbol of being married, like a pennant, but I did.

I was seething, but I kept my lips sealed for the sake of my husband. I was sure my husband would have done the same for my family.

The night of Diwali, my mother-in-law asked me to wear a new sari she had bought for me. I stood staring at six yards of the beautiful red silk with golden zari borders that had been laid on the bed in the guest bedroom that my husband and I were allotted. I had never before dressed in a sari without anyone's help. I struggled to wrap the sari around my body — tucking it in and securing it with safety pins, but it did not cooperate.

An hour had passed already. My husband knocked. Everyone was waiting to start the Diwali puja. I asked him to help, but he demurred. It would be too embarrassing for him to be locked in the bedroom with his new wife at that time of the day. Tears ran down my face.

Then, my mother-in-law knocked gently. I let her in. She was resplendent in her maroon silk sari and matching mina jewelry. My eyes told her my story, and the look I saw in her eyes was not that of disgust, but of kindness. She helped me with draping the sari, forming each pleat with her expert fingers.

When she helped me pin the pallu of the sari on my shoulder, I could smell the faint onion and garlic on her fingers just like my mother's fingers.

She told me to ask her for help, woman to woman, through my one-week stay at her place. My relationship with her was starting to germinate.

With my sari in place, my head felt lighter by 100 pounds, at least. I emerged from the guest room, youth glowing on my cheeks, bangles adorning my arms and jhumkas dancing in my ears. My husband looked handsome in his traditional kurta-pajama, and he gave me a look that reinforced his promise of love to me.

For the Diwali Lakshmi puja, my father-in-law collected some token money from all the men present to put in the puja thali, so that the Goddess Lakshmi could bless their earnings. My mother-in-law asked me to fetch a few rupees from my purse to put in the thali.

"My daughter-in-law is an earning member of the family, too," she announced with palpable pride. "She even travels abroad for work."

My mother-in-law had spoken for me, for my equitable position in the family. She was my voice at that time when I chose to keep mum. My gratitude must have shown on my face.

After the puja, all of us went to light firecrackers on the terrace. Soon, it was dinnertime, and my mother-in-law excused herself to lay the table with all the dishes she had cooked. I volunteered to help, but she asked me to stay back and enjoy. That was so like my mother. I realized that mothers everywhere are one and the same.

My mother-in-law also kept reminding everyone to speak in Hindi so I could partake in the conversations. All the relatives were not fluent in Hindi, but they were trying their best for me. I tried to correct their grammar, and everyone laughed at each other's mistakes. They did not coerce me to speak in Marathi or to learn the language.

Thanks to my mother-in-law, I was enjoying the familial revelry and camaraderie.

I learned that the next day of Diwali, called the Padva, symbolized the love between a husband and wife. It was marked by some special rituals. The wife was supposed to touch her husband's feet, and the husband was to give her a gift in return as a blessing. My mother-in-law went first and was awarded a sari by my father-in-law. One of the aunts followed. She earned a gold necklace.

My heart thumped furiously. I whispered to my husband that, in my religion, we bowed down only to God and not to humans.

I saw him whispering something to my mother-in-law. She looked at the unease in my eye and nodded reassuringly. Now, she and I were reading the language of each other's face and eyes.

When it was our turn, my mother-in-law gave her verdict. "This couple is special. They were friends before they became husband and wife. They can only shake hands with each other." Everyone applauded and approved.

I shook my husband's hand, and he gave me a pair of gold earrings with a wink. He had been holding them as a surprise for me. A big smile, which is captured in the albums, broke out on my face and then was joined by tears of happiness and gratitude.

My mother-in-law had taken care of my concerns with such grace, without making me feel alien. She was so like my own mother.

— Sara Siddiqui Chansarkar —

21

Happy Birthday to Us

To me a birthday means celebrating the presence
of an individual in our lives.
~Meena Bajaj

It was just what I wanted, the perfect present, a one-size-fits-all — something that I'd long thought of buying for myself but never did. But somehow, my mom — with her special maternal instincts and motherly radar, with her uncanny ability to glean information from snippets of overheard conversations — figured it out all by herself and gave me that one gift I truly wanted.

Nothing else could ever say, "Happy Birthday, Son," like a large gift-wrapped box containing a brand-new Sawzall reciprocating saw.

Two months later, I put my newest tool through its paces while volunteering on a mission trip to Appalachia with my church. We were helping to make homes warmer, safer and drier. My trusty saw and I quite capably resolved a plethora of challenging cutting circumstances with ease and efficiency. One night, as I was reflecting on its versatility, I suddenly wondered what I had done to deserve such an awesome birthday present. Then came an even greater question: What does anyone ever do to deserve any special recognition for nothing more than having been born?

It occurred to me that aside from being the blue-eyed, blond, babbling bundle of joy that caused my parents' world to change, I'd done nothing to merit becoming the recipient of birthday cards and gifts.

It also occurred to me that if anyone truly deserved to be recognized for enduring nine long months of discomfort that included morning sickness, indigestion, anemia, and swollen ankles — if there was any one person who'd earned kudos for my birth — it was my mom.

It seemed so wrong for her to have done all the work and for me to receive a lifetime of birthday celebrations!

So, it was on that night in Appalachia, as I packed away my saw, that I knew I was going to do something about this.

The following year, on my birthday I surprised Mom with a beautiful floral arrangement. I would do this several more times over the coming years as we'd mutually note the anniversary of my birth.

Getting these annual arrangements to her should have been easy, but in truth, it wasn't. This mother and grandmother filled her life with a whirlwind of activities. While some of her flowers were dispatched to her home, not all of them were. Once, I surprised her by placing them inside her car outside the deli where she often stopped for a midmorning cup of coffee. Another time, I had them delivered to the hospital information desk where she was volunteering. Still another year, she found them at the food pantry where she helped out.

Although the delivery locations, as well as the arrangements themselves, would differ from year to year, the one thing that never changed was the verbiage on the enclosed card. My handwritten message to her was always the same: "Happy Birthday to Us, Love Steve."

My mom is no longer with us, but "my" birthday will always be "our" day.

— Stephen Rusiniak —

22

The Queen of the Special Project

Mothers are the only ones that think nothing is beyond
their control when it comes to their children.
~Ali Fazal

It didn't seem like a big deal when I landed in Mrs. Wilson's fifth-grade class. I wasn't even concerned when I learned she would require us to give oral reports and presentations. I liked her and accepted the fact that I would be spending my days with the "Empress of the Special Project." What I dreaded, however, was my mother's reaction to these assignments. I may have been hanging out with the Empress by day, but I was in the Queen's court at night.

Mine was the mother who read *Green Eggs and Ham* and followed it up with a special "green-egg breakfast." She took me horseback riding after I read and fell in love with *Black Beauty*. A rainy day was the perfect opportunity to cook or do art projects; a breezy day invited kite flying in the park. A creative monster lived inside my mom, and I feared it would rear its imaginative head every time I came home with a new assignment.

As it turns out, the fear was well founded. She had a lot of suggestions about what I could do to add "depth" to my projects. I balked at the idea of approaching experts in search of that "depth." There were battles and tears, but in the end my mother sent me out into the world with the single goal of making every presentation a great one.

Upon hearing of my assignment to give an oral report on the life of Vincent van Gogh, my mother said, "Wouldn't it be more fun for the class if you gave your report from the viewpoint of a family member?" Once I discovered that van Gogh had a sister named Wilhelmina, Mom helped me assemble a costume and listened as I rehearsed my biographical material. On the day of the report, I moved among my classmates, telling stories of "my brother's" depression, alcoholism and suicide. I don't know if my friends had "fun," but Mrs. Wilson was thrilled with my effort.

Next came the assignment to write about drug abuse in my community. "Do you know what you can do to make your report better?" Mom asked.

"Pass out samples to the class?" I quipped.

"Not what I had in mind. How about a visit to a drug-treatment facility?"

"I'd rather pass out drugs."

"When you call," she said, handing me the phone book, "tell them your name, explain your assignment, and ask to schedule an interview with a counselor."

A week later, a very nervous ten-year old — with her mother at her side — carried a tape recorder into the center like a gangly cub reporter. The therapist patiently answered all my questions and added insights of her own. Some clients even spoke with me about their addictions and gave me permission to use their gripping personal stories in my report. Mrs. Wilson marked my paper with a bold, red A.

"Pick any topic that interests you, learn all you can about it, and prepare a fifteen-minute oral presentation for the class." I chose the Special Olympics because I had a genuine interest in the organization. Somehow, my mother knew that the state headquarters were housed at a nearby college, and she quickly turned that knowledge into a "field trip." Before I knew it, I was knocking on their office door, seeking to glean what I could from them. Hours later, I came away with the history of the Special Olympics, their annual budget, fund-raising strategies and a video to show my classmates. I was also recruited to volunteer at the track-and-field event the following weekend. Mrs. Wilson was effusive as she praised the thoroughness of my report.

My next assignment was to give an oral report on India and the caste system. Mom was sure that our neighbor, Mrs. Patel, would be very happy to speak to my class about her culture. As I stood on her doorstep, making my request, Mrs. Patel looked anything but "very happy." She wore a traditional sari and had a small dot on her forehead. She was a shy, soft-spoken woman, and although the idea of speaking in front of a room full of children did not seem to excite her, she promised to recruit some of her more "outgoing" relatives to help.

On the day of the presentation, my mother and Mrs. Patel arrived with several other family members in tow. As it turned out, Mrs. Patel's sisters were thrilled to speak to my classmates, who were amazed at the invasion of vibrant silk saris, long black braids and lyrical Indian accents. Our visitors told us about daily life in India, the architecture and religious customs. They taught us a traditional dance and led an art project. As they cooked an authentic Indian meal for everyone, our classroom filled with the wonderful aroma of chicken stewing in exotic herbs and spices. I glanced toward the back of the room, where my mother and Mrs. Wilson looked on with identical expressions of delight.

Many years later, Mom and I laughed about my fifth-grade experiences. I lamented the fact that I didn't remember her "torturing" my brother and sister in the same way. "They had their own strengths," she explained. "You were such a creative thinker; it was my job to cultivate it. Mrs. Wilson just gave me the perfect opportunity to do it."

As the challenging — and often exhausting — fifth grade drew to its inevitable close, the "Empress" assigned one last project. We had been studying character development in literature, and she explained that cartoon characters were notoriously one-dimensional. Once we drew the name of a famous character out of a hat, we were to add an interesting backstory and fun details to help breathe life into them.

I was excited as I explained the assignment to my mother after school. "I drew Charlie Brown's name!"

"I wonder," she pondered, "if you could find the contact information for Charles Schulz!"

—Vicki Kitchner—

Tough Love

When you are a mother, you are never really alone in
your thoughts. A mother always has to think twice,
once for herself and once for her child.
~Sophia Loren

It was summer break, and my children and I were visiting my mom at her home in New Jersey. My mother and I sat at the table as usual updating each other on what was going on in the extended family — who was married or engaged, sick or promoted at work, the usual. Then my teenage daughter came in and interrupted, "Mom, can you do my hair today?" she asked.

"Sure, let me run out this afternoon and pick up the relaxer," I answered.

My mother smiled. "I don't miss those days," she said. Instantly, I flashed back to all the times my mother had to find the money to get my sister's and my hair relaxed at the salon. The hairdresser would charge sixty-five dollars per person for a relaxer, wash and set. As a single mother, that was not small change. My mother somehow managed, though.

I started retelling the story of one particular day when my mother sent my sister and me to the beauty parlor by ourselves on the public bus. My sister was thirteen, and I was ten. We had a 3:30 appointment, and my mom couldn't take us because she worked until 5:00. She told me to wait outside the school for my sister to pick me up so we could take the bus to the salon. Then she would pick us up there after she got off work.

I was scared. What if someone tried to follow us? What if we missed the stop? I had never ridden the bus without my mother before. My mother took one look at me and said, "You'll be just fine. Listen to your sister and help her look out for your stop." Then she gave my sister the bus fare and went off to work.

All day at school, I kept looking at the clock, dreading the end of the school day. When the time came, I went to the front of the school and waited for my big sister. She got there in a few minutes, and we walked quietly to the bus stop. A few high-school kids and a woman stood at the bus stop. My sister asked the woman if this bus was the Number 2 headed toward Clinton Avenue. The woman said, "Yes." I could tell that my sister relaxed a little.

We boarded the bus and stood in the aisle so we could look out of the windows for our Clinton Avenue stop. When we were almost there, the woman who spoke to my sister earlier tapped her on the shoulder and told her our stop was next. We thanked her and pulled the string to ring the bell. When we got off the bus, my sister took my hand and led me across the busy street to the salon. We called our mom from the salon's phone as soon as we got inside.

My mother sat there smiling while I retold the whole story. I asked her what was so funny. She said, "You know, that day I was a nervous wreck. I went to work, but the whole time I kept looking at the clock, thinking about my girls. I actually left work at 2:30 that day and came to your school. I waited in my parked car to see that you two got on the bus okay. I followed the bus all the way down to make sure you got off at your stop. I was so proud of you both that day."

"But Mom, if you were there the whole time, why didn't you just take us and save me the drama? I was so scared that day."

"Because, as scared as I was for you both, I was more afraid of not teaching you how to overcome fear in your life. My mother, your grandmother, was born in Jamaica and came to America by herself when she was twenty-two to make a better life for her family. She taught me that life is not lived without fear. Instead, it's the fear that pushes you to live and make the right choices. I needed to find a way to teach you and your sister that life lesson."

And I knew she was right. That day, I sat in the beautician's chair and forgot how scared I was; I grew more confident and daring. My heart filled with gratitude for my mother. I hope I can find a way to teach my children this important life lesson as well.

— Cherise Payne —

Mom Turned Mentor

One of the most important relationships we have is the
relationship we have with our mothers.
~Iyanla Vanzant

I'm ashamed to admit it, but there was a time when I thought my mother was stupid. I look back and wonder what in the world I was thinking. But the honest truth is, I disagreed with just about everything she said. I was offended by her tone. I didn't like her dinosaur-era beliefs. I wondered why she didn't "get" me. And I was convinced I knew more than she did during my angsty teen years.

Oh, boy. Did I ever have some growing up to do.

Mom not only worked, but she raised three kids and took excellent care of my dad, who commuted two hours a day for twenty years to a job he disliked. Oh, and we lived on a small farm in the middle of nowhere. So Mom took care of the animals when we didn't, which was most of the time. She drove us to school so we didn't have to take the bus. When I was busy pouting because she didn't show up for my volleyball games, she was canning peaches or making quilts or hanging our laundry on the clothesline.

Suddenly, I was in my twenties and facing brand-new responsibilities. Now *I* felt like the stupid one. Being an adult was hard. Paying my own bills and making my way in the world was not as much fun as I thought it would be. Sometimes, I secretly wished I was back at home, where my mother had always taken care of me. It was then that I realized just how good I'd had it.

I hit my thirties. By now, I thought my mother was a bona fide genius. Every bit of advice she gave me was spot-on, especially when I got married and had my sweet baby Emily. I felt so lucky that Mom was a registered nurse, for I was a very nervous first-time mother. I could call her about anything and everything. She was my safety net as I raised my own daughter. She became my mentor as well as my mom.

When I was in my forties and facing a divorce, I realized my mother was not only a wise woman, but a staunch ally. At this juncture, I recalled how she had always defended me, even back in high school when I was a smart-mouth teenager. And she was certainly there for me as I adjusted to the reality of single motherhood. Oh, the conversations we had.

"Mom, I'm scared," I confided.

"You're smart, and you're strong," she'd tell me. "You can do this."

"Mom, I think I'm losing my faith," I whispered.

"Hang on to your faith. God will get you through this. You'll see."

"Mom, I'm so angry at my ex," I exclaimed.

"Me, too," she said. "I want to strangle him."

It felt so good to have someone on my side, no matter what. I could vent, and she would listen with unconditional love. But it felt even better to have a fiercely protective "mother bear" who was once again my safety net. She let me know I could always come home. Emily and I would never be without a roof over our heads. But the real icing on the cake was that she raised me with enough *chutzpah* to make it on my own.

Having an emergency resource named "Mom" was empowering. It gave me the courage to leave corporate America and start my own business. It allowed me to stretch, take risks and chase dreams. I knew if I failed, Mom would catch me, and that gave me wings.

We've always lived near each other, usually within an hour's drive. Over the years, we developed a friendship like no other. Now that I'm in my fifties, Mom is relaxed enough to take off her "mom cap" and do a little venting herself. I'd never heard her say a cross word about my dad — she was always protective of him. But now she fussed a bit, knowing I wouldn't say a word. And get this — she actually apologized for anything she did to hurt, offend or bug me, stretching back to high school.

Wow. That knocked my socks off. I should have been the one apologizing for being such a pain in the neck. But to Mom, I was a joy. She didn't dwell on my annoying behavior or bad attitude from thirty-plus years ago. She simply reveled in my accomplishments and spoiled her granddaughter. She might not have had the luxury of attending my volleyball games, but she certainly attended Emily's. She didn't miss an awards ceremony, graduation, or birthday party for that child.

I'm so proud of my mom, and even prouder to be her daughter. I thank God for her unending support, her wit and wisdom, and especially her advice. But the biggest blessings are the lessons I learned from her — how to forgive, ask for forgiveness, focus on the positive, and overcome.

My mom taught me how to count my blessings. I can never repay her for the many roles she has played in my life, but I can reciprocate. Now, she never has to worry about a roof over her head. She can always come to my home. I will advocate for her, defend her, and protect her in her golden years. It's the least I can do for my mom — my mentor and my friend.

— Melanie Saxton —

25

The Gift of Spontaneity

Surprise is the greatest gift which life can grant us.
~Boris Pasternak

My pink duffle bag hit my calf as I walked. Other children laughed and screamed around me as I trudged across the school lawn toward my after-school babysitter's street. I almost didn't hear my mother and grandmother yelling my name from the curb.

My mother was standing beside our big red station wagon, her face shining bright, waving me over. My grandmother, sitting in the front passenger seat, was leaning through the open window and smiling with an eagerness I'd never seen from her.

"What are you doing here?" I asked in awe, surprised to see my mom before 6:00 p.m. I didn't remember her being at my elementary school after the first day of kindergarten. She was the first generation of working moms, and while I was proud of her, I never expected to see her after school.

They were there to whisk my older sister, a third-grader, and me off for a weekend trip to an amusement park. They had packed our bags, and they both exuded such excitement that I felt a rush I'd never known before.

We drove into the night toward our destination, crossing two state borders along the way. There was confusion in the front seat as it grew dark, a map rustling as it was folded and refolded, and adult conversation I couldn't quite follow. But in the back seat with my sister, who at that age still liked me enough not to make me miserable, I felt adventurous and unafraid. I leaned my head against the window and watched the scenery until it grew into only passing streetlights.

I awoke as we drove up to the hotel, and the four of us lugged our bags into our room. I'm sure a dinner occurred at some point, but I don't remember. What is vivid from that first night in the hotel is a bright red swimsuit and splashing and jumping amid the smell and fogginess of an indoor hotel pool.

Snippets of the weekend remain — waiting in lines, getting splashed by jumping whales, and Richard Simmons, who was a guest star at the park. It was a good time, we all got along, and the activities were amusing. But it was that first night of travel, of the unexpected, that stuck with me — the surprise of being picked up after school and whisked away for an adventurous weekend.

More than thirty years later, I woke my eight-year-old daughter before dawn to whisk her away on a surprise weekend trip to an amusement park. With her bag already packed in the trunk, snacks already in the cooler for the road, and the GPS ready to instruct, we were off on our own adventure. My own child is much more well traveled than I was as a child and, I'll be honest, she'd been to this amusement park no less than a hundred times before. It really shouldn't have been a big deal, but it was likely the best visit ever because it was a spontaneous event, an adventure.

As far as childhood memories go, it doesn't get any more vivid than that weekend, which had a huge influence on the adult I became. I'm sure my mother had no idea what she'd done for me. I would never quite be satisfied with staying put. I'd move during my adulthood, over and over and over again. She ignited a passion for travel, for the unexpected, for change.

My mom is in her seventies now and travels all over the world, usually by herself. I am in my forties now, and I travel all over the world with my teenage daughter. Occasionally, the three of us meet up, and it's always a gloriously good time, but it's the best when it's spur-of-the-moment. Nothing ever quite compares to the unexpected trip. The spontaneous adventures in life continue to thrill me. My

26

Enriched

One good mother is worth a hundred schoolmasters.
~George Herbert

My mother's family was so poor she didn't know what Halloween or Valentine's Day were until she was an adult. People in her region had no time for such frivolities. Born in 1930, Mom grew up in Oklahoma's Dust Bowl amid the Great Depression. Her grandparents reared eleven kids of their own and then cared for Mom off and on throughout her childhood. They struggled as farmers even under the best of circumstances and were no-nonsense folks. But they loved their granddaughter and instilled in her a strong work ethic.

Mom graduated from high school and went on to work in a bank where she met my dad, a photographer. They married, and she determined to give her three daughters more than she'd had. Though she could have continued working, Mom felt it was important that she stay home while her children were young. Our family wasn't poor, but neither did we live the high life on a photographer's pay. So she looked for ingenious ways to enrich our lives without using much money.

One of my earliest memories is of Mom asking if I'd like to take art lessons. I loved to draw and color. Mom noticed and found a small, inexpensive class taught by students at the local college of art. It soon became apparent I had no natural talent, but she gave me the opportunity to explore the possibility.

We often spent family time watching nature shows such as *Mutual* of Omaha's *Wild Kingdom* and *The Undersea World of Jacques Cousteau*. One year, near my birthday, Mom learned that an adventurer who had explored the Galápagos Islands was scheduled to appear at a local auditorium. She and Dad took me to the lecture for my birthday. Was I upset at not getting the latest plaything or a new dress? Far from it. I was elated to know my parents wanted to share this exotic new world with me. For another birthday, they took me to see a live production of Jane Austen's *Pride and Prejudice*. I reveled in the poetic prose re-enacted on the stage, my first exposure to theater.

Though we weren't Jewish, Mom once arranged for me to hear Israel's military leader and foreign minister Moshe Dayan speak. I knew little about politics or Israeli history, but I was fascinated by the man with the thick accent and the black patch he wore over one eye.

Visits to museums and the zoo were a staple of our childhood. Most were free at that time, and we made the rounds regularly. We knew and loved the historic old homes in downtown Memphis. And, of course, we toured the art gallery on many occasions.

One of our forays into the world of culture didn't turn out so well. When my music teacher offered to take our class to see *Aida*, my mom signed up to chaperone as she'd never attended an opera. The singing was impressive, but listening to incomprehensible Italian arias until midnight made us wish for a boring TV show. We agreed those were the longest four hours of our lives. The highlight for me was when Mom pointed to the teacher's husband, who had fallen asleep. We laughed when his wife elbowed him, and he popped up straight in his seat. Apparently, operas weren't his favorite form of entertainment either.

Not all our activities were centered on educational pursuits. Mom became expert at squirreling away nickels and dimes, and she led us in redeeming soft drink bottles and other fundraising activities so we could enjoy more amusing pastimes. Once a week during the summer, we packed a picnic lunch and left our inner-city home to travel to north Mississippi where we visited a swimming area with a white sand beach. We spent glorious days there honing the skills we learned at YMCA swimming lessons. During the winter, Mom scanned newspapers for upcoming Ice Capades shows. After performances ended, local kids could use the temporary rink to learn to ice skate, something our warm southern winters never permitted.

Mom took advantage of any opportunity she could find to help us develop skills or explore options we might never have considered. After I spent a couple of days in the hospital following an accident, I decided I wanted to be a nurse, something most little girls say at one time or another. But Mom took me seriously and arranged for me to spend the night at a nursing students' dorm and tour the school the next day. Thanks in part to my mother's encouragement, I became a registered nurse.

Today, when I study an old picture of my mother, I understand the term "dirt poor." Mom looks to be about five and wears a colorful shift over a white blouse. A jaunty hat sits to one side atop her curly hair. Her attire contrasts sharply with her grandparents' drab clothing and sturdy work shoes. They are standing in front of their home, a wood shack of rough boards that never saw whitewash, much less paint. The Oklahoma dust creeps up to the knees of her grandfather's pants and blows through the open doorway onto what appears to be a dirt floor. It is the picture of abject poverty. It is also the picture of hope.

Most survivors of the Depression wanted their children to have a better start in life than they did. It wouldn't have taken much for our childhood to be easier than our mom's, but she didn't stop there. She made sure we experienced as much of the world as possible. We weren't rich, but we were enriched, thanks to Mom.

— Tracy Kirk Crump —

27

Letting Go of Fear

Action cures fear, inaction creates terror.
~Douglas Horton

Jumping out of a plane at 10,000 feet to do a tandem skydive was not on my to-do list. I've done a lot of adventurous things in my life, and I have been quite a daredevil, but I've always been terrified of heights.

Boarding the small, single-engine, door-less plane dressed in my purple, one-piece suit, adorned with goofy goggles and a multicolored foam, pointy hat, was not quite what I had pictured myself doing when I went to New Orleans, but my host April had other ideas. A couple of weeks before my visit, she booked us for tandem jumps as part of our three-day side trip to The Big Easy. I might have said "no," but when I realized the date of the reservation, I knew that I had no choice but to do it because it was going to fall on what I feared would be my mother Denise's last birthday.

My relationship with my mother was confusing to me, as it is for many adoptees. As far as my mother was concerned, there was nothing to be confused about. I was her child, and she was my mother, even though she didn't conceive or carry me. I came home to her from The Good Samaritan Agency at seventeen days old, and from that moment on she made a point of making sure that I wasn't treated any differently than my brother or sister, who were her biological children.

She loved me enough that when I asked for her help in finding my birth parents, she gave me her blessing and provided me with enough information that I was able to locate them just a few days after my search began. When I met them at age twenty-five, she welcomed them into her home and our family.

She celebrated with me when I found out that my birth father was a member of the Passamaquoddy Tribe of Maine. She was so happy that we finally had an answer to the question that I had been asked my entire life, "Is she part Native American?"

Before she adopted me, in a four-year span, my mother had lost her sixteen-year-old brother in a swimming accident, her husband from complications after back surgery, and carried two babies full-term, only to have them die within twenty-four hours. She eventually adopted me because she wanted another child. As a baby, I brought her healing after all of those losses. We had a special bond.

As a result of my mother's losses and traumas, she had many fears. Mostly, she feared losing someone or something terrible happening to her or someone she loved. She did not get to enjoy the fullness of life. Often, her fears kept her from doing new things, going to new places, and meeting new people.

I have been quite the opposite of her, in part because I saw how much she missed out on in life. My mother didn't take risks or expand her horizons because she was held captive by her fears. She always thought of me as her daredevil because I wasn't afraid of much, and she called me her "wanderer" because I was always off on some kind of adventure.

One of the positive things about her Alzheimer's diagnosis was that eventually she let go of most of her fears. Though she had spent much of her life worrying about what might happen or what could happen, those worries were lost as her mind began to empty its memories.

I almost didn't take the trip to Louisiana. Right before I left, she took a turn for the worse, but my friends, family and the nursing-home staff encouraged me to go because they all knew that I had dedicated four years of my life to her. They encouraged me to take a break to gain strength for the final stretch.

I made the jump that day to honor her life and to acknowledge that she had raised me in such a way that I have been able to overcome many fears and live an adventurous lifestyle.

Just before we plunged out of the plane, I whispered, "Mum, I know you are in the process of crossing over, so if you can, please keep me safe because I'm not ready to cross over yet."

A second later, we rolled out of the plane into a forty-second free fall. My suit fluttered in the wind like a flag in a hurricane as the force pulled back the skin of my face. There was the sharp jerk upward when the parachute deployed, followed by the slow seven-minute descent.

The first thing I said when I hit the ground and unbuckled my harness was, "What would my mother think if she knew what I had just done?"

The next morning, I received a call that she was close to death, so I cut my vacation short and flew home. I got to her bedside in the middle of the night and was alone with her for the last three hours of her life. I held her hand, sang her favorite hymns, and stroked her forehead as she left this world and went to whatever may lie beyond this place.

As I shared that moment with her I realized that she was indeed my mother in every sense of the word. Her love, encouragement and life story helped me to overcome many fears in life in order to travel to far-off places, meet many interesting people and take risks.

The life lessons my mother taught helped me to believe in myself. That confidence has helped me many times before and after my jump. It will no doubt lead to many more adventures.

— Wendy Newell Dyer —

28

That Darn Work Ethic

If you want children to keep their feet on the ground,
put some responsibility on their shoulders.
~Abigail Van Buren

When I was twelve, my parents wanted a pool. A concrete pool with blue tile around the edges. We lived in not-so-sunny Tacoma, Washington, where we reveled in our four days of summer each year, but this didn't faze these sun worshipers. No, we would carve out a slice of Palm Springs in the North and bask in whatever heat the stingy sun would impart to its disciples.

This was long before the days of credit cards and home-equity loans. Dad was a teacher, so there wasn't a lot of money. But we had the nicest lawn in the county, and Mom's roses looked as gorgeous as any on the cover of her magazines. So we started a yard-care business. It was a good match. Dad bought a truck — a metallic green Chevy — and tossed a mower and tools in the back. He took out a classified ad and was immediately swamped with customers. I was expected to traipse along on weekends and during the summer to help out.

On most days, I loved it. We left early with fat lunches that Mom packed the night before. We might stop for a shake and eat lunch together on the tailgate, swinging our legs to some country song on the radio. Dad paid me twenty bucks a week. I was rich and got to spend all day with my dad. Life was pretty good.

One day, however, I didn't want to go. While I worked all day, bleeding and sweating my way to wealth, my friends played baseball at the field or rode their bikes to the Safeway. I was twelve. I wanted a little bit of summer. So, one morning, I said, "No." It was weird. I kind of expected the seas to part. I absolutely expected lots of yelling. At the very least, I expected to be dragged to the truck by my ear. But Mom and Dad just looked at each other. Dad walked out to the truck. "Fine," Mom said. "Stay home if you like. Sheesh. We're not slave drivers, you know." Dad came back in and phoned one of my friends to help for the day. That was it, and everyone was happy.

Dad left, and I got dressed. Mom got me breakfast, and I was feeling good about my place in the world. I made my way to the front door and yelled to Mom that I was going to Doug's. Before I had even reached for the doorknob, the world hiccupped. My mother's head spun a full one-eighty while she kept washing dishes. "Oh, no, you're not. You're not going anywhere." That part about not being slave drivers? That was out the window.

"But… I don't have to go to work. You said so."

"You don't have to go to work with your father, but you are not going to play." There was a heavy emphasis on *don't, father,* and *not.* "You are darn well going to work around here all day. You'll get the same breaks you get with your dad, and I'll make your lunch. You can start with weeding the back rhodies, and we'll keep going until your dad gets back."

It was a genius plan. I worked all day without the breaks I usually got driving from yard to yard with Dad. There was no milkshake. No cooling off in the shade for a minute. And Mom? Until she died, there were no two men on the planet who could keep up with her when she started working. She defined "taskmaster."

I pulled weeds. I swept the garage and the drive. I cleaned my room. I vacuumed. I worked right up to break time and lunch and kept at it until Dad drove up the driveway with the truck. Mom made sure that I was in the front when Dad drove up, too. He hopped out of the truck and made a big show of pulling out a crisp five and handing it to my friend. With money in his pocket, my buddy waved as he ran home, yelling over his shoulder that Dad could call him anytime.

He never needed to. I learned my lesson. I never skipped a day again. And we got our pool. Which I enjoyed on my few days off.

— Dennis Mitton —

29

Mom's First and Last Vacation

Creating memories is a priceless gift. Memories will
last a lifetime; things only a short period of time.
~Alyice Edrich

A s a child, I hoped, dreamed and prayed to vacation someday with my parents, but my mom was agoraphobic. Therefore, it never happened.

Then I grew up and married. My husband was happy to take me to see the things I most desired, like mountains, oceans, nature and lovely historic places, but I still longed to take my parents on a vacation with me. I'd go home and give Mom all the details and say, "You would love it, Mom!"

"You must begin dialysis soon," her doctor informed her in February 2004. We walked slowly to the car, both of us in our own world of thoughts.

Our drive home was quiet. Mom was sixty-nine. Finally, she broke the silence. "I am not going on that machine. God will decide when to call me home." She sighed deeply. "My only regret is that I've never seen the ocean, never gone on a vacation."

I thought of all the things I was busy doing and wondered if we could change any of them. Then I heard a small voice saying, "Business will always be there, but your mother may not." The following week, while working, I heard the same words again. "Business will always be there, but your mother may not."

Could I interrupt my busy schedule to take my parents to the ocean? Would they go? I shared my feelings with my husband. He had his doubts, too. He asked, "Would we be able to talk her into really going?" We both agreed we must try.

To lessen her fear, I waited until two days before we were to leave to tell her our plans. My siblings didn't think I'd pull it off without having her in the hospital somewhere along the way. But she surprised me. She began packing that very night.

We headed to the beaches of Charleston, South Carolina, via the Great Smoky Mountains. She admired the picturesque scenery along the way and marveled at the majestic mountain beauty. I'd never seen her smile so much.

The most breathtaking moment came at her first view of the endless blue of the Atlantic Ocean. Her eyes shone, and then she gasped, "Isn't God awesome!" as joyful tears flowed down her cheeks. She picked up a seashell and examined it reverently. The ocean sunrises and sunsets thrilled her beyond measure. In fact, she viewed every new sight with awe. She was like a child on her first major adventure. Many people told me that, when she arrived home, she called and gave them all the details of her first vacation and how much she loved it.

Mom died in her sleep only two weeks after our return from her dream trip. Had I placed business first, this opportunity would have been lost forever.

— Linda J. Hawkins —

Take a Bow, Mom

I can no other answer make, but, thanks, and thanks.
~William Shakespeare

We were driving over a hundred miles — one way — to attend an annual awards ceremony for state newspapers. I'd been informed I was among the finalists in my category, and Mom had decided to accompany me on my road trip.

"You must remember to thank me and also tell them you got your sense of humor from me," she said.

"Uh-huh," I said absentmindedly. We drove on in silence for a few minutes. It was an unfamiliar road, and I needed to concentrate fully on my driving.

Meanwhile, Mom pretended to pout. "Where else would you have gotten it?"

"I don't think there will be any speeches made," I said. "These awards are for the entire state, for many circulation sizes, and hundreds of first-, second-, and third-place winners will be announced."

"Then why are we going?" asked Mom.

"Well… uh… I just thought it would be cool to be there when my name was announced."

"Right," said Mom. "And I'm going with you because I just thought it would be cool to hear my daughter's name announced, and then hear her thank her mother."

I grinned. "Thanks for coming with me, Mom."

Just as I'd suspected, the venue was huge, with hundreds of chairs crammed into a slightly darkened room. Three large projectors were strategically placed, aimed at three large screens.

Apparently, there were so many awards to announce for each circulation size that the only way to get through them all in less than four hours was to project the category, circulation size, home newspaper, winning names, and a few of the judges' comments on the screens.

Third place was projected to the left, second place to the right, and first place appeared in the middle. I could tell right away there would be no time for anyone to say much of anything, and I relaxed a little.

We quickly found good seats, and then I went to the bathroom while Mom saved our places. When I returned, she got up to go.

"Notice that I let you go first," she whispered as she passed my chair. "Don't forget how much a mother sacrifices for her children."

I snorted ice water out my nose and grabbed a paper napkin.

It seemed to take forever before they got to the "Humorous, Personal Experience Newspaper Column" category, but my moment had finally arrived. Mom reached over and squeezed my hand.

Third place appeared on the left screen, but it wasn't my name. After a few seconds, second place followed on the right-hand screen, and it also wasn't my name. Mom squeezed my hand tighter.

Then my name appeared in the center screen, and the announcer even pronounced it correctly!

And so help me, I could not restrain myself. With my big, booming, former elementary-schoolteacher voice, I yelled at the top of my lungs, "THANK YOU, MOM!"

The audience erupted into laughter. I leaned over and whispered in Mom's ear, "How was that?"

She let go of my hand, took the paper napkin out from under her water glass, and wiped her eyes. "It's so nice to feel appreciated."

Then I started crying, too, grateful that the room was fairly dark, that the awards continued to be announced, and that no one was paying any attention to us.

And ever after, I made sure I frequently told my mom how much

Chapter
4

Role Models

31

Mom's Spark

*If I have done anything in life worth attention, I feel
sure that I inherited the disposition from my mother.*
~Booker T. Washington

All my life, I have been a creative person. It's one of my best qualities. People ask me all the time how I come up with the things that I do. It didn't come from thin air. My mother had a lot to do with it. She was special, and everyone was aware of it.

Mom was a brilliant woman who held a bachelor's degree in English and two master's degrees — one in Women's Studies and one in Education. Although qualified for a career in higher education, she felt the need to teach where she felt most needed and could make the greatest impact on her community.

As an elementary schoolteacher, she shared her vast knowledge with the neighborhood children, and I was no exception. She taught me the same things she taught the older kids so that I could have an advantage when I became their age.

We weren't well-off or even middle-class. A teacher's salary in the inner city could only buy so much, but my mother did what she could. One thing she did was bring home books to read to me. She read to me every night when I was growing up.

One day, we both realized something: Mom had literally read to me all the books from the school's library. So, she decided to reread some of the more entertaining books we had.

I don't know if she felt that I was bored, or if she herself was the one thoroughly unentertained, but one night she changed my life with a simple act. I asked, "Mom, are you gonna read the story about the pig that ate too much again?"

She replied, "Know what? No, I don't think I will. I… I think I'm gonna tell you another story."

My mother began to tell me a story about a boy with a magic notebook; anything he wrote in it became reality. She went on for what seemed like thirty minutes. It was so exciting. The characters were relatable, the descriptions were vivid, and the story was unlike anything I'd ever heard.

For the next few weeks, my mother's stories were magical and extraordinary. At school, I couldn't wait to tell my friends about the new stories I heard. I even told my teachers about the stories and asked if they had the books that went along with my mother's wondrous tales. My teachers tried and tried, but they couldn't find any books from which my mother could have taken these amazing stories. I was ridiculed by my classmates for lying, which made me upset with my mother for setting me up to be the butt of so many jokes.

One night, after a particularly rough day of peer cruelty, I went to bed after dinner. I didn't watch *Who's the Boss?* or *Growing Pains*. Mom knew something was wrong. She walked into my room after cleaning the kitchen and asked why I was in bed. I told her it was because the kids at school were making fun of me for lying about the stories she told. I remember asking why she would tell me stories from books that didn't exist. My mother laughed in her warm way and sat next to me on my bed. She rubbed my head to comfort me because, at this point, I was crying.

"Son, there's something you need to know about the stories we read. Those stories don't just come from a machine that makes the stories, like a doll or an action figure. They come from inside a person's head; that person puts those thoughts and ideas on paper. A publishing house then turns them into a book.

"Do books exist with my stories in them? No, baby, they don't. It's because they are my stories, and they come from my own thoughts and ideas. They're just not on paper. But you can be that person whose thoughts and ideas are put on paper. Maybe they can be the book that someone else's mother will read to their child. That is, if you want to. I make up my own stories all the time. You can too, you know? All you have to do is find interesting people who do interesting things, and describe what they do in an interesting way. Put it on paper, and you've got yourself a book."

As I grew up, I took my mother's advice and found that a world of my own imagination was much more entertaining than a world that had been created for me. I also learned just how remarkable my mother truly was. Even the greatest writers of all time suffered from writer's block and took years to come up with an idea for a story. My mother was able to stretch the limits of creativity by coming up with a different story with new characters, settings, and plotlines every single night. There were no days off or resting between deadlines. She was able to deliver every time she opened her mouth.

My mother died when I was nine. The sadness drove me into a hole from which I never thought I'd escape. However, in all that darkness, as I drowned in the tears of losing someone so special, I still had her with me. I had her stories. I had all the times she made up a tale to comfort, uplift, or inspire me. Not only did I take those times to help me get through one of the toughest times of my life, but I turned them into something special, something real. With her watching over me, I became an author of science fiction.

When I opened the box containing copies of my first published novel, my wife asked what was wrong because I was crying. It was so bittersweet. I replied that I just wished my mother were there to see this happen. Although the book says "by Weston L. Collins," I still see my mother's name. It's funny that, after all this time, she still takes care of me, and she still reads to me. Only this time, I make sure her stories become novels everyone can read. Now the world can share story time with my mom.

— Weston L. Collins —

32

Teaching by Example

*We are not put on earth for ourselves, but are placed
here for each other. If you are there always for others,
then in time of need, someone will be there for you.*
~Jeff Warner

I was six years old the summer a new family moved into the house next door. There was a mother, three teenagers, and a girl about my age. One day I noticed the girl was watching me shyly as I played with my dolls on our front steps.

"Hello, I'm Julie," I said with a smile. "Do you like dolls?"

She nodded and came closer.

I held out a rag doll. "Her name is Molly. What's yours?"

"Frances." She took Molly, tucked her under her chin and cuddled her soft body.

Frances and I became best friends. We both loved playing with all the wonderful accessories that went with dolls. I had lots of tiny clothes and a toy baby carriage, and our imaginations were limitless. We never disagreed about any game, and she seemed to be the perfect friend. I was too young to notice what was really going on in her life, but my mother did.

Mom noticed that we always played at our house, and Frances never invited anyone into the rooms her family rented in the house next door. Her mother went off to work very early in the morning and came back looking very tired. Her teenage sister, who was supposed to be watching Frances, spent more time smoking cigarettes and laughing with boys. And her two older brothers were a bit wild and never at home. Mom also noticed that Frances never brought any toys with her, she was always hungry, and her clothes were often too small and not very clean.

Mom never mentioned any of that to me. But she did ask, "Would you mind if I gave Frances some of the clothes you have grown out of? You are so much taller than her, and you can't wear last year's trousers or skirts anymore."

Frances was thrilled with the new clothes, and her mother came to our door for the first time to thank us.

Mom began to spend more time with Frances and me, taking us on shopping trips and errands around town. She and I had always done kitchen jobs together, but now the three of us were baking cookies, making lunches and washing up together. Frances was always eager to help with anything, as long as Mom was there. And sometimes they would just sit together and chat while I was off doing something else.

Dad began including Frances in our weekend activities as well. She still went home every night, but she was with us all day. She had become more like a sister than a friend. And sometimes, after Frances had gone home, my parents joked that they had almost adopted her!

We went to different schools, so we didn't see each other as often when the summer ended. But we still spent weekends together, all four of us! And when the next summer came, we were inseparable again.

That routine continued until we were both young teenagers. But then her mother announced that she was moving back to Ireland, where they had come from originally. Frances was devastated and begged to stay here. But the decision was made, and they left Canada. We wrote for a while, but we both found new friends and our letter writing dwindled to nothing.

Ten years later, my mom called to say that a letter from Frances had arrived. She had a good job and had married a wonderful man. She wondered if I would like to start writing again. We picked up our friendship as if we'd never been apart. I could "hear" her voice through her written words, and we had years of news to catch up on. Her letters were filled with optimism and happiness.

Then Frances had a baby, and suddenly everything went black. She wrote that the doctors thought it was postpartum depression, and that might have been part of it. But Frances knew it was far deeper than that. The dark void she felt overwhelmed her. She felt helpless. Then one day she telephoned me and poured out the whole sad story. I will never forget what she said.

"The deep and abiding love that I feel for my baby reminds me of how unloved I was. My father had been ill and unemployed for years before I was born, so I was the last straw. My mother was already struggling to survive. I understand that, but my father died when I was just four, and from then on I was their scapegoat. Everyone took their frustrations out on me."

Then Frances's voice broke. "My mother hated me and told me once that I should never have been born."

I struggled to find words of comfort and support.

She continued, "I've spent years trying to erase that pain, and now I am trying to concentrate on loving my tiny daughter. Your letters are so important to me. I hope you can continue to write even if I am not always able to write back."

I wrote constantly, rarely receiving a reply. Then one day a letter from her husband arrived saying that Frances had been admitted to a psychiatric hospital for treatment.

He wrote pleadingly, "I have hired a nanny for the baby, but I'm at my wits' end. I don't know what to do to help her, but your letters are the only things that seem to keep her going. She reads them over and over, and tells me all about your mother and the things she did for her. If you could possibly continue to write, I would be eternally grateful."

So I did. I wrote about those wonderful summer days so long ago and all the things we did with my mom and dad.

Frances fought a long and brave battle against her mental demons, and she eventually won. When she was able to write again, she told me something marvellous.

"Your mother saved me. Without her love and attention when I was little, I would never have survived my awful childhood. And

I would never have been able to dig myself out of this pit of despair I've been in. I have used your mother's example as my guide to be a good person and care for my daughter as your mother cared for you and me. She was my guardian angel."

Before Mom died, Frances was able to return to Canada for a visit with me and to see Mom one more time. They had a tearful and wonderful reunion. Frances and I are both in our sixties now and e-mail regularly.

My mother taught me many things, but this was her most valuable lesson: Always be kind to those you meet and don't underestimate the little things in life. Watching her gentle example and seeing the life-changing results decades later were powerful. We will never know how or when our acts of kindness will affect others, but it's always better to try.

—Julia Lucas—

33

My Hallmark Mom

What a wonderful thing is the mail,
capable of conveying across continents
a warm human hand-clasp.
~Author Unknown

You know those sappy Hallmark commercials you hate to love? Those moments that tell a teeny, tiny story of someone who "cares enough to send the very best" expression of their love? Those commercials always remind me of Mom.

Mom was an avid and wonderful card giver. For as long as I can remember, she spent hours searching for just the right birthday card or the perfect anniversary card. She'd find get-well cards to match the personality of someone who needed a little love, encouragement, or kindness. On Valentine's Day, everyone got a unique and touching card that was always a keeper. Then there were the cards for St. Patrick's Day, Easter, Thanksgiving, and even Veterans Day for my retired Lt. Col. husband.

At Christmastime, Mom would set up the card table in her bedroom and spend hours choosing and signing and addressing Christmas cards. I came to realize that for her, Christmas cards weren't just a social expectation or a holiday tradition. They were her way of giving a little piece of herself and acknowledging that she valued friendship and family. They were a gift from her heart, not just an obligatory tradition.

When someone died, she'd find just the right card for those left behind, and then she'd personally deliver it to the funeral home or memorial service. My phone visits with her often consisted of her talking about attending a wake or funeral, sometimes several in a week. She seemed compelled to show her love and support in a time of need.

When I got married fifteen years ago, I revisited my special box that held all the cards Mom had sent me through the years. I spent some time reading them again and realized that she was not only a thoughtful card giver, but also an eloquent writer. Her notes were full of personal, loving, encouraging comments written in prose so meaningful and memorable that, even years later, they bring tears to my eyes. As I closed the box, I dubbed her my Hallmark Mom and have called her that affectionately ever since.

When she needed to move into an assisted-living facility, her many boxes of cards were spared. Some went with her. Others went into storage. We found hundreds of pieces of cardstock that were chosen with love and care for others. She never got to send them all, but she bought each and every card with love — to bless someone and show she cared.

Mom passed into heaven three weeks shy of her ninety-fifth birthday, but she will always be my Hallmark Mom. And to all whose lives she touched with her cards, she has become the Hallmark Queen of Hearts.

— Susan G. Mathis —

34

In My Genes

As the purse is emptied, the heart is filled.
~Victor Hugo

I've always thought of my mother Lee-Ann as a superhero. Not that she can fly or shoot lasers out of her eyes, but because she never runs out of room in her heart for anyone or anything.

I could write about all of the wonderful things she has done, but I want to focus on the one project she does every year that has shaped my whole family and everyone around us: She collects money she finds in the washer and dryer, and she puts it in a little jar that we refer to as "The Charity Jar." Every year, she takes this money and puts it toward something—a cause, an act of kindness, anything that can help someone. Sometimes, she buys coffees for the next people in line at a coffee shop. Other times, she buys something for an organization that needs it.

If you ask her about this tradition, she will tell you that she is carrying on something that her mother used to do around the holidays. If you ask anyone else who knows her, however, they will tell you that she has a huge heart. She manages to get our whole family involved in this movement every year. Last year, she helped an organization where I volunteered—Ruth's Place—a homeless women's shelter in Wilkes-Barre, Pennsylvania.

I had been helping a professor run a writing workshop in the shelter when I noticed the wish list on the wall: comforters, a DVD player, a coffee maker and supplies. I told my mom, and within a day she had already asked if our family wanted to help Ruth's Place. We all agreed and decided that the coffee maker and supplies would be the best things for our family to work on together. A few days later, Mom found a coffee maker online, showed it to us, and with a few clicks it was on its way. We gathered the rest of the supplies and called the shelter to find a day that we could deliver them.

I drove my mom to the shelter — very slowly because she had baked fresh chocolate cupcakes for the women, and they were sitting on my clean leather seats. She had never been in the shelter before, but the whole way she talked about how excited she was to be able to check off something on their list.

When we took the gifts inside, the women were so happy. My mother was bright-eyed, carrying chocolate cupcakes into a shelter full of women she did not know. She stood by the front desk, thanking women for their compliments on her baking and talking to the volunteers as I filled out the donation sheet. As we left, I wished the women "Happy Thanksgiving," and we were met with a chorus of "Happy Thanksgivings" and "Thank Yous." My mother teared up as we walked through the rain to my car. I did not have to ask why; I knew that she did not cry out of pity. She did not cry out of sorrow or commiseration. She cried because she was thankful to have the opportunity to help someone.

I am thankful for my mother and the lessons she has shown me in love and compassion. I can say with certainty that I am not the only one whom she has made a better person.

— Cheyenne H. Huffman —

35

Chicken Soup for the Soul

The Path You've Paved for Me

Mothers and daughters are closest,
when daughters become mothers.
~Author Unknown

I've always loved the bond I've shared with you from the start,
You've taught me to be strong and how to see with my heart;
As my journey toward motherhood is about to begin,
I hope to be even half of the mother and leader you've been;
As I prepare for my role as a mother, I reflect on the path you've
  paved for me,
And I want you to know the lessons you've taught that I now
  hope to repeat;
I hope my daughter knows that she is loved despite her faults,
I hope that she is always proud of her effort despite failed results;
I hope she is kind and loving to those who have less,
I hope she doesn't settle and always gives her best;
I hope she is independent and paves her own way,
I hope she finds joy and seeks laughter each and every day;
I hope she finds friendship with women who are strong,
I hope she recognizes that judgment and prejudice are wrong;
I hope she finds value in her education and her mind,
I hope she recognizes that loyalty is sometimes hard to find;
I hope her confidence increases through her mind and not her
  looks,

I hope she learns the power gained through learning and through
  books;
I hope she values family and finds comfort in our arms,
I hope that I protect her from those who mean her harm;
I hope she finds me funny and that I make her laugh,
I hope she has the courage to speak up on her own behalf;
I hope she becomes someone who makes the world a better place,
I hope her world is not divided by gender, beliefs, or race;
I hope that she knows the difference between what is real and
  what is fake,
I hope she recognizes the power of those who give vs. those who
  take;
I hope she never falters in her journey to reach her dreams,
I hope she goes her own way, no matter how difficult it seems;
I hope she never doubts my love and care for her,
I hope she asks me questions if she ever is unsure;
I have so many hopes and dreams with her I plan to share,
I hope she knows that when she needs me, I'll always be there;
I am nervous on this journey as there will most certainly be stress,
However, I know I am capable of doing this; after all, I've learned
  from the best.
All of these dreams I have for her are not original or new,
All of the dreams I have for her, I've been lucky to learn from you.

— Katie Wright —

36

Go to Them

No act of kindness, no matter how small,
is ever wasted.
~Aesop

Freshman year of high school, I was new in town, and I knew no one. One of the first friends I made asked me to the homecoming dance. Brian was a model kid — polite, kind and quiet. One very sad day, a year or so into our friendship, Brian's dad passed away unexpectedly. I had not met his dad, but it didn't stop me from feeling heartbroken for my friend. When I told my mom about it, she asked when the service was so we could go.

"What?" I said. "I never knew him. I shouldn't be there."

I was sure that Brian would think my attendance was weird or offensive. Being young and (thankfully) having little experience with death personally, I thought it would be grossly inappropriate for me to show up having not known his dad. Despite the fact that I wished I could do something to show Brian I was sad for him and be there for him, going didn't feel like an option. I felt frozen, upset and unsure of what to do.

Mom explained that such services are not just about the person who's passed away, but so much more about the people left behind. She said it makes a difference just to show up for people, to take time to be with them in their darkest hours. Her words seemed to make sense, but I was still wary that I could make any kind of difference. Reluctantly, I agreed to go.

I was so nervous walking toward the building. I felt I had nothing to offer, even though Mom had told me otherwise. It felt all wrong, like I was trespassing into the most sacred "family and friends only" space for Brian's dad. However, Mom was totally natural — sad, but relaxed and confident in her stride. The steady *click, click, click* of her heels on the pavement kept me steady enough to not run back to the car.

We didn't do anything extraordinary that day. We didn't have fond memories to share with Brian. We didn't make food or even take flowers. We were just there. And, somehow, that was enough. Watching my mom hug Brian made all her words come alive. Then, when I felt the warmth of his hug, it was rewarding for me to share that space, to be so close and convey my pain at his pain, even though I couldn't fix it or take it away. Brian thanked us for being there, and it was clear that he was touched by our presence. I wouldn't and couldn't have gone without Mom encouraging me and teaching me that day about compassion.

The lesson I learned that day has always stayed with me: If friends are grieving, go to them. My mom was there to guide me for so many moments like these, when people were grieving, or sick, or needed a safe place. It came so naturally to her; her life's work was being a nurse, after all. She used to say that compassion could be taught, and in her field, it *should* be taught. It was a fascinating concept to me. Little did I realize that she was in the midst of teaching it to me! Mom was right. You *can* teach compassion. She taught me, and I'm sure many others along the way. For that, I thank her.

— Lisa Solorzano Petit —

37

Plates of Compassion

Without a sense of caring, there can be
no sense of community.
~Anthony J. D'Angelo

om and I were putting the finishing touches on dinner, and my five-year-old niece Jessica came in to set the table. Instead of going to the dish cabinet, she went into the pantry where there was a foot-tall stack of old, mismatched dinner plates on the bottom shelf.

For years, Mom had picked up odd plates from yard sales and thrift stores for a nickel or a dime apiece. Jessie carried one plate at a time to the table, using great care as if she were holding a treasure. When she had set all six places, she stood back and admired her work. She sighed, "Oh, Grandma, your plates are so beautiful. Ours are all alike!" We had a good laugh at her innocent remark, but as I think back to all those years ago, I believe she was right. Those plates were beautiful.

Mom worked for the local council on aging as a housekeeper/aide. She did many of the little things that allowed older people to stay in their own homes. Most of her clients got Meals on Wheels, a service that was new to our town in the 1970s. They received a hot lunch and a cold snack to have later in the evening. This is really not very much food. Every evening after we finished dinner, Mom would make to-go meals from our leftovers on these mismatched plates covered with aluminum foil, and either she or Dad would deliver them to the people she knew didn't get enough to eat.

This was about ten years before microwave ovens became common household appliances, so it was important that the food be on a plate that could be reheated in a regular oven. Instead of a cold deli sandwich and macaroni salad, Mom's clients dined on Beef Manhattans, pan-fried chicken or meatloaf, along with veggies and a piece of pie or cake. Mom and Dad did this even after Mom left her job, and Mom continued after Dad's death until all her former clients had either passed away or moved out of their homes.

When I was cleaning out Mom's house after her death, I found that stack of mismatched plates shoved to the back of the pantry. I kept one as a souvenir and donated the rest to the church rummage sale. That plate is a sweet reminder of the lessons of generosity and caring for one's neighbor that were modeled for me by my parents.

— Brenda Keller Robertson —

38

Chicken Soup for the *Soul*

Making Peace with Grandma

It is as grandmothers that our mothers
come into the fullness of their grace.
~Christopher Morley

Every day, I understand my mother a little more. And, conversely, every day, I understand this woman called "Grandma" a little less.

My mother raised seven children under what can only be described as martial law. She had bedtimes, chores, rules and consequences, and she rarely made exceptions.

My mother not only had eyes in the back of her head, but she possessed an entire set of supernatural powers. She could hear a cookie jar open from two floors away and knew something was wrong by the slant of an eyebrow. She never seemed to sleep.

My mother said things like, "I'm your mother, not your playmate." "If you want a new Barbie, I have a toilet that needs cleaning." And, "I don't care who started it; I'm finishing it."

My mother was in the business of raising productive human beings, and "no" was her go-to word.

Then there is this woman whom my children call "Grandma." Grandma not only lets them open the cookie jar, but she lets them drag it in front of the TV and call it breakfast.

Grandma would never leave so much as a gas-station store without buying a "treatie for my sweeties." Grandma lets them have tea parties with Coca-Cola while they're taking a bath.

Grandma will triple her gas bill to warm the pool water in May so her grandson can swim on his birthday.

Grandma says things like, "Finish your Happy Meal, and then we'll get a Blizzard," and, "Don't worry about the mess. Grandma will take care of it."

Grandma would rather surrender to the Taliban than use the word "no."

Naturally, my children adore her. They sing songs about her and fight over the phone to talk to her. When we moved across the state, farther from her, one would have thought I sold their dog.

My youngest, during her kindergarten screening, could not shut up about Grandma, even when she was supposed to be naming her shapes. When I asked her why she was not listening, she said, "Grandma is my favorite person. I just can't help it."

And why should she? Grandma is never too busy to play. No story is too long, no board game too tedious, no idea too wacky for Grandma.

Grandma is the Kiddie Court of Appeals. No matter how reasonable and appropriate my actions are, Grandma will wonder aloud, in front of the children, why I was so cruel as to refuse my daughter a $125 doll.

My youngest calls her "Fairy Grandmother." It doesn't take a genius to figure out who the "Wicked Queen" is.

The truth is, I'm jealous. I love kids; that's why I got into the family business. But my job, as my mother's job before me, is to raise productive human beings. This means bedtimes, consequences and the word "no."

My mother did this for thirty-three years. It is, to quote the Peace Corps, "the toughest job you'll ever love." No wonder she is redefining the "grand" in grandma. It is her retirement. My children are the fruit of her labor, her chance to have fun with the kids instead of checking their breath for toothpaste.

And that I can totally understand. Besides, if I do my job right, one day I'll be the Fairy Grandmother.

— Nicole L.V. Mullis —

39

Badger Fierce

*The art of mothering is to teach
the art of living to children.*
~Elaine Heffner

My mom is happy to share her strong opinions. Once, when I told her I planned to skydive, she replied, "Oh, great! You will probably fall out of your harness and hang upside-down by your panties." This prophesy was accompanied by a YouTube video of an unfortunate grandma in that exact situation.

In the grocery store, mom caught a man leering at me. "Hey, you. Watch it, buddy. Yeah, I see you," she called out, in fierce protective-mom mode. His face reddened and he looked away.

Mom is also fiercely helpful. I experienced this when she cared for me post-surgery. My medications were administered with the efficiency of a drill sergeant. My couch-bed was plumped and cleaned, with stacks of books and the television remote within reach. She protected me from pushing myself too hard, and guided me with gentleness and patience to the porch for much-needed Vitamin D. On top of that, she was a fun nurse, which led to one of our oddest schemes yet.

It all started with a rumor.

Judy told Peggy, who told my dad, which I overheard in a post-surgery stupor, that Judy's husband Mike saw a badger in an irrigation pipe at the front of our horse pasture. The Bureau of Land Management was called to set humane traps to capture and relocate the fierce creature.

"A badger? In our pipes?" I blinked away my Percocet cloud, and then grinned. "Finders keepers."

Mom and Dad offered tolerant smiles. After two weeks, they were unfazed by my pain-killer-induced ramblings. Their trivial discussions were a blur of noise behind me. I pondered how to reach this badger. When Dad left for his office, I seized my chance.

"Wanna have an adventure?" I asked my mom. I couldn't hide my grin.

"Maybe?" Mom said warily.

"Let's go look at the badger!"

"You can hardly walk!"

"Hardly walk?" I protested. "I am more upright than yesterday. Besides, I need to see the sun and feel the wind on my face. I am going crazy!"

"Badgers are fierce animals, and you can't run away. What if it's rabid?" she cautioned.

"It's probably hiding in the pipe until it can escape tonight." Badgers were not uncommon in the high mountains of Wyoming, but they rarely ventured down to our valley homes. I couldn't miss an opportunity to see one.

"You will be exhausted if you walk that far." She referred to the mere distance of seventy-five yards from couch to pipe.

"We will drive. We can just peek from the window."

Mom chewed her lip, caught between common sense and a willingness to make me happy. My newfound eagerness after listless days on the couch was too great for her to deny. Without Dad or my husband to convince her otherwise, we began the laborious process of loading my bloated carcass into the truck. Mom supported me, never rolling her eyes at my piteously slow state.

"What if it won't come out of the pipe?" she asked.

"We should take a peace offering," I said, even as guilt gripped me. All nature lovers follow a staunch don't-feed-the-wildlife code. Apparently, Percocet had loosened my morals. "Deli ham?" I suggested.

Thusly armed, we drove to the pipe. Mom parked the truck, and we waited. And waited. Nothing happened. We waited some more. Surely, I earned my *National Geographic* Wildlife Photographer

Patience Badge.

"Try the ham," I urged.

Mom rolled up a slice and tossed it out my window into the dirt. It landed about a million miles away from the opening of the pipe.

"Good one."

"Oh, kiss my grits," Mom grunted as she released another blob. It also landed remarkably off-target.

"Try underhand?"

She did, and five pieces later, the ham landed with a satisfying plop near the entrance of the pipe.

My eyes widened at a slight movement. There was indeed a fierce, scary badger in there. Then, a little nose emerged, quivering as it sniffed. A flat face peeked from the shadows, striped black and white. It had large, liquid black eyes and was the size of a loaf of bread.

"Oh, my goodness," I squealed. "It's just a baby!"

Moments later, a truck rattled past, its side emblazoned with Bureau of Land Management. The vibrations scared our sweet baby badger back into its pipe.

The Fed gave us a friendly wave, but terror washed over me.

"The ham!" I shrieked. It was lying all over the ground in incriminating piles. We could be fined, imprisoned or, worse, splashed across the front page of the local tribune.

"You have to pick it up."

"It's too dangerous," Mom protested.

"We can't leave it!"

"I am not bending down with my face near that pipe."

"Use the rake."

"Do we have time?" Mom glanced up the road. The federal officer would realize he missed the correct pipe and turn around soon.

I looked her square in the eye and summoned my gravest superhero face. "We don't have a choice." Mom nodded and leapt from the truck, grabbing a rake from the bed.

I caught one more glimpse of the badger's nose before Mom sailed around the front of the truck. She flipped dirt-coated ham into the sagebrush-filled ditch.

"There are rake lines. You have to make it look more natural!" I yelled.

She groaned and kicked dirt into a great cloud, clarifying the lines with evidence-linking footprints.

"Never mind, I see his truck," I wailed.

Mom let loose a curse word, and I gasped with laughter. This was even more of an adventure than I imagined.

We charged back to the house, slamming the front door just as the man's truck pulled parallel to our driveway. We leaned our heads back, panting and laughing.

I looked in her eyes. "Thank you," I said seriously. "I really needed that." Mom hugged me with half her normal strength, mindful of my stitches.

We found out later that the precious baby badger was safely relocated to the mountains. I thought of his hesitancy to enter the big world, mingled with curiosity for its delights. All he needed was ham to pull him from the safety of his irrigation pipe. Mom lured him, however momentarily, into the great world.

She does the same for me daily. She assuages my doubts. She encourages me to work for my dreams. I am still in my baby-badger stage, learning and growing into the person I wish to become: fiercely loyal, kind, and humble; fiercely sassy, fun, and hilarious. Fierce like a full-grown badger. Fierce like Mom.

— Shelby Kisgen —

40

The Can-Opener Queen

The same way one tells a recipe, one tells a family history. Each one of us has our past locked inside.
~Laura Esquivel

I was a child in the 1950s when mothers wore aprons and routinely prepared homemade meals. My mom was not typical, and she never wore an apron. She earned her moniker, The Can-Opener Queen, because she wasn't much of a cook. She didn't bake cookies or cakes either, but we always had pastries—selected from the day-old rack at the neighborhood bakery.

When Mom wanted to impress us with a robust dinner, she didn't make a roast. She poured sliced roast beef and gravy right from the can onto a mound of mashed potatoes quicker than we could say, "Instant spuds." She and Chef Boyardee made great spaghetti and meatballs, and her buddy, Dinty Moore, helped her cook up an awesome beef stew.

She always topped off the evening meal with a sweet treat, but she did better when she bought those. Mom's one and only attempt at baking cookies resulted in a mess that resembled a charred chocolate-chip lava flow. It happened when she discovered slice and bake cookies.

"Look at this, kids." She waved a log of refrigerated cookie dough at us as she unpacked the groceries. "Now what could be easier than this? I'm going to make you warm, gooey chocolate-chip cookies like other mothers do."

She gave a cursory glance at the instructions, picked up a knife and began to slice the dough into one-inch medallions. She laid them on the cookie sheet that she did not grease lightly because she did not read beyond the first step of the directions. She preheated the oven to 350 degrees.

"Well, this sure didn't make many cookies," she mumbled. "You'd think for the price, you'd get more than a dozen cookies out of this roll."

She shook her head as she shoved the cookie sheet with twelve discs into the oven. My brother and I sat at the kitchen table and tried to make one another laugh until Mom told us to settle down or there would be no cookies. Five minutes passed, and the delightful aroma made our mouths water. Ten minutes passed, and our eyes began to water. Mom opened the oven door, and the acrid smell nearly choked us. She grabbed a dishcloth, yanked out the smoldering cookie sheet, and slammed it down on the stovetop. Since Mom never used the oven, she had no idea the thermostat was stuck on broil.

"Well, they sure took me for a fool. Cookies that run together in one big mess! I thought they were supposed to be round," she grumbled. "You kids saw when I put them on the tray. They were round, weren't they?"

Tears flowed — hers, not ours.

"It's okay, Mom. They're not so bad," my brother and I said.

"Might as well scrape them into the trash!"

"No way, Mom. We'll eat them."

She wiped her tears and blew her nose, and then she pried a piece of the magma-hot dough from the center. She poked the rock-hard, charcoal-colored edges and shook her head.

"I must have done something wrong. Let me see that package," she said as she snatched it from the garbage.

She read the instructions aloud. "Slice dough into one-inch sections. Yes, I did that. Cut one-inch sections into quarters. Hmmm. I really didn't think it would make that much difference if they were the size of silver dollars rather than quarters."

She was talking to herself.

My brother and I, nine and ten at the time, nearly snorted our milk.

"Mom, that means four pieces. Don't you know fractions? We're learning fractions in math class. A quarter means one-fourth; four pieces make a whole."

"Oh, I know all that." She whisked the tray away and flung it into the trashcan, and then she made an offer we couldn't refuse. "You kids want to walk with me to the bakery?"

At times, I felt cheated that my friends' mothers prepared fabulous food, and my mom didn't. But after the rock-hard lava cookies, I honestly didn't care anymore. I had acquired a taste for burned-to-a-crisp, fried bologna, but I didn't want to chance any more varieties of blackened foods.

No, The Can-Opener Queen didn't make homemade soups, stews, or desserts, but she nourished us with a heaping helping of Bible stories when we sat down to eat. Mom never stopped preaching and teaching us about God's love, forgiveness, and kindness. To this day, I use Mom's favorite recipe. It has only two basic steps: generously season everything you serve with love, and always do unto others what you'd have them do unto you.

The other day, at the grocery store, I walked down the baking aisle. I considered buying a bag of semi-sweet chocolate chips for homemade cookies. No, I reasoned, it would be much easier to stop by the cookie aisle and grab a package of Soft Batch chocolate-chip cookies. Better yet, I moseyed to the bakery department to pick up a dozen freshly baked chocolate-chip delights for when my grandkids came over later that day. Then I had a flashback.

I pushed the cart to the refrigerated case, selected a slick packaged roll of chocolate-chip cookie dough, and thought, *This one's for you, Mom. I'm going to show the kids how to bake chocolate-chip cookies. And I'm going to sprinkle them with love and share your recipe with them.*

— Linda O'Connell —

Chapter
5

Like
Mother, Like
Daughter

41

Tea for Two

There are few hours in life more agreeable
than the hour dedicated to the ceremony
known as afternoon tea.
~Henry James

My mother taught me about tea when I was young. How chamomile soothes. How herbals heal. How black tea warms up a body.

The first time I shared a mug of tea with my mother, I was a bullied ten-year-old in the fifth grade. I stayed up late reading most nights, and as a result I often fell asleep in class. My teachers complained, but my solution was to read every book in their classrooms before midterm. That usually appeased them, along with the fact that I was a good student.

This particular evening, I had no book to comfort me. I'd finished every single one I owned. I couldn't sleep.

I picked at a hole in the plastic tablecloth on our kitchen table and complained to my mom about the kids who teased me for being smart. During evenings like this, she'd advise me to ignore them, or talk to a teacher, or even just make friends instead of spending my recess time in the school library. I would nod and agree, even while I knew I couldn't do that. Mice don't make friends with the big, loud cats. They get eaten by them.

My mother saw my anxiety, tilted her head, and sighed. "What you need, my little reader, is tea."

She meant, of course, Sleepytime tea from Celestial Seasonings. I'd watched her make it for herself often enough. She took hers with milk, and so this evening I also took it that way.

We sat together at the table, sipping and talking about nothing. I went to bed soon afterward, with a warm belly and a warm heart to match. From that evening onward, if I had a bad day at school, or life at home became a little too tough for my sensitive heart, my mom and I would share a cup of tea late at night.

Years passed, and I grew up, got married, and moved overseas. In a country where I didn't speak the language and had no friends, I missed my mother and how she reassured me that it didn't matter if I wasn't normal.

She confessed recently to me that, back then, she'd actually had no hope of me ever fitting in or making friends. And, to my surprise, this pleased me greatly. I like being different.

I think, as children, we find our identities however we can. Some of us take our identities from the people with whom we surround ourselves. Some of us find identity in rebellion. And some of us savor our solitude. I took comfort from being left alone with my books, papers, and journals. It was the only peace I found in a six-person family of adopted, special-needs children.

Often, the teen years can be characterized by rifts between girls and their mothers, and perhaps the same could be true of us. But tea proved to be one of our bridges back to one another. No matter what kind of day or what fight we had, when one of us suggested tea, the other would never refuse.

My home now boasts three shelves full of a variety of teas: assai, green, chai, spearmint and lemongrass, Earl Grey, and so on. It would be almost unhealthy if it weren't so nourishing for my soul. I can't pass up a teashop while I'm out. I'll overpay for a subpar green tea from a paper cup at a café. It's more than an antidepressant or a nostalgic salve. It's a way to feel connected to my mother, despite the ocean between us.

Tea fixes everything. This has become a mantra in my life, and I repeat it often to friends. My son is growing up with a mother who often has a mug of tea in one hand and a book in the other. I wouldn't have it any other way.

I still drink Sleepytime, only now I drink it with honey; my mother still drinks hers with milk. And if we're in the same place for just a while, digitally or physically, we smile, sip our fragrant favorites, and talk of nothing.

—Kati Felix—

42

The Nurse

*The more a daughter knows the details of her mother's
life, the stronger the daughter.*
~Anita Diamant

My mother was a stay-at-home mom. She cared for my brother and me, making many of our clothes and my fancy ribbon barrettes, and carting us off to birthday parties, dance classes, and soccer practices. As a result of my father's good job and her ability to stay home with us, Mom decided that she would start taking some classes at the local university so that, eventually, she could pursue her dream of becoming a nurse.

I have cloudy memories of her coming home from college, making sure my brother and I were taken care of and staying up late studying. Often, her studying included bringing home anatomy specimens and using our washing machine and dryer in the basement as her laboratory. I was never horrified of these labs; I was intrigued by them and proud of her for chasing her dream.

My father left us not long after my mom started taking classes. He left two days before Christmas, walking out the door and leaving us with no money in the bank, no way to pay bills, and no way to find him. I remember being called to the school office to be told that the check for my lunch tickets had bounced. With the Christmas holiday looming, my mother called her parents and let them know what was going on. Together, they gave my brother and me a spectacular Christmas. Soon after, the car was repossessed, and the bill collectors started calling day and night. Somehow, Mom managed to hold it together, even though her world was collapsing around her.

When my father left, he informed my mother that he was gay. Out of fear for herself and concern for my brother and me, my mom visited the local health department and got an HIV test. Thankfully, her test was negative, and she could focus her energies on how to move forward with no husband, money, or job, and nothing more than a high-school diploma.

I remember the day that my mom told me we were going to move in with my grandparents. I had just come back from visiting the middle school that I was supposed to attend, that all of my friends were going to. I was so angry with her. How could she take me away from my friends? How could she let me go on the middle-school field trip when I wouldn't be going there? I did not want to move to another state, move in with my grandparents and leave my life. Selfishly, my ten-year-old self did not even consider that this was not what my mother wanted either.

We moved out of state. I started at a new school with people I did not know, and Mom was able to start taking classes at the local college while she looked for some part-time work. Things were not easy at my grandparents' house. The differences between Depression-era parenting styles and baby-boomer parenting styles clashed all too often. After less than a year, my mother found a job back home and an affordable apartment. My brother and I were thrilled to move back. In order to return home, my mother had to put her dream of continuing classes to be a nurse on hold indefinitely.

Fast-forward about six years. Mom was remarried, and I was getting ready to graduate from high school. My dream was to go to college and become a nurse. Little did I know, but my mom was planning to go back to school and get into the nursing class ahead of me. She knew I would not want her in my class, and she wanted to give me the space and freedom to spread my wings without her. As fate would have it, we were both accepted into the university's nursing program, and we were placed in the same graduating class.

Four years of classes, clinical rotations, and highs and lows ensued.

We were in some of the same lectures together and even sat beside each other most of the time. Having the same sense of humor, when one of us would start giggling at something, the other would start giggling, too. We would make a conscious effort not to look at each other for fear of uncontrollable laughter that would be sure to draw an evil eye from the professor. We never did have clinical rotations together, as the nursing faculty wanted to make sure that I would not rely on my mother for help.

People often ask me who the better student was. I always respond the same way: Mom. She was a much better student. It meant more to her. She had waited longer, sacrificed more for it, and had to go through so much more to get it.

We are coming up on our twentieth nursing-school reunion. For much of that time, we have worked in the same academic medical center, though in different departments. Mom will retire soon, a hard-earned retirement that she has been looking forward to for some time. I will miss knowing that she is in the building. I will miss our commonality in our daily work. I will miss this journey we have been on together for so long. My mom has always told me how proud she is of me. I hope she knows how proud I am of her.

— Jessica Gray —

Turning into My Mother

Mirror Mirror on the wall, I am my mother after all.
~Author Unknown

When I was eight years old, I had a terrible stomachache at school and felt like I was going to throw up. My third-grade teacher sent me to the office, and the secretary called my mom to pick me up.

About five minutes later, I heard an obnoxiously loud car horn. The entire office staff heard it, too, and shook their heads collectively in disgust. The principal came out from behind closed doors and screamed, "What kind of lunatic is honking a horn at 9:00 a.m. in front of a school?"

It turned out that the "lunatic" was my mother. The secretary went out to investigate. My mother asked if I could be sent out, but the secretary explained that school rules required she come inside and sign me out physically.

My mother walked into school wearing a floral housecoat, curlers and slippers. I can't be 100 percent certain, but I don't think she wore a bra. Between the honking and the outfit, I vowed right then that I would never be so embarrassing to my children when I was a mother myself.

Not leaving my house dressed like a crazy person was just one of the many ways I planned never to be like my mother. I was not going to insist that beds got made daily because what was the point? It was a stupid rule. I wouldn't say "because I said so" when my kids asked why we couldn't get more than one pack of Oreos, even though Dad was going to eat half the box before any of us could get one. I would cook elaborate dinners from actual recipes, not just chicken with ketchup four times a week. I'd be able to work a VCR. I'd keep current on music, not stay stuck in the decade of my youth and insist that the last good song written was "All Shook Up" by Elvis Presley.

I would not become increasingly annoying as my children became teenagers, unlike my own mother who seemed to kick the annoying behavior into high gear when I entered high school. I remember once walking through the mall with my friends, and she happened to be there along with my grandfather. She started screaming, "Yoohoo, Randi-Boo!" from a few stores away. I pretended not to hear her and started walking in the other direction. She shouted louder and came toward me. Didn't she understand I was with my friends and did not want to chat?

It was bad enough when I brought friends over to the house, and she asked them a million questions even when I asked her not to. She'd peek into my room and pretend to just be on her way to get the laundry. "Oh, Elena," she'd say. "I didn't know you were here. How are you? How's your mom? Is anyone hungry? You girls need to eat." When I was a mom of teens, I wouldn't interfere so much in my kids' lives. I would listen to them and respect their need for space and privacy.

I had the best intentions not to turn into my mother. Then I had my own children. I found out that turning into your mother is sometimes inevitable.

When I was a kid, I didn't understand my mother's motivations, but now I do. Making beds makes me feel in control when my world is chaotic. Cooking gourmet dinners is virtually impossible when I am running around all afternoon, picking up kids at sports, religious school, debate club and music lessons. Sometimes, the only answer I have is "because I said so" because I don't have the energy to explain myself, but I know I am right. Nobody needs two bags of Oreos because processed foods aren't healthy. Better to limit the sugar and eat an apple or a tangerine. VCRs were not as confusing as today's technology, so sometimes I do need a tutorial from my kids. And there is no reason

I should stop listening to 1980s music because I enjoy it, and Sirius has a whole channel devoted to it. Listen to a few Madonna songs; Cardi B is nothing compared to her.

That day at the mall, my mother shouted my name because she was genuinely excited to see me, even though she had just seen me that morning. The fact that our worlds had randomly intersected outside the house made her happy. She asked my friends questions because she was interested in their lives. It's not that she didn't respect my need for privacy. She did. But she also missed me. She had given birth to me and taken care of me for so many years. And as she watched me grow up, she was letting go — just not as quickly as I was.

My mother didn't walk into my school in her pajamas to embarrass me. She did it because I was in trouble, and that superseded everything else — even her personal appearance. I have never worn a housecoat or curlers, but I have run into school wearing my exercise pants and a ratty T-shirt (possibly braless) when one of my children has needed me. So, yes, I've turned into my mother, and my kids are darn lucky I have.

— Randi Mazzella —

44

A Journey Twice Taken

Vitality shows in not only the ability to persist
but the ability to start over.
~F. Scott Fitzgerald

"I can't believe my baby is going to become a mom today," my mom said, handing me another ice chip.

"Hopefully, it will be today," I said. "At this rate, it might be tomorrow."

Mom smiled. "No matter how long it takes, when they put that baby in your arms, it will all be worth it, honey."

Many hours later, my baby was born, but they didn't put him in my arms. He was born with the umbilical cord wrapped around his neck, and he wasn't breathing. The doctor placed a respiration bag over my son's nose and mouth to force air into his tiny lungs.

"Thank you, God," I whispered when I finally heard his first cries.

Later, when I was holding him for the first time, Mom returned to my bedside. "He's beautiful," she murmured.

"I can't believe how much I love him already," I said.

Mom smiled through tears.

"It's hard to imagine that you used to love me this much."

"Used to?" Mom said. "I still love you that much."

"Really? But he's still perfect. He's never disobeyed or disappointed me. He's still perfect, and I'm definitely not."

Mom's tears spilled over. "That doesn't matter. A mother's love never changes. We love and protect our children, no matter how old they get."

And while I didn't know it at the time, Mom was protecting me at that very moment. Just two days before, a woman had stopped by my parents' home. She was a stranger to Mom, but my father knew her quite well.

In short, my parents' thirty-year marriage was over, but Mom was protecting me from the heartbreaking news. Of course, that didn't stop it from breaking her heart.

Over the next year, Mom and I talked on the phone nearly every day. We cried a lot, and I spent a lot of time wishing I could do more to help her. But I lived three hours away, and I had a job and a new baby.

Mom insisted that I was helping her just by listening. But I'll never forget that feeling of powerlessness as I listened to her cry into the phone day after day. All I could do was listen to her pain, and it never felt like I did enough.

It was the hardest thing either of us had ever been through — until seven years later when my own marriage fell apart.

By then, I had two children. For financial reasons, my kids and I moved in with Mom and her wonderful second husband, Doug. Their home was 150 miles from mine, so my kids had to change schools, give up their friends and extracurricular activities, and leave the only home they'd ever known. I had to resign from my job and move away from the life I'd built for ten years.

Sitting on Mom's couch one day, I felt utterly hopeless. "I hate this," I told her. "I'm an adult, and I can't even take care of my own children." I stared at her through teary eyes. "I don't see how things will ever get back to normal."

Mom shook her head. "Things won't ever get back to your old normal. You have to find a new normal."

"I don't know how to do that." My shoulders slumped. "Right now, my new normal is depression and dependency on you and Doug."

"Do you remember the advice you gave me when I was in your shoes?"

I shook my head.

"You told me to find the good in each day. No matter how small it was, I needed to find some tiny good thing in every day. Honey, that's how you find your new normal."

"Find the good? My husband left me. How do I find the good?"

"That's what I thought when you told me to do it. But please try it."

I nodded. It looked as though I was going to have to follow my own advice.

The next morning, Mom made my favorite pancakes for breakfast. When I thanked her, she said, "I just wanted to make sure you could find something good in today."

Over the next few weeks, Mom made sure I could find something good in countless days. She took me shopping for a new outfit, made my favorite meals, and brought me novels from the library.

One night, we were watching a movie, and I laughed. Mom looked at me and said, "I'm glad to hear that sound again."

After months of finding the good in small ways, I began finding it in bigger ways, too. I found a new job that I loved. My children and I rented a small house, and I felt stronger living on my own again.

Although I didn't live with Mom, we still saw each other frequently. One day, we met for lunch, and Mom commented on how much I'd grown.

"Recovering from something as painful as a divorce takes so long," I said. "I don't think I see the growth because it's been so gradual."

Mom nodded. "I felt the same way when I was going through mine. Sometimes, I determined that I was healing because you seemed to be in less pain while listening to me."

I thought about her words for a long moment. I remembered those phone conversations and how painful they'd been for both of us. But I could recall moments when Mom said something positive, and I realized that she was going to be all right. The relief I'd felt was immense.

I realized that Mom must feel that same way now. Seeing me living on my own with my children, working at a job I enjoy, and even occasionally smiling must set her mind at ease.

"For months, I've been saying 'I'm going to be okay someday,' but just now, I realized that someday is now." I smiled at Mom. "I'm okay now."

Mom reached for my hand across the table. "You're more than okay, honey. You made it through this."

I nodded, a lump in my throat. "We both did."

Walking my mom through her divorce and then having her help me through mine was painful — sometimes excruciatingly so.

But it was also beautiful at times. Mom knew how I felt without me saying a word.

It was a journey twice taken. First, for Mom, and then, for me. And although I wouldn't have chosen it, since it happened, I'm glad I had Mom by my side.

— Diane Stark —

45

Role Reversal

We are at our best when we cheer each other
on and build each other up.
~Author Unknown

My mother was a constant presence at my cross-country meets in middle school and high school. I remember thinking that she must have been bored. For most races, the majority of the course was in the woods or behind the school, so my mom would usually only see me running at the start and finish. But she still insisted on coming to my meets, sometimes even traveling to other towns around the county to watch. And I had to admit that it was always exciting to emerge from the woods and hear my mother's cheers as I approached the finish line.

Years after my high-school cross-country days were over, I started running marathons and eventually became a coach for long-distance charity runners. Around the same time, my mother had started to become more active and was walking a few days a week. One day, she told me that she had started to run instead of walk. She loved it and wanted some running tips. The day after Thanksgiving, we went out for a run together, and I noticed the shoes she was wearing — a beat-up pair of canvas sneakers. I told her that if she was going to run, she needed to get a real pair of running shoes. She didn't seem convinced, almost as if she thought running shoes were only for serious, hard-core runners. So that Christmas, I gave her a brand-new pair of Nikes.

Once she tried them on, she quickly embraced the comfort of

her new shoes. She was so excited about them that she kept running outside, despite the blustery winter weather in her suburban New York town. After a few months, she told me that she was running three miles at a time.

"You know, Mom, you're totally ready to do your first race," I said.

The look of astonishment and fear on her face told me that she definitely didn't think she was prepared. "I don't think I could do a race," she said.

"Mom, you're already running a 5K," I said. "The only differences are the start and finish lines, and some other people running along with you."

She was not persuaded, but I continued to push the idea. I picked out what I thought was the perfect race: a women-only 5K at a local state park on Mother's Day. I told her that she, along with my sister Cindy and me, would all run it as a mother-daughter team. She still had her doubts, but I filled out her application form and said I would pick her up that day. "If you keep running the way you have been, you will be more than prepared," I told her.

When I walked into my mom's house on Mother's Day morning, I heard the roar of her blow dryer. I looked down the hallway and saw my mom standing in the bathroom, drying her long, blond hair in the mirror. "Well, if I can't run well, I might as well look good!" she said with a laugh.

We got to the race early, so there was plenty of time for my mother to pepper Cindy and me with typical pre-race questions. "What if I don't finish? What if I'm the last person? Should I wear pants or shorts?" she asked. We assured her that she was going to finish, she wouldn't be last (the race was open to walkers, after all), and it was too warm to wear pants. Fortunately, we were able to distract her for a little while when we picked up our race numbers and goodie bags. "Wow, we get a T-shirt? How exciting!" she said, as a race volunteer handed her a shirt.

As we approached the start, I thought back to my first race in middle school and remembered that my mom was there to support me. I hoped that she was feeling the same comfort I felt that day.

Mom told my sister and me that she wanted to run at her own pace, so we should go ahead. "Okay, good luck, Mom," I said to her. "See you at the finish line."

The course started out on a road and then turned onto a wooded trail. For the last half-mile of the course, we ran out of the woods and onto a road that led to the finish line in a parking lot. After I crossed the finish line, I grabbed my camera from my car and positioned myself along the road. I watched as runners appeared from out of the woods onto the straightaway. Cindy finished the race, and we both kept looking to catch a glimpse of our mom's signature stride and her light blue shirt.

I started jumping up and down as I spotted her in the distance, her blond ponytail bouncing behind her. "Here she comes!" I yelled, as I pointed her out to Cindy. We started cheering, "Go, Mom!" as she approached us. She smiled and waved to us as she passed.

I raced back to the parking lot to snap a picture of her crossing the finish line. She was elated as I gave her a big hug and handed her a cup of water. "Great race, Mom," I said. She was definitely not the last person to finish; in fact, her time would be part of an award-winning performance in the mother-daughter category.

As we sat eating brunch later that morning, I looked at my mom — proudly wearing her race T-shirt — and smiled as I thought about the morning's events. Now I understood why my mother came to all those cross-country meets. The pride and excitement we feel when watching someone we love reach the finish line is actually more thrilling than crossing it ourselves. Back in high school, I never thought in a million years that one day I would be standing on the sidelines, waiting for my mother to re-emerge from the woods. I feel lucky that I was able to return the favor.

— Christine Many Luff —

46

A Waffle at Breakfast

A daughter may outgrow your lap,
but she will never outgrow your heart.
~Author Unknown

S he sat across the kitchen table from me, watching my every move. I was eating breakfast. Surely, it could not be that fascinating. It was just a toaster waffle. I cut off a piece, swirling it around to capture the sweet syrup as her eyes bore into my very soul. Good lord, this was so irritating. *Stop staring at me*, I screamed in my head while reaching for my glass of milk. I put down my glass and looked into her eyes. "Mom... you are staring at me," I stated with the bereaved tone of a teenager.

"Sorry," she said and looked away, taking a sip of her coffee.

Now here I am, a mother of two daughters of my own, and I'm seeing the world from a whole new perspective.

My older daughter plays quietly in her room. Her imagination runs wild, and her play is vigorous and captivating. I put down my basket of laundry in the hallway and take a seat on the floor, leaning my back against her bed and watching. I look at her face, how her eyes change with the tone of her voice. I watch her hands busily bounce her dolls from room to room in their playhouse as the narrative inside her head plays out with excitement and emotion. I watch every facet of her being and soak it up, knowing it will continue to change. She is only four, but my whole world revolves around her and her sister.

"Mom," she says, "why are you staring at me?"

"I'm sorry, honey. I just like to watch you sometimes."

I don't know if my mom watching me eat breakfast could compare to me watching my daughters, but I can imagine that the premise behind it is the same. As I was sitting across the table from my mother, getting ready for another day of high school, wishing away my adolescence to race into adulthood and all the "freedoms" I thought that would entail, my mother was watching her little girl grow into a woman, and inevitably feeling her little girl pull away with each bite.

The inertia of growing up and the self-absorption that often goes along with it couldn't prepare me to understand why my mother watched me eat my breakfast. And I assume the same will apply to my daughters as they continue to grow away from me with each passing day, each moment of play, each waffle they eat.

I try to drink in this moment, pull my daughter close to me and breathe deeply. She is anxious to escape my embrace and return to her play, so with a kiss on the forehead, I release her, rise from the floor and walk toward the door. I take one more look and smile, appreciating that I still have many days ahead to soak in all these moments.

— Patricia Wood —

47

A Sweet Goodbye

All sorrows are less with bread.
~Miguel de Cervantes

om never claimed to be a good cook, but everyone in our family knew better. Her homemade pies and cinnamon coffeecakes were delicious. Her crispy buttermilk fried chicken was the best. But her made-from-scratch sweet rolls were heavenly. She'd baked them for holidays and special occasions for as long as I could remember.

After I married and had children of my own, I asked her to teach me how to make the rolls, but she insisted she didn't have a recipe. She just threw the ingredients together until the dough felt right.

When my children were teenagers, Mom was diagnosed with a rare, fast-growing cancer of the pituitary gland. She fought a hard battle, but her tumors continued to spread.

Early one morning, she called and asked if I could come over right away. My heart pounded as I raced to her house, thinking the worst.

I pulled in her driveway, jumped out, and dashed in the back door. The look on Mom's face mirrored mine.

"What's wrong?" we both asked at once.

"It's time for you to learn how to make my rolls."

"Jeez. You scared me half to death."

Mom was so weak that she had to sit down as she recited the ingredients. Rather than provide a precise measurement, she instructed me to add flour a little at a time. Then she taught me how to knead the dough.

"Push it forward and then pull back with both palms while you count to a hundred."

"Seems like a lot of work," I mumbled.

"Remember, you get out what you put in," she quipped.

While we waited for the dough to double, she told stories from her childhood that I hadn't heard before. Her mother had sewn identical dresses for her and her sister, with the exception of different colored buttons. Only a year apart, everyone thought the girls were twins. She recalled sitting next to her own mother and watching her make rolls and bread every Monday, Wednesday and Saturday. By the time she was a teenager, the job belonged to her. Mom said the best part was spreading the hand-churned butter onto a steaming roll and savoring every bite.

The afternoon flew by as we talked and laughed. When it came time to punch the dough and form the rolls, she reached over and pinched a section, showing me how to shape and smooth the top with my thumbs. My first few didn't look great, but I soon got the hang of it and formed each one to near perfection before placing it in the muffin pan.

After covering the pans with a cloth, I set the rolls aside to rise once more. All too soon, it was time to place them in the oven. When the tantalizing smell of yeast wafted throughout the room, I snuck a roll, broke it open and lathered it with butter that dripped down my chin as I devoured the slightly doughy roll.

Mom grinned. "You should see your face!"

When the rolls turned a golden brown, I held one up for inspection. Her eyes glazed over. "Perfect."

While I tidied the kitchen, she placed the rolls in a sack for me to take home. When I got ready to leave, Mom tapped my shoulder.

She whispered, "Can you drive me to the hospital tomorrow? It's time."

I nodded and rushed outside, tears spilling down my face. Mom had fought to stay home as long as possible, but cancer had now spread throughout her body, and she'd grown weary of the daily struggle to stay alive.

The next morning, a deep sadness overtook me as I watched my mother shuffle through her house one last time. In the living room, she stopped and grabbed a family photo off the mantle to take with her to the hospital. Then she walked slowly out the door. A lump formed in my throat as I trailed a short distance behind. She took one last stroll around her flower garden. When she stopped to smell a yellow rose, I turned my head so she wouldn't catch me crying.

"I'm ready," she whispered.

I thought to myself, *I'll never be ready*.

We rode in silence, and somehow I managed to hold it together. Hospitalized for over a month, Mom never once complained. She lost her battle surrounded by loved ones.

That first holiday without Mom, when I placed her scrumptious buttery rolls on the table, a hush came over my normally boisterous relatives. I hadn't told anyone about the day she and I shared in the kitchen. Eyes teared up as the sweet aroma rose from the platter, along with memories of our mother.

My youngest sister broke the silence. "They look like Mom's rolls, but do they taste like hers?"

I tossed one to her and said, "See for yourself."

Soon, rolls sailed around the room, and laughter replaced our sorrow. Everyone agreed they were delicious. From that first holiday after she died, I gladly made the rolls for all our family gatherings. Mom would be proud to know that her heavenly hot rolls will forever be a part of our family tradition.

— Alice Muschany —

48

Just Like Grandma

We often take for granted the very things that most deserve our gratitude.
~Cynthia Ozick

O ne word. That's all it took to throw my family into a frenzy. It began one night during dinner. One of my girls made an innocent comment. I blurted out my response with one little word: "Well!"

The tone of my voice surprised even me. Where did that raspy drawl come from? For a moment, the room was silent. Then, suddenly, all three of my daughters laughed.

"What?" I asked, folding my arms.

My oldest caught her breath. "You sound just like Grandma."

"What? Grandma? No. No way."

My husband joined in the fun. "Oh, yes, you did." He gave me a playful grin. "You must be turning into your mother."

"You're all crazy," I said.

The next morning, I woke to the sound of two girls arguing while getting ready for school. One girl shouted out a cutting comment. The other came back with sarcasm. Back and forth. Louder and louder. Finally, I'd heard enough. I threw back the covers, jumped out of bed and marched down the hall to the bathroom.

"Girls, stop it. If you can't say something nice, don't say anything at all."

I stopped in my tracks, mildly disturbed. Memories of my mom declaring those same words flashed through my mind. What in the world? Without even thinking, my mother's words had jumped out of my mouth.

Later, as the school bus drove away, I reasoned with myself. *It is just a cliché. Lots of moms have said those words. It doesn't mean anything. I'm not turning into my mom.*

Within a few minutes, my cell phone rang. I checked the caller ID: Junior High. Why were they calling? Instantly, three scary scenarios slipped into my mind.

Did she get hurt during PE? Maybe she's feeling sick — what if she threw up during class? Then I remembered a recent note from school. *Oh, no, head lice.*

I took a deep breath and answered the phone.

"Mom? I forgot my lunch money."

Relieved, I hung up the phone. But I couldn't help but wonder, *Why am I such a worrywart?* Over the years, I'd received dozens of calls from the school. *Why do I always worry?*

Then it hit me. If there's one thing my mom excels at, it's worrying. *Just great,* I thought. *Now I am worried about worrying.*

I assured myself it didn't mean a thing. All moms worry. But when I returned home from the grocery store later that day, I found clues everywhere.

Like Mom, I collected an ever-practical bag full of bags. No sense throwing away those plastic grocery bags when we might use them for something. My mom's words echoed in my head. "Why buy bathroom trash bags when these fit perfectly inside the wastebasket?"

I grabbed a head of lettuce and opened the crisper drawer. More proof glared back at me from inside the drawer. How had I accumulated so many leftover packets of ketchup, mayo, and mustard from fast-food restaurants?

Suddenly, it wasn't just plastic bags and packets of ketchup. I stared into a drawer full of empty containers. Cool Whip. Cottage cheese. Sour cream. Yogurt. My kitchen drawer had more plastic dishes than a Tupperware catalog.

Just then, my daughter burst through the door. "Bad day?" I asked.

She exhaled and plopped down on a chair. Over the next few minutes, she shared the dramatic details of life in middle school. I tried to encourage her. Apparently, it worked.

"Thanks, Mom. You give pretty good advice."

"Junior high can be tough," I said, "but this too shall pass. Seems like a long time ago when I told Grandma all about my problems at school." I patted my daughter's leg. "Grandma gave good advice, too."

"See, we told you," she said, beginning to smile. "You're just like Grandma."

I thought for a moment, and then replied with a familiar raspy drawl. "Well," I said, "maybe that's not so bad, after all."

—Sheri Zeck—

49

Reunited

A mother's love for her child is like no other love. To be
able to put that feeling aside because you want the best
for your child is the most unselfish thing I know.
~Mary, American Adoptions Birth Mother

There I stood, blurry-eyed, looking at a face so familiar I could mistake it for my own if I didn't know better. We embraced and then stared at one another in disbelief.

It felt like an out-of-body experience, like living in an alternate universe where you aren't quite awake, but you aren't asleep, either. I hugged her again. She was real, a living, breathing person with skin and hair like mine.

Adopted at a very young age, I grew up surrounded by people whom I loved as family and still do to this day. The faces weren't like my own, nor the personalities, but they were mine to love nonetheless. As I got older, the curiosity to learn more about myself took hold and didn't let go. Who was I? Where did I come from?

With the support of my adoptive parents, at the age of twenty-one, I was given the chance to find out. I contacted the adoption agency and started the process of reaching out to my birth mother through the agency's reunion services. The process was convoluted and often frustrating. I didn't anticipate the many hoops to jump through and the caution with which the agency had to move to ensure the privacy of both parties should my birth mother choose not to meet me.

After several nerve-wracking days, I received a call from the social worker handling my case. They had located my birth mother, and she was willing to be in contact with me. I called my adoptive parents right away and told them the good news. They seemed to be just as excited as I was. My mom was especially looking forward to thanking my birth mother for the sacrifice she had made, which allowed my parents to start a family that wasn't possible on their own. I'm not sure if my mom cried, but I know I did.

I had created an image in my head of what my birth mother might be doing or what she might look like, and I was on the precipice of finding out. The process continued with e-mails between the caseworker, my birth mother and me. We went back and forth for what seemed like an eternity, but was only a few weeks. When the caseworker felt the relationship could stand on its own, without issue, she allowed us to exchange more personal contact information to continue our communication. After a series of e-mail exchanges and phone calls, the moment had finally come — we were to reunite.

So, there I was, in the private room of a bakery and sandwich store, looking at my birth mother who, twenty-one years before, had made the brave and difficult decision to put her faith in someone else.

"How are you?" "I can't believe this!" "We look so alike." She laughed; I laughed. We shared a sense of humor, which was comforting. It felt like catching up with an old friend whom I had never met. She had kind eyes, a warm smile, and a family of her own. I had siblings who were there to meet me, too. A smile spread across my face so wide that I thought my cheeks might never stop hurting. I had a new extension to my family, a younger brother and sister. I had never had a sister, and I promised myself that, given the chance, she would never have to steal my clothes, shoes, or make-up. I would gladly give them to her without fuss.

My mother was wearing a gray shirt, and so was I. Later, I learned that neither of us is too fond of bright colors. We compared old pictures, both aghast to see that the way we stand and pose is identical. She apologized for any problems I've ever had with my frizzy, crazy hair and blamed herself. We laughed out loud and confessed we both are in a committed relationship with our flatirons to keep the wildness of our hair at bay. Our lives seemed to intertwine in ways we could never have guessed.

We introduced our families to each other, shared more than a few hugs and shed more than a few tears. I understood that my life would be different after this, but different in a good way because I had a unique story to tell. I watched as my birth mother and adoptive mom interacted and shared tales of motherhood. My mom told my birth mother about my active childhood and rebellious teenage years. My birth mother smiled, laughed that familiar laugh, and said she understood since she had been just as active and rebellious in her youth.

I was one of the lucky ones. Lucky that my adoptive family loved me, cared for me and supported me. Lucky that my birth mother had been strong and brave, watching me be whisked away with only the hope that another family could provide what she couldn't. Lucky to see the smiles and laughs as we all interacted and agreed to spend more time together, making future plans for dinners and theme-park visits. I knew my story was special, and the twenty-one years waiting to learn it were all worth it. I found the missing piece to complete the puzzle, fill the hole in my heart and make palpable what once was just an image contrived from my imagination. I didn't need to imagine anymore — it is my reality.

— Michelle H. —

50

Learning from the Best

*Being a mother is learning about strengths you
didn't know you had, and dealing with fears
you didn't know existed.*
~Linda Wooten

My mom worked part-time in our local library and had a few hobbies, but she devoted the vast majority of her time to raising my siblings and me. From our perspective, that was both good and bad.

Mom was an excellent cook, and she was always willing to play a game or read with us. She was liberal with the yeses when we asked to have friends over, too.

While having Mom around so much was great for those reasons, she did other things that really bugged me.

There was this weird counting thing she did when my siblings and I did not comply immediately with her requests. It usually went something like this:

Mom (in a cheerful voice): "Time for bed, kiddos."

Us (whispering to each other): "She doesn't sound mad yet. I'm sure we can stay up at least ten more minutes."

Mom (less cheerfully): "Kids, it's bedtime. You need to brush your teeth."

Us (shrugging): "I think we've still got time."

Mom (angry now): "Kids, this is your last warning. If you aren't in the bathroom brushing your teeth by the time I count to three, you're gonna be sorry. One… Two…"

Us (decisively): "I think it's time now."

And we'd run to do whatever it was she'd told us to do minutes earlier. I hated that counting-to-three thing. It worked every time, and it drove me nuts. I decided that when I became a mom, I would never, ever do that to my kids.

When I became a teenager, Mom did something else that bugged me. Anytime I asked to go to a party where the kids' parents might not be home, Mom would say "no." Not only that, she had this super cheesy line to accompany it. "I'm not trying to control you," she'd say. "I'm trying to protect you. The rules I make come from a place of love, not a desire to control."

"My mom's not too strict," I'd tell my friends. "She just loves me an awful lot."

"If your mom loved you less, would you be allowed to go to Brian's party this weekend?" my friends would tease me.

While I didn't like missing out on things, I believed Mom when she said that it was love, not control, that dictated her parenting decisions. I didn't like it, but I understood it, and in my wiser moments, I even appreciated it.

Nevertheless, I vowed that when I had kids, I would be a cool, laidback parent who trusted my kids to make good decisions without a lot of rules to govern their behavior.

When I became a mom, my laidback attitude lasted an entire fifteen months — and then my baby learned to walk.

I figured out quickly that being a cool mom was far easier when my only child was incapable of moving from the spot where I'd last seen him. But once he was mobile, he could get into things. He could make messes. He could hurt himself.

Gone was my super-chill attitude. I became that little boy's shadow, following behind him to make sure he didn't drink Windex or go swimming in the vat of Crisco I kept for chocolate-chip-cookie emergencies.

By his second birthday, things got worse. That sweet little baby started testing the boundaries. *Mommy said not to touch the light socket, but is that a hard-and-fast rule, or is it negotiable?*

So I did the only thing I knew to do: I pulled out Mom's secret weapon. Yes, it's shameful but true. I became a mom who counts at her children.

Although I hated it, the counting worked like magic. This little person who could care less about what I said at "one" and "two" suddenly became compliant the second before I said "three."

I decided that having a child who did not drink household cleaners or swim in lard was more important to me than being a cool mom.

I had another child and counted at that one, too. I'd hear other moms counting at their children, and it would make me feel better. If it works, it works, I decided finally.

My kids got older and began asking permission to go to other kids' homes. "Invite them to our house instead," I'd say every time.

Suddenly, I realized why Mom almost never said "no" when we asked to have friends over. "If our house is the hangout house, we'll always know what our kids are doing," I told my husband. "It's a genius plan."

I stocked up on pizza rolls, microwave popcorn, and earplugs, and our house became the place to be.

Just when I thought I'd mastered this parenting thing, everything changed again. "Mom, can Jessica come over this weekend?" my son asked.

"Jessica? That's a girl's name, and you're a boy," I said with a calmness I didn't feel. *How could this be happening already?*

And with the onset of opposite-gender friends, I became even less of a cool mom. We laid out an entirely new set of rules, which included things like ensuring that all dates remain on the first floor of our home since all the bedrooms are on the second floor.

When the kids protested these new rules, I said, "It's only because I love you, and I don't want you to make decisions you'll regret later."

"But don't you trust me?" they asked.

"Yes, I do trust you, and I love you more than life itself. And that's why these rules are in place. I love you, and I want to protect you."

As soon as the words left my mouth, I realized the awful truth: I'd turned into my mother. And then I realized a greater truth: Turning into my mother wasn't a bad thing.

My mom raised four great kids. My siblings and I are all college graduates. None of us has ever been arrested or struggled with an addiction. We're all married and have families of our own.

Mom has a good track record in this parenting thing. If turning into her means my kids will turn out well, then count me in.

Turns out, I'm not a laidback, super cool mom. I'm an old-school, count-at-my-kids-until-they-listen kind of mom. I'm also a love-them-with-everything-I-have kind of mom.

If it works, it works.

And I learned from the best.

— Diane Stark —

Chapter
6

Wise
Words

51

Why Not Be Both?

No influence is so powerful as that of the mother.
~Sarah Josepha Hale

To the young boy that I was, the world was binary. Everyone played a singular role. My schoolteacher was a teacher. My dad was an engineer. The cashier at the store was simply a cashier. Everyone had a single path to follow. So when I was about to leave elementary school and I thought I needed to figure out my own future, I asked my mother, "Should I become a writer or an artist?"

"Why not be both?" she answered, calming the whirlwind of worries inside me within an instant.

I could be more than a single thing? A writer *and* an artist? My mother's simple words changed my future.

"If you enjoy both, then pursue both," she continued.

It was exactly what I needed to hear. It wasn't just the fact that I could pursue two different roles, but that she believed in me, in my ability to attain both dreams. I could be more than I thought.

It went beyond my potential career options, too. She opened my mind to a whole new view of life. Anything seemed possible at that moment. I was free to chase any and all of the dreams I had.

Whenever I face a defining decision in my life, I return to those words of wisdom spoken to me more than twenty years ago. Like a comforting hand upon my shoulder, my mother's perspective eases my anxiety. I know that even if I fail at one path, a plethora of other routes remain open for me to follow.

—Brian Danforth—

52

A Different Path

The mother's heart is the child's schoolroom.
~H.W. Beecher

My hand trembled as I answered the phone call that would change my life forever. "Jill, this is the doctor's office. I'm sorry to tell you that your procedure was not a success. You are not pregnant."

I could feel the blood drain from my face. All my dreams of becoming a mother came crashing down around me. Fred and I had tried to get pregnant for three years, with no success. In-vitro was our last hope, and now all the surgery and treatments were for naught. All I ever wanted was to be a mother, and now that wasn't going to happen.

I felt like a failure.

I wanted to cry my eyes out, but I was in the middle of a big box store, shopping with my mom.

As soon as I ended the call, my mom looked over at me questioningly.

"Oh, Mom," I cried. "The in-vitro didn't work. I'm not pregnant."

She hurried over to me and gave me a hug. "It's okay," she said. "You can try again."

I leaned into her. "No, Mom, we can't try again." My voice broke. "We've spent all the savings we had. I'll never be a mom. The dream is dead." We stood there for a few seconds, letting my words sink in.

When the teacher would ask the class what they wanted to be when they grew up, I was the one kid in the class who wanted to be a mom. I wanted to be the type of mom who played with her kids outside. A mom who would spend one-on-one time with them, asking about their day. A mom who would teach them to read. A mom who would love them and give them all the skills they needed to be the best they could be. I wanted to be like my mom.

Then Mom said the words that still stay with me today. She said, "It's not the end of the world."

I looked at her in shock. She had six kids! My friends all wanted to have a mom like her. Standing before me was the epitome of motherhood, and she was telling me it wasn't the end of the world? It was *her* world!

"I always wanted to be a schoolteacher, ever since I was a little girl," she explained patiently. "I didn't want to get married and have kids. I wanted to teach kids. That was my dream. Then, when I met your dad and got married, the dream of teaching school was gone. My life is very different than I imagined it would be." Mom grabbed my hand. "Your life will be different than you imagined it. Not better or worse, but different. You still have a purpose and a path to travel. So travel it."

I thought about Mom's words of wisdom for the next few weeks. If my dream of having children was over, what purpose did my life have? What was in my future?

That's when I started to volunteer, and my purpose became clearer. Perhaps I didn't have children to love and nurture, but I had seniors in the seniors' residence who needed a friendly visitor. I had cats and kittens in my neighbourhood shelter who needed me to love them, care for them and find them homes. I also had children's groups that would come into a museum where I volunteered so I could teach them about history. Was it the same as having my own children? No, but in the process of healing and moving forward in my life, I was making a difference in other people's lives. In turn, I was growing and learning and creating a different path on which to travel.

My life has been very different and, thankfully, very fulfilling. I often wonder if I would have come to this epiphany about life without Mom's wisdom. Would I have continually mourned the loss of a dream, and by doing so, hurt my marriage and the people around me? I'll never know because I was blessed with having a wise, loving person in my life who put aside her dream of becoming a schoolteacher to be my mom.

—Jill Berni—

53

The Strength of Forgiveness

Forgiveness does not change the past,
but it does enlarge the future.
~Paul Boese

My father was killed by a drunk driver when I was nine weeks old. At nineteen, Mom was a newlywed, a new mother and a widow. After several months of being consumed by grief, my mother decided to enroll in the local university. That's where she met Stephen. By the time I was three, they were married.

Although my mother and I were very close, Stephen was extremely hard on me. I never felt loved or accepted by him. At the end of my junior year of high school, he informed us he was quitting his job and opening a small business in a town 250 miles away. I felt as though the rug had been pulled out from under me. I was just about to start my senior year, and I wanted to graduate with the friends I had gone to school with since kindergarten. The day we moved, he literally dragged me kicking and screaming out of the house. I vowed that day I would never forgive him.

For the next ten years, it seemed like our family dissolved into nothing. My mother and stepfather got divorced and halfheartedly dated other people. After many years of loneliness, they started dating each other again. They began to attend church together, and they dedicated their lives and their relationship to God. After a year, they remarried. I was thankful I was 2,000 miles away so I didn't have to pretend to be happy for them. Just because my mother could forgive him didn't mean I could.

My mother tried to explain why she had allowed my stepdad back into her life. She told me why forgiveness is so important. "I didn't just forgive him for *him*," she said to me one day. "I forgave him for *me* because the unforgiveness was too much to bear." She explained how important it is to let go of resentment and live in love and forgiveness instead. I didn't listen.

In 2011, my mother was diagnosed with an extremely rare brain disease called corticobasal degeneration. It started with her losing her balance and progressed to her being confined to a wheelchair and living in a nursing home.

Mom had been in the nursing home for six months when I went to visit her. I didn't want to stay with my stepdad during my visit, but I couldn't afford an extended stay in a hotel, so I decided to put my feelings aside and make the best of it for my mother's sake.

I had planned on staying only two weeks, but when I witnessed how gravely ill she was, I promised her I'd stay until the end. The first few months with my stepfather were extremely uncomfortable. My resentment kept the wall up between us.

Every day when I visited Mom, she would ask me how my stepdad and I were getting along. I didn't want to disappoint her, so I made it sound like we were getting along better than we were. Many times over the next several months, Mom would ask me to reconsider forgiving my stepdad, as she had, but I ignored her.

Then my mother became extremely ill with a virus and was moved to a local hospice facility. Family flew in from all over to say their goodbyes. During one of my visits, Mom reached out and took my hand. Her voice was weak, but she spoke with strength when she told me it was time to let go and open my heart to my stepfather. "I want to leave this world knowing that you still have a parent you love and can rely on," she said.

She told me stories that illustrated how he had changed. He built the wheelchair ramp in front of their house so Mom could stay home a little longer. He helped her dress, bathe and get to doctors' appointments. He cooked and cared for her. And after she was admitted to the nursing home, he never missed a daily visit.

She told me that he encouraged her when she wanted to give up, comforted her when she was in pain, and showed her, as well as told her, how much he loved her every day. "This is the man I forgave and fell in love with again," she said. "The man you hate doesn't exist anymore."

When I walked in the door that night, he was sitting in the living room reading the Bible with his cat on his lap. In that moment, I saw the man my mother saw, and I realized she had been right all along. I was flooded with love for a man I had despised all my life. He looked up and saw that I had been crying. With a fearful look, he said, "Is your mom okay?" I told him she was sleeping comfortably when I left, and then the words I had kept locked up for years tumbled out of me.

I thanked him for taking such good care of my mother throughout her illness. I thanked him for allowing me to stay with him indefinitely so I could be with her. I told him I was sorry for all the years of distance and animosity. His eyes filled with tears as he apologized for the times he was cruel to me when I was a child, for moving me away from our home and friends, and for never being the father I needed. And he told me how much he loved my mother, how much he had always loved her, and how sorry he was for his part in the failure of their first marriage.

My mother didn't die that day. She's still in the nursing home. Every day is a struggle, but my dad (no longer "stepdad" in my eyes) and I work as a team to care for her. Now, I consider him to be one of my closest friends. I'm so thankful my mother didn't just tell me how important forgiveness is — she showed me. I feel as if I've shed a ton of bricks and lightened my soul. Proof that Mom really does know best.

— Kim Carney —

54

Happy for No Reason

Taking care of yourself doesn't mean me first,
it means me too.
~L.R. Knost

I saw the last guest out the door and then, exhausted, flopped on the sofa. It had been a good birthday party; everyone had enjoyed it. My one-year-old son loved it, too.

I looked around at everything I had to clean up. The glow of the party vanished, but as I was preparing mentally to get started, I heard my mother call out to come in and sit with the family to unwrap gifts. Reluctantly, I joined them. My son was really enjoying tearing off the paper and seeing a new toy emerge from each package.

In due time, I grew restless and was about to leave when Mom pulled me aside and gave me a small box. "This is for you. Don't worry, I have given away the eatables. Everything else can wait until tomorrow. Now you go and catch up on some sleep." I hugged her and went upstairs.

In my room, I opened the gift and inside was a card with the word TODAY on the cover. Puzzled, I opened the card and found a note: "Enjoy your day tomorrow. Cab will pick you up at 7:00 a.m. Read this letter when you are there." I wondered what this was all about, but that was Mom: mysterious as always. How could I go tomorrow anyway? It was Sunday, but there was so much to do. I'd skip the trip, I decided, and I made a mental note to tell my mom. But before I could do so, I heard my son cry and went to him.

I forgot all about the gift until morning when a reminder on my phone announced that the cab had arrived. I went out and saw Mom giving instructions to the driver. I told her I wouldn't go; there was so much to do. But she would have none of it. Handing me a bag she had prepared, she sent me off to spend a full day at a park and resort.

I wasn't happy because I wanted to get through my to-do list before going back to the office on Monday. Nevertheless, once I arrived, I went in. As a child, I had spent many a happy day in this park at this resort. Though not perfectly timed, it was a welcome break. I sat down on a bench, soaking in the view. I searched the bag for my phone but realized that Mom had deliberately removed it. Instead, I found the gift box and opened it to read her letter.

Remember, when you were young, you were happy for no reason. Just happy to be.

Yes, I remembered. Those were the days when happiness was so natural.

The letter continued:

Of late, you have put so many terms and conditions on your happiness. So, I thought I would send you here to rekindle your memories. You know, after so many years, I have realized that the perfect day, the perfect future, never arrives. When we are young, we think we will be happy when we grow up. When we are in our teens, we want to be adults so we can have financial freedom and make all our decisions. When we are adults, we think we will be happy when we get married, and then when we have our own house and then when we retire. So on and so forth. But you know what? Life is a journey. The destinations will arrive with their own problems. It is very important to enjoy the journey, now and today.

I knew what she meant. My life had become a big to-do list. At the office, I would think of home. When home with my one-year-old, I wanted to run to the order of the office. Afraid I would lose out, I hit the gym with a vengeance. Determined that having a child would not change my life, I committed myself to all social engagements. In the process, I was just burnt out.

The letter further read:

These are precious moments of life with Dhruv and your husband.

Your worry is unwarranted. Time is not running out. Different stages of life require different adjustments, and that is okay.

I could see why Mom had sent me here and written all this in the letter. If she had told me the same thing at home, I would not have had the patience to listen, and I would have argued with her. Brilliant! Grudgingly, I acknowledged that she was right. I was indeed fighting to keep everything in order. In trying to be everything, I was enjoying nothing. I was on a constant treadmill of reaching toward the future but never enjoying the present.

The letter concluded:

Okay, enough for today. Now, enjoy your day.

My mom had unusual ways, but I was glad I was here. "Happy for no reason" — without terms and conditions. With nothing to do, I soaked in the feeling for a long time. I could feel the joy bubble up in me. I must have fallen asleep after that. When I woke up, I was completely refreshed and had so much more clarity, as if a light had been turned on inside. I was grateful to Mom.

Looking back, it was a very memorable day for me. I returned home in the late evening and saw my son and Mom rolling with laughter. Suddenly, I could decode the mystery of the gift box. It meant, "Today is a gift."

I smiled at Mom. She understood that I really liked her gift and perspective. Every day is indeed a gift, which is why it is called the "present." I could see that clearly now.

—Anju Jain—

55

A Strange Sound

In the sweetness of friendship let there be laughter,
and sharing of pleasures. For in the dew of little
things the heart finds its morning and is refreshed.
~Khalil Gibran

My parents decided to start fostering soon after I was born, so I don't remember a time when our house didn't have a revolving front door that was continually bringing in and taking away new and exciting people. During the first eighteen years of my life, I had more than fifty brothers and sisters. It's hard to admit that, although I think I remember all of their faces, I struggle to remember all of their names, especially from the earlier years.

I can recall special moments, though: A young boy who would play peek-a-boo with me for hours on end when I was a toddler. An older girl who patiently taught me how to put on blush and eyeshadow when I had to perform in a school play. A teenager who would get into trouble sometimes but would always take the time to help me pass any video-game levels I got stuck on. All of them hold a place in my heart, but some of them affected me in a way that shaped how I viewed and interacted with others for the rest of my life.

Such was the case with one little girl named Charlotte. I was six years old when Charlotte came to stay with us. She was sweet, she loved animals, and she happened to be the same age as me, which made us instant friends. Charlotte also happened to have severe heart disease. This meant she was very tired a lot of the time, and she couldn't really go outside and play without becoming tired and lethargic within moments. But there was a light at the end of the tunnel for this young girl carrying such an unfair burden: She was scheduled for major heart surgery in a few weeks.

She had come to stay with us because her mother, who loved her very much, had been mentally unwell and was unable to deal with the stress of the situation, which resulted in a nervous breakdown. Charlotte was to stay with us for the duration of the surgery and healing time so that her mother could get well.

We shared a bedroom and would spend hours lying on the floor, making up elaborate stories about our stuffed animals and dolls. We would watch movies together and listen to music. So, when it was time for Charlotte to finally make her big trip to the hospital, those few days she was gone felt like an eternity.

My parents kept me informed as much as possible, but it was a very hard concept for a child to understand. I can only imagine how it felt for Charlotte, having to go through such an ordeal with just a basic understanding of how it all worked.

When Charlotte finally returned to us, there was a joy throughout the house. The surgery had gone spectacularly, and she was recovering so quickly that they felt confident enough to release her sooner than planned.

She had our room all to herself for the first bit of home recovery. Although she was weak at first, she was a fighter. We watched her grow stronger every day. Once she began to feel better, I moved back to our shared space. It seemed like things would be getting back to normal, but Charlotte didn't seem quite herself. When the night began to draw in, she suddenly grew distant and quiet. This was understandable considering the circumstances, but with that special way in which children can read each other, I knew that something was wrong.

Nothing came of it until later, when we were both tucked in our beds with our pajamas on and our favorite stuffed animals clutched in our arms. I could hear Charlotte tossing and turning in her bed, and her small voice finally squeaked out at me from under the covers.

"Ever since I got back, I feel like something's not right in here...."

I keep hearing this loud sound, and I think it's coming from under my bed."

I couldn't hear anything myself, so I tried to calm her down. We talked about different things as a distraction, but I found myself conjuring up all sorts of strange and bizarre explanations for what could be hiding in our room. When we tried to clear our heads and fall asleep, I could still hear Charlotte moving around. I knew it was time to call Mom.

I told Charlotte to sit tight and then tiptoed down the hallway toward my parents' bedroom, where I woke up my mother and shared our predicament with her. She slid out from the covers and wrapped a robe around herself, following me back down the hallway.

When we got back, I stayed by the door, peering in, as my mother flicked on the lights and began to search the room. She peeked inside the closet and then got down to check under both beds. Finally, upon finding nothing, she sat on the edge of Charlotte's bed. Charlotte was sitting up against the pillows with her knees pulled up against her chest. I watched as my mother placed a gentle hand around hers and inquired as to what was going on.

They talked softly for a few moments. I heard Charlotte explaining what she had been hearing and when it had started, and then I saw my mother place a soft hand on Charlotte's chest, right where her heart was. Finally, I saw my mother turn her head to the side for composure, and her cheeks shone with tears.

She explained to Charlotte that the sounds weren't coming from the room at all, but from inside her. Her heart was finally strong enough. She was hearing it beat for the first time.

Charlotte stayed with us for another month before she went home to her family. I remember crying at the loss of a sister and a friend when she left. But I understand now how wonderful it must have been for her to go home. I will be forever grateful for the time she shared our home with us, and for all the foster children that my parents brought into my life.

— S. Chamberlain —

56

The Letter

To send a letter is a good way to go somewhere
without moving anything but your heart.
~Phyllis Theroux

My mother, though a warm person, rarely expressed her emotions outwardly. As I was growing up, I knew that she loved me, but I couldn't always feel it in my heart. Therefore, as an elementary student off to summer camp in Jeju (an island off the coast of South Korea) for the first time in my life, I did not expect anything from my mother except encouragement to do my best and be a good girl. And in the beginning, I was right. At least, I thought I was.

During the summer camp, I got an extremely bad case of homesickness. I was okay during lessons and activities, but at night I was overcome with loneliness. I couldn't stop crying. It got worse when my allowance was stolen from me. My roommate made fun of me by hiding my possessions and treating me like a baby. It got so bad that I almost told the staff that I wanted to go home. Almost.

The thing that changed my mind was a letter that my mother sent me. My mother sent me letters almost every day, mainly to tell me to work hard, to learn and to ask how I was. However, one letter was different from the others, containing more than encouragement.

Dear In-Young, how are you doing? I wonder which stuffed animal you're sleeping with today — your unicorn or your teddy? I hope they will be a source of comfort to you, away from home for so long.

I was puzzled at this start of the letter, since my mom had never begun her letters like this before.

When I saw you off to camp, I was proud of how much you've grown, but I was a little sad because you've become old enough to go away from home for such a long time. I don't know how you must be doing, since you don't let on much during your phone calls, but knowing you, I think you must be feeling lost and alone in the world, so far away from home.

I choked up a bit here since she had brought up the very thing that had been bothering me for the entire camp.

I know it must be hard for you to be in a foreign place with only strangers for company. Still, I believe in you, and I know you will succeed in everything you try during camp.

This made a lump form in my throat as I read. I savored the wonderful words, "I believe in you," as I read on.

To be honest with you, I'm still quite worried about sending you to camp for the first time. Jeong-Yoon [my younger sister] has been telling me that the house seems strangely quiet and dull without you here, and I agree with her. I was so used to having my little baby next to me all the time that I didn't realize how much I would miss her if she went away. I expect you must be feeling the same way about us, being so far away from your family, who loves you very much.

The lump in my throat grew larger as I read these words. I hadn't realized my family was missing me as much as I missed them.

Still, we'll see each other soon once you come home from camp. Don't worry about us. Just remember that we love you, and we believe in you to do a good job in camp. I wonder what you'll be dreaming about today. I think I'll be dreaming about you coming home, with a smile on your face tonight. See you... in your dream.

With love,

Mom

The effect of this last part, of seeing my mother in my dream, made me burst into a new stream of tears.

That was the last time I ever cried at camp. After that letter, I joined in the activities with gusto, even winning second place in the spelling bee. I managed to have a good time and went home triumphant, having made new friends.

Today, as a college student writing this story, I still carry my mother's letter in my heart. It helps me whenever I face an obstacle that overwhelms me. I remember that my mother loves me and believes in me, just as she did all those years ago when she sent her little girl off to summer camp. With this in mind, I get up, dust myself off, and plow on through everything life throws at me, with my head held high and a determined smile on my face.

— In-Young Choi —

57

The Triple B

Children are mirrors, they reflect back to us
all we say and do.
~Pam Leo

W hen she spotted flashing lights in the rearview mirror of our powder-blue station wagon, she muttered, "Blankity-blank-blank."

"What is it, Mommy?" I asked.

"Duh! She's getting pulled over," said my brother Danny.

"It's okay, kids," Mom said, her voice cracking. She began digging madly through the vehicle's overflowing glove box for registration papers.

Danny shouted a warning. "Mom, here comes the cop!"

"Blankity-blank-blank!" Mom repeated as beads of sweat formed on her brow.

Clearly, Mom was irked. And anxious. And hot.

Suddenly, the advertisement for Dry Idea deodorant popped into my head: "Never let them see you sweat."

I tapped Mom's arm and handed her one of the crumpled tissues she had just hurled my way as she poked through the glove box.

"Quick! Wipe your face and look innocent!" I said, having no clue what she had done wrong.

The officer knocked on the glass of the driver's side window.

"License and registration," he barked.

No greeting. No pleasantries. Not even a tip of the hat.

After another moment of digging, Mom unearthed the papers

that were wedged between the owner's manual and a dusty road atlas.

"Here," Mom said.

The officer marched back to his squad car. Mom sat quietly, her thumbs nervously drumming on the thin blue steering wheel.

"Why is the fuzzy after you, Mommy?"

"It's the fuzz, dip wad," Danny corrected me. "She got busted for speeding. And it's all your fault, Christy," he continued, poking me in the ribs. "If we hadn't been rushing to get you to your stupid dance class, Mom wouldn't be going to jail now."

"What? Jail!" I shrieked. "Mommy, no!"

I hurled myself into the front seat, draping my body across Mom's lap and, in the process, banging my forehead on the gearshift.

"I won't let him take you!" I proclaimed.

"Honey, I'm not going anywhere," Mom said. "Stop scaring your sister, Danny."

He snickered as I positioned myself in the back seat, rubbing my sore head.

After jotting down our license plate, the husky cop sauntered back to the window and handed Mom a slip of paper. He cleared his throat and said gruffly, "In the future, slow down."

Mom read the ticket, and when he was out of earshot, muttered "Blankity-blank-blank" again.

My mom was not one to use expletives. Not that she didn't let one fly occasionally when my brother and I weren't within earshot, but for the most part, she kept her emotions in check.

Still, she was human, so sometimes anger, irritability, and aggravation got the best of her. For instance, the day she dropped a glass jar of canned tomatoes on the tile floor and it shattered into a million shards, steam blew from her ears and she blurted out, "Blankity-blank-blank!"

The blustery morning she stepped onto our driveway in sub-zero temperatures to scrape the station wagon's windshield and slipped on a patch of black ice, she shrieked, then whimpered, and then grumbled, "Blankity-blank-blank!"

The time she got the whole family dressed in our Sunday best for a portrait at Olan Mills and then realized, upon our arrival at the studio, that she had the dates mixed up, she took us by the hand, gritted her teeth, and whispered, "Blankity-blank-blank."

It should come as no surprise to learn that I grew up thinking that "blankity-blank-blank" was a super long cuss word. Therefore, I made sure never to utter it under any circumstance — not even if my brother was irritating me.

Then one day, after enduring a tiff with said brother, I stomped up the stairs carrying my Barbie case, which was stuffed to the gills with doll paraphernalia. When I reached the top step, the latch that held the case together unhinged, causing it to pop open and expel hundreds of tiny Barbie shoes, accessories, and items of clothing.

Without even thinking, I exclaimed at the top of my lungs, "Blankity-blank-blank!"

Instantaneously, my face turned beet red. I cupped my mouth with my trembling hands and awaited my reprimand from Mom, who had come running.

"Oh, sh*t!" I uttered. "I'm sorry, Mommy!"

Mom's eyes grew wide.

"What did you just say?" she asked.

No way was I going to repeat the odious phrase again, so I hung my head in shame and apologized once more.

"Sorry, Mommy," I said sheepishly. "I got mad and said the 'B word.'"

"The what?" Mom asked. "It sounded to me like you said the 'S word.'"

No, I was sure of the phrase that had tumbled out of my mouth, and I most certainly had declared, with utter abandon, the Triple B.

"You do know that's a profanity, right?" Mom asked gingerly. It was clear she was trying to educate me without humiliating me.

"Oh, yes, Mommy. I know."

"So, where have you heard that word before?" Mom asked.

"From you."

Mom's eyebrows shot skyward.

"That can't be," she insisted. "I never use that language."

"Sure you do, Mommy. You used it just the other day when you got pulled over by the fuzzy."

Mom's expression turned from bemused to amused as she fit together the pieces of the puzzle.

"Are you referring to 'blankity-blank-blank'?"

"Mommy! Watch your mouth!"

"Honey, that's not an actual curse word. I use that phrase in place of swearwords. You know, like a fill-in-the-blank kind of thing."

At that moment, I experienced my greatest childhood epiphany.

"There are quite a few profanities in the world, and until someone tells you what they are, you may not even be aware," Mom said, getting down on her hands and knees to help me retrieve my Barbie gear. "Let me clue you in while we clean up."

She proceeded to let me know that the "S word" was one such example. I must admit, I could certainly see why it was so widely used. It was easy to say — just one syllable — and it rhymed with everything: fit, lit, bit, hit, quit. What fun! Plus, let's face it: "Blankity-blank-blank" didn't roll trippingly off the tongue, so I didn't see incorporating it into my vernacular. Not now. Not ever.

Suddenly, I had a new appreciation for my mom, who had developed her own secret code of cursing that enabled her to shield me from obscenities while still being able to release her emotions out in the open.

After offering a brief rundown of curse words, many of which I had already heard on the bus or playground, Mom asked if I had any questions.

"Just one," I said. "Doesn't dance class start in ten minutes?"

— Christy Heitger-Ewing —

U-Turn

People appreciate and never forget that helping hand
especially when times are tough.
~Catherine Pulsifer

Several years ago, my mom was driving us home from church. My sister and I were busy talking about a new game we were going to play, so we were startled when Mom made a quick U-turn.

We both asked her what was going on, but she didn't say a word as she pulled up next to the curb of an apartment building. She hopped out and rushed up to an elderly lady.

We watched in awe as Mom helped up the lady, who had fallen on the sidewalk. Mom picked up her groceries and then reached into her purse to retrieve a tissue, which she used to wipe off a small cut on the lady's forehead. Then she placed a Band-Aid over the cut.

Then Mom smiled and gave the elderly lady a hug and kissed her forehead. We could see Mom talking to her and then waving goodbye as she got back in the car.

Mom said, "Always be watching how you can be helpers now because one day you will be her age and may need help."

I have never forgotten those words. To this day, I still watch out to see if anyone needs my help, especially the elderly.

— Jana Bernal —

An Ordinary, Special Day

Always pass on what you have learned.
~*Yoda*, Star Wars

My nine-year-old son came into his room where I was filling his clothes organizer with outfits to wear to school in the days ahead. But for the last three weeks, the same outfit had remained in the organizer. I didn't understand why. "Nathan, why haven't you worn your new *Star Wars* shirt yet?" I asked. "You were so excited when we bought it. I figured you'd wear it right away."

Nathan shrugged. "It's brand-new, so I'm saving it."

"Saving it for what?"

"I don't know. Like a special day."

"Okay, honey," I said. "The reason we use the organizer is so you can choose your own clothes each day, so it's up to you when you wear it."

He nodded. "I'll probably wear it on my birthday. That'll be a special day."

"Your birthday is still several weeks away. Go ahead and wear the shirt, and I'll wash it before then. That way, you can wear it now and then again on your birthday."

He thought for a minute. "No, I think I'll save it. It's such a cool shirt. It needs to be saved for a special day."

I smiled, knowing I wouldn't change his mind. "It's up to you, bud." I patted his shoulder. "I'm going to start dinner now. I'm making chicken quesadillas."

I went downstairs, still musing at my son's "old soul" attitude toward wearing his new shirt. I found it funny that a kid who loves instant gratification was saving his favorite shirt for a special day.

I opened the refrigerator to get the ingredients I needed for dinner. I grabbed a bag of shredded cheese and smiled at what I found underneath: a package of pre-cooked, grilled chicken strips. They were expensive, so I didn't buy them often, but I loved the convenience of having half of the dinner prep work done for me.

I held the package of chicken in my hand, debating whether I should use it that night or not. Because of the extra expense, I tried to save it for nights when I was especially busy or tired. I decided that tonight didn't qualify, and I could make the chicken strips myself the old-fashioned way.

I started to put the package back in the refrigerator when the expiration date caught my eye. The chicken strips had expired two weeks ago.

I sighed, irritated with myself. I hated wasting food, especially a pricey item like this.

I thought of all the nights when I could have used the chicken, but instead I'd decided that I wasn't busy enough or tired enough to deserve the convenience. Now, I had to throw it away.

As I set about making dinner, I realized how often I'd put off treating myself well, even when it was easily within my ability to do so. Television shows I enjoyed watching sat unviewed on our DVR for weeks because I didn't allow myself to watch them until my to-do list was complete. And since I never completed everything on my to-do list, I never got to enjoy my shows. The same thing happened with novels I wanted to read and friends I wanted to meet for lunch or coffee.

Somehow, I'd developed a thought process that required me to earn time to relax. When had self-care become something I had to earn? Why did "me time" always come last on my to-do list?

I'd gotten into a bad habit, and worse, I feared I'd passed the pattern onto my son.

The phone rang. It was my mother-in-law.

"What's wrong?" she asked. "You sound upset."

I sighed and told her what was wrong. Ten minutes later, I got off the phone, feeling much better. I looked at the shredded cheese and rethought my dinner plan. I remembered that, three weeks ago, I'd made a double batch of taco meat. I'd frozen the extra meat so that I could take another night off from cooking.

Normally, I'd save the taco meat for a dinner emergency — just like I had the chicken strips that were now in the trash — but no more of that. Tonight was the night.

I tossed the frozen container in the microwave and then called for Nathan. "Bring a book," I said. "We're going to read together while dinner thaws."

He came running with a smile on his face. Reading together was his favorite thing. We snuggled on the couch, reading instead of cooking. It felt terrific.

When the taco meat was thawed, we ate, using the paper plates I save for busy nights when I don't have time to wash dishes. I grinned, realizing that using paper plates made me as happy as some people feel when they pull out their fancy china.

"We're eating on paper plates so we can read some more after dinner," I told Nathan.

He grinned. "All of a sudden, today feels like a special day."

I grinned back. "I know, and we have Grandma to thank. She told me to stop saving the good china for a special day that may never come. She said we should enjoy the little things each day, and that can make every day feel special. Grandma said we can't wait for someday." My smile grew. "Nathan, someday is today."

My mother-in-law raised eight kids in an era when self-care wasn't even thought about. But her wise words taught me that treating myself well isn't something I should have to earn. We all deserve to relax and enjoy small pleasures, even if what makes us happy is eating tacos on paper plates so we have more time to read.

The following morning, Nathan chose to wear his new *Star Wars* shirt. When I asked him about it, he said, "I decided to take Grandma's advice. It's silly to wait for a special day when we can just make our own special day."

I hugged my son, so grateful for this ordinary, special day and

What Words?

Making the decision to have a child—it is momentous.
It is to decide forever to have your heart
go walking outside your body.
~Elizabeth Stone

When I was expecting our first child, I missed my mom—maybe more than I'd missed her since she died. As an adoptee, my birth was never shared with her, and my greatest wish was that I could have her in the delivery room with me while I gave birth to my daughter, to share that experience with her.

I appreciated my mother-in-law's presence during that bittersweet time. She had two daughters of her own, but she never made me feel less important to her. She shared my excitement over my pregnancy and seemed to understand the loss I felt.

When my daughter was born, I was overwhelmed. Maybe it was the fact that she was the first person I'd ever seen who was biologically related to me. Or maybe it was the amazing love that only a parent can feel for a child.

After my husband and I returned home with our new baby, his mother visited. She was very excited to meet the first child of her only son. She threw herself into the role of helper, doing dishes and laundry, cooking and tidying up. She helped with the baby, but seemed more interested in letting us learn how to be parents. Whenever I thanked her, she brushed off the sentiment, making some lighthearted joke.

She didn't want gratitude. She was happy being of use.

A few days later, I worked up the nerve to ask the question that had consumed me since my daughter's birth. I expected she'd make light of it as well.

"Why didn't you tell me it would feel like this?" I asked.

"What do you mean?" she responded.

"Why didn't you tell me the depth of love I would feel for this tiny person? It's all consuming. I didn't know I could love anyone this deeply."

She put down the dishtowel and turned to me, her expression serious. "What could I have said?" she asked. "What words would I have used? How could I have possibly conveyed it? There's no way to explain it. You had to find it out for yourself. I knew you would. I knew the feeling would hit you both the minute you set eyes on her. And that's exactly what happened." A fleeting smile crossed her lips.

Moment over. She started chopping onions for the meatloaf she planned to make for dinner, an excuse to cover the tears in her eyes.

—Audrey RL Wyatt—

Chapter
7

Embracing
Change

61

Tattoos for Two

To describe my mother would be to write about a
hurricane in its perfect power. Or the climbing,
falling colors of a rainbow.
~Maya Angelou

"My mom will talk me out of it for sure," I said with confidence. "She just about flipped out when I got a second piercing in my ears."

"It sounds like you almost want her to talk you out of it," Katie said.

I thought about that and shrugged. I certainly was being indecisive.

I was twenty-something and had already lived in Europe for several years. I was looking forward to my first visit back home where I would indulge in all the things I missed about being in the States — shopping malls, American bookstores, and my favorite chain restaurants. And I'd gotten it into my head that I might want to get a tattoo while I was back home. At the time, tattoos were not that popular, especially among preppy girls like me.

I waffled daily about whether or not this was something I wanted to do. It was permanent after all, and I didn't want to regret it later.

I decided I would toss the idea out in the next phone conversation with my mother. I fully expected her to rant about the dangers and how nice girls didn't do such things. I expected her to put an end to the discussion with the ominous warning that I would regret such an irreversible action.

During the call, we chatted about the fun things we had planned, and then I casually dropped the bombshell. Contrary to my expectations, she didn't say much in response. I imagined her so horrified that she didn't know what to say. I pictured her giving me the "mom look" that could instantly quell any thoughts of rebellious behavior. I let the subject drop, taking her silence for an extreme form of disapproval. I resigned myself to abandoning the tattoo plan.

Finally, the time came for the trip. My mother and I spent our days catching up and reconnecting, indulging in plenty of retail therapy. One night, after a dinner out, Mom turned to me and said, "I have a surprise for you."

I expected we would be heading to our favorite ice-cream parlor or maybe renting a favorite movie. We got into the car, and she started driving without revealing where we were going. I kept trying to guess, but nothing looked familiar, and there were no clues to help me out.

Finally, we parked in front of some shops on a side street, and she proclaimed excitedly, "Here we are!"

I looked around but still could not figure out what the big surprise was. She waited a moment to build the suspense and then blurted out, "I made appointments for both of us to get tattoos!"

I could only stare at her, speechless. Was my conservative mother not only permitting me to get a tattoo, but getting one herself?

The rest of the evening moved along like a dream running on its own momentum, dragging me along. Mom picked out a hot-air-balloon design. I requested one of the angels from Michelangelo's Sistine Chapel, thinking the tattoo guy wouldn't have a clue what I meant and would never be able to execute such an intricate design. But Bruce pulled out a sample sheet of the famous artwork and asked which angel I wanted. Stunned, I picked the one resting his head on his folded arms. The next thing I knew, needles were piercing my shoulder.

As we left the shop with our new body art, Mom said, "Well, that was fun." And then she asked me if I wanted to go for ice cream.

— Donna L. Roberts —

62

Road Trip

*Sometimes the most scenic roads in life are the detours
you didn't mean to take.*
~Angela N. Blount

My mom is a road warrior with whom I've journeyed many miles. She and Dad were snowbirds who followed sunshine and seventy-degree temperatures between Pennsylvania and Arizona. Maintaining their lifestyle required four road trips annually, and I was their driver for many of those years.

We knew the route by heart, but Mom still insisted on giving me turn-by-turn directions from their trusty *Rand McNally Road Atlas* while Dad read or napped in the back seat. Dad's objective was to arrive at our destination in the fewest number of hours possible, despite Mom's suggestion to take a scenic detour or stop at the gift shop shaped like a giant candle.

In the glove box, Mom also kept a travel log and a sharp pencil with which she'd note the car's mileage and our precise time of departure. She'd jot down what time we passed each landmark, how long we'd stopped, the price of gas, the weather, what we ate, and our arrival time. I always attributed her attentiveness to the strong black coffee, which she'd sip continually, even after it had marinated for two days in the big Stanley Thermos. Mom's journal served as a ready review of each motel, hotel, breakfast bar, or public restroom we'd ever patronized. And her memory, in those days, was impeccable.

"Don't pull into that station!" she'd warn. "I remember the last time we stopped there, I saw roaches, and the door wouldn't lock. It was 1954."

"I don't remember that one, Mom. I wasn't born yet."

"Well, why take chances?"

Mom often read aloud from notes of previous trips, as well. "Last year, we left the house at 4:07 a.m. and passed this same exit at 5:35." Then she'd look at her watch and sigh. "It's already 7:00." At times, I felt like a contestant on *The Great Race*, one of Mom's favorite shows.

After Dad passed away, traveling our old familiar route was like a yellow-brick road of memories, and a 1,000-mile ribbon of mourning, too. So, Mom and I began to venture on roads less traveled, stopping along the way. Only then did she allow my GPS to navigate our route, but the *Rand McNally Road Atlas* stayed close at hand.

When Mom downsized to one small home in the Midwest, we began to enjoy shorter adventures closer to home. Somehow, in the shuffle, the atlas went missing. But on a spontaneous weekend trip to Hot Springs, Arkansas, we sure could've used old Rand McNally.

The reason for our weekend jaunt was two-fold: to enjoy the fall foliage and to relocate an old friend of Mom's. We meandered through the Ouachita Mountains and over black iron bridges that carried us across gushing white streams. We strolled along Bathhouse Row, enjoyed dinner at a historic hotel, and found a cozy room overlooking Lake Hamilton.

The following afternoon, I chose a more direct route for our return trip. Forests and valleys glowed crimson and gold against a deep blue sky. Our car handled the mountainous highway without incident until I shifted into reverse after stopping at a rest area outside of the Ouachita National Forest, and the transmission hesitated. A few miles down the road, the "check engine" light came on.

I pulled onto the first wide shoulder available, activated the car's flashers, and dialed for help on the car's built-in emergency-service provider. A woman's voice responded to my SOS.

"My check engine light is on," I offered. "Feels like the transmission."

"I can help you, ma'am. I just need to ask a few questions first."

Mom's eyes targeted me. "Who are you talking to, honey?"

"I'm speaking to you, ma'am," the voice answered her. "Are you in a..."

"Who's talking...?" Mom interrupted.

I pressed a finger to my lips while pointing to the car's speaker, and then asked, "Could you repeat the question, please?"

"Are you in a safe spot while I run diagnostics on your vehicle?"

I glanced at the steep ledge, trying not to sound frightened. "Yes."

"No," Mom chimed.

"Which is it, ma'am?" the voice asked.

"We're fine," I conceded. While on hold, I gave Mom a layman's tutorial on satellites and navigation systems. Within minutes, the voice returned.

"Your check engine light is on, ma'am, indicating your vehicle's transmission may be affected."

Seriously? Mom's eyes rolled. "That's what my daughter just told you!"

"Thanks," I piped up. "Can you tell me where we are and how far to the closest garage?"

"You're in Booneville, Arkansas."

Booneville? We hadn't passed any signs for Booneville, and neither my smarter-than-me phone nor my fading-in-and-out GPS showed Booneville on our route. I assumed the mountains were to blame. "Are you sure we're in Booneville?"

Mom unbuckled her seatbelt. "Where's that atlas?" she mumbled as she leaned toward the back seat.

"I'm sure you're in Booneville," the voice replied. "You're eight miles from the closest dealership that can provide service. I can program turn-by-turn instructions over your radio, or I can transfer you to roadside service. Which would you prefer?"

A logging truck roared past, shaking our vehicle. "I think we're safer on the road than teetering on its shoulder. I'll drive to the dealership. Eight miles? Straight ahead on Highway 71?"

"The dealership is on Broadway Street, ma'am. Not Highway 71."

"You said eight miles straight ahead."

"Yes, Ma'am. You're not on Highway 71. You're in Booneville. I can send you directions."

"Miss," Mom interjected, "we most certainly are on Highway 71. Didn't you see that truck?"

"I can't see you, ma'am," the voice answered.

Mom directed her gaze at me. "You told me she could see us."

I gave Mom's hand a gentle squeeze and further queried the voice. "Are you absolutely certain we're in Booneville? Can you actually see our location?"

"I know where you are, ma'am. You're in Booneville. The dealership is eight miles straight ahead on the right. Would you like me to program your turn-by-turn directions or not?"

I inferred "or not" to mean "or else," so I didn't press the issue. Soon, another female voice, more automated and less condescending, told us to continue our route.

Within moments, however, we passed a Highway 71 marker, confirming my suspicion. I swerved into a quick mart, veering from the pre-programmed directions, which initiated an onslaught of recalculated directions from the radio's speakers.

"Cancel," I instructed, while also explaining to Mom why I was stopping.

"Recalculating. Please follow directed route."

"Cancel."

"Recalculating. Please follow…"

"Cancel!" I repeated, irritation rising in my own voice. I knew I was listening to a computer, but apparently Mom did not.

Like a gunshot, my mother's hand smacked the car's dashboard, startling me. "Miss," Mom yelled at the radio, "would you please be quiet and let my daughter drive!" Then she pointed a finger inches from my nose and scolded me with her best "mom look."

"I told you not to get rid of that atlas!"

— Julia M. Toto —

63

My Mother the Feminist

Furnish an example, stop preaching, stop shielding,
don't prevent self-reliance and initiative, allow your
children to develop along their own lines.
~Eleanor Roosevelt

M y mother was a feminist ahead of her time. But I didn't know that as a child. It was just one of hundreds of things I didn't know growing up and have only come to appreciate as a middle-aged adult.

I grew up in Peoria, Illinois, in a middle-class neighborhood where the houses were either split-levels or ranches, and the owners were accountants, managers, and entrepreneurs. Most of the women did not work outside the home.

My mother was the epitome of what I didn't want in a mother. I wanted a 1950s-era mom in a pretty dress who kept the house spotless, braided my hair with ribbons that matched my outfit, and packed crustless sandwiches cut on the diagonal in my lunchbox.

When other mothers wore housedresses and pedal pushers, my mother wore blue jeans and sweatshirts. Other mothers went to the beauty parlor regularly, and sometimes I'd see them with a head full of plastic curlers. My mother chopped her hair short and barely owned a bobby pin. Mrs. Stewart went golfing with her daughter; Mrs. Miller had "the girls" over for coffee and cards; Mrs. Opal sewed fashionable outfits for her daughter. My mother taught me how to hold a bat and run the bases; our card game of choice was gin rummy; and, somewhere in the house, there might have been a needle and spool of thread.

Magazines like *Good Housekeeping* and *Ladies' Home Journal* did not come to our mailbox. Instead, we got *The New Yorker* and *Psychology Today*. My mother owned a single cookbook, Adelle Davis's *Let's Cook It Right*, whose pancake recipe called for wheat germ. Other mothers cut recipes out of the newspaper and had homemade cookies on the table after school. Mine, in the 1960s, had a compost bin on the kitchen counter. The contents were tossed into our garden — organic, of course.

Instead of Donna Reed, I got a beatnik, hippie, tomboy, free thinking, ahead-of-her-time woman. I got a mother who, along with my father, made sure I understood the reason for a college education was to be able to support myself, not to find a husband. I got a mother who nurtured my hobbies of baking and sewing, even though both were anathema to her. I got parents who opened my eyes to racial inequities, volunteerism, and social injustice. My mother encouraged my siblings and me to pursue any careers we wanted, not just those that were expected. My brother was a stay-at-home dad in the early 1990s, something he probably couldn't have done successfully had he been brought up in a non-feminist home.

Yes, it's not only women who benefit from being brought up in feminist households. It's men, too — men who don't cringe at the thought of a female boss, who don't have to be the primary breadwinner, who can raise their own strong daughters.

My mother saw the world through the eyes of an artist and talked about art and music therapy twenty years before they were mainstreamed. She mixed flour, water, and food coloring, and let us use the concoction to turn the living-room windows into stained glass. On Halloween, she guided us through the rag box as we created our own costumes. She believed creativity is the foundation for an open mind, and that an open mind is imperative for a just society.

This year, my mother turns ninety-one. She rarely leaves her house or, on many days, even gets dressed. But she still challenges her children, grandchildren and great-grandchildren to think globally,

64

Chicken Soup for the Soul

The Matchmaker

The art of love... is largely the art of persistence.
~Albert Ellis

We are in a playground fueled by the energy of city kids desperate to climb plastic tree houses, while their parents, grandparents, and nannies watch. We see a slightly stooped gentleman in a well worn but tidy blue blazer. He smiles as he admires the children. He looks like someone's grandfather. My five-year-old daughter likes him. So does my eighty-six-year-old mother, who is visiting me from Florida.

"Some people think he's dangerous," says my friend Anne, the old man's neighbor. "But he likes to come to the park and be around children. He lost his wife two years ago, and he's been devastated."

My mother spots an opportunity. Even though the man has come to the park to be cheered up by children, my mother is hoping he's ready to meet an octogenarian who is fit, far from feeble, and alone.

"He seems awfully nice," she tells me later, back in my apartment.

I thought his hair looked greasy, and his teeth were in bad shape. "My friend says he's a very sweet man," I say.

"I'd like to meet him," says Mother. "I miss companionship, you know."

For forty-nine years, she was with my father; after his death, she spent the next decade living with a man who turned her into a lovesick teenager with mushy cards and flowers. A year after his death, Mother is dissatisfied attending the ballet with groups of women; she's always preferred the company of men — from selecting golf foursomes to what she now calls "companions."

I call Anne, who lives around the corner from me. This is going to sound odd, I apologize, but my mother wants to meet that man from the playground.

"Mr. Meltzer?" Anne is slightly amused. "At least, I think that's his name. I called him Ned for a long time. I can't always understand him. He doesn't hear well."

"Neither does my mother," I say. "How can I get in touch with Ned? Or whatever his name is?"

"He lives on the third floor. I'm almost positive his name is Meltzer."

"I'll write him a note," I say. "The doorman is sure to know who he is."

That night, as Mother reads a book on meditation, claiming, "Meditation can cure lots of things," I struggle with a letter to Mr. Meltzer: *My mother, Sylvia, and I enjoyed meeting you in the park. She's visiting from Florida. She enjoyed talking to you and she said she would enjoy your company.* I feel foolish, but I plod on. *Have a nice day,* I sign off cheerfully.

On the way to the grocery store to buy dinner, I leave the note with Mr. Meltzer's doorman.

Every morning, Mother soaks her ginger crystals in water to remove the excess sugar, repeating how marvelous ginger is for digestion. She swallows a dozen vitamin pills, including ginkgo. Holding up the pill, she says, "It's for memory — that is, if I remember to take it!"

She laughs. I hide in the corner of my kitchen, surreptitiously smearing butter on my toast as if inhaling some illegal drug.

"I never eat butter," Mother says. "You shouldn't either. Haven't you put on a few pounds?"

She points to my multi-vitamin bottle, which I keep on an open shelf so I don't forget. (I need ginkgo, too.) "Vitamins should always be kept in cool, dark places."

She removes the now sugar-free ginger crystals from the glass of water. I remember feeling unnerved when I saw my grandmother's false teeth in a glass, which she always left out on display. Thanks to dental implants, Mother still has teeth. Instead of old-fashioned housedresses, she wears jeans and sneakers. I have a mother who sits with me at my computer as I retrieve weather forecasts, stock prices, and e-mails. Yet she speaks with regret about the world gone by.

"We all lived close to each other," she says. "Every Sunday, we had dinner with Aunt Mimi."

She lives thirty miles from my nieces and nephews, her grown grandchildren in Florida. They visit her on holidays.

"Maybe it would be better if you moved closer to them. That way you could see them more," I say, tearfully thinking of my mother eating dinner alone on Sundays.

"They have their own lives. And I have mine. I can't make new friends at my age."

"It must be difficult to meet male companions," I say.

"You mean ones who are walking and above ground?" Mother nods.

"Maybe you should look for younger ones," I suggest.

I glance at the phone. What must Mr. Meltzer have thought when he read my matchmaking letter? I haven't told Mother about dropping off the note. I don't want her to be disappointed.

I've been spoiled all these years with my strong-willed, strong-bodied mother, racing from museums to movie theaters. I've always had difficulty keeping up with her energy, but lately when we walk together on crowded streets, I must decrease my pace, reminding myself to back up into first gear. I'm used to chasing after my five-year-old daughter, who sprints to every corner; it's a race I always lose.

Now, Mother lags behind me as she used to when I was a child and she was tireless. After an afternoon gallivanting around the city, she needs to nap. I peek in on her, in the rocker where I once nursed my infant daughter. The meditation book is open, upside-down, on her lap, and her mouth is agape. I can see every bone in her face, and she suddenly looks much older in sleep. Tiptoeing inside, I listen for her breathing and am relieved to hear the regular rhythm.

The phone rings, startling her awake. I answer it, hearing Mr. Meltzer's voice. Mother smiles when I pass the phone to her.

"Hello?" she says. "Yes, yes, of course I remember meeting you.

How nice of you to call."

She winks at me, her matchmaker. Quickly shaking off the grogginess of her nap, she makes plans with the stranger on the phone. Her voice is lighter, her complexion flushed in a healthy glow.

"Do we have plans tomorrow?" she asks me, covering the receiver.

I shake my head, even though we had talked about taking my daughter to a children's museum. But I don't mind being ditched by my mother for the possibility of a new companion.

"Yes," she breathes excitedly into the phone. "I'd love to. What time will you pick me up?"

— Candy Schulman —

Bonding over the Kitchen Sink

*Some people arrive and make such a beautiful impact
on your life, you can barely remember
what life was like without them.*
~Anna Taylor

M y mother-in-law was never a fan of her son's girlfriends. For that reason, he didn't bring many of them home to meet her. She was the type of mom whom you only see on sitcoms. In fact, her son's friends nicknamed her "Mrs. Cunningham" based on the TV show *Happy Days* because she always welcomed them into her home with tea, cookies, or whatever else she had baked for company, while ironing, doing the laundry, cooking meals, gardening, and holding down a full-time job. She was the epitome of an ultra mom.

When I first started visiting my boyfriend, I was terrified of being in the presence of his mother. She never greeted me warmly, and we only exchanged a few words. There was always a sense of tension in Mrs. Cunningham's immaculate bungalow, and I avoided eye contact and confrontation at all costs.

When my boyfriend and I had our very first Christmas together, something amazing happened. My boyfriend's father was there, even though he had moved out. That made the atmosphere even more tense and awkward than usual.

His mom had cooked in the kitchen all day, creating a delicious turkey feast with all the trimmings and two decadent homemade pies for dessert. The kitchen was in utter disarray, and after everyone polished off full plates of her wonderful meal, the family all rose from the table and retired to the comfortable, overstuffed sofa and recliners in her living room. She stayed in the kitchen to tidy up the mess.

My boyfriend was seated on the couch and patted the seat beside him, indicating that he was saving me a spot to sit, digest and mindlessly watch whatever was on the TV with his sister, her children and his dad. Instead of getting comfortable beside him, I took a deep breath and walked bravely into the kitchen, grabbing a tea towel from the hanging towel rack beside Mrs. C.

Neither of us said a word for quite some time, and the air seemed too thick to breathe. But instead of panicking and walking back out to the living room to sit down beside my boyfriend, I pulled a pan out of the sink and began to dry it.

"That was a delicious supper. Thank you." I could barely get the words out.

"You are very welcome, dear. You don't need to help me," she replied.

"It's the least I can do. You worked so hard on supper and feeding everyone here today. I really appreciate it." I sighed in relief as these words came out in my normal voice. I stopped trembling inside, and for the first time in that house, I was not afraid of her.

She was a tiny lady, with thick red hair, pale skin that appeared almost flawless, and striking blue eyes. She was always dressed in pretty blouses with matching dress pants, and pearl necklaces draped down her chest, with matching pearl earrings in her tiny earlobes. She was beautiful, yet for someone of her stature, she was quite intimidating.

As she put the dirty dishes into the hot, sudsy water, she started asking me questions about my family and genuinely listening when I replied. In turn, I asked her about her work, recipes, and various other topics. Her tightly pursed lips loosened, and her eyes, although not looking directly at me, began to shine when she spoke. Within the hour it took us to wash, dry and put away all the pots, pans and dishes, we had developed a new understanding. Dare I say, we bonded.

From that day forward, when I came for a visit, she greeted me warmly and offered me tea or her baked delights. She always chose to talk with me, rather than go off to her room to read books alone.

Over the years, she and I became very close. She cried at our engagement, and she was beside herself with joy when we married and had our daughter. I don't think anyone besides us was more proud and in love with our baby girl than she was. Her joy bubbled over at every visit she had with us, and she was always full of warm hugs, love, support and understanding. We spoke on the phone daily, even if we had no specific reason to call each other. We always made time for a "visit," even by phone when my husband and I moved far away from her for a few years.

She and I could spend an entire day simply talking as we had coffee, prepared meals or just sat on the sofa. We would play endless games of *Yahtzee* and *Scrabble* together, and the majority of our time was spent chatting about anything and everything. No one on the planet knew more about me, or I about her. We shared every thought and opinion, and made many plans together. Every opportunity we had to spend time together, we took it.

During one of our very lengthy conversations, we talked about when I first started coming to her house. She told me that she resented me then because she had never seen her son fall for a girl so hard before. She loved having him living at home, and since she and her husband were splitting up, she feared being alone in the house if her son moved out to be with me. She said she always felt bad for treating me the way she had. It melted my heart to hear her say those words.

She taught me how to be a mom, a wife and, in many ways, a daughter. She taught me to bake bread and make pickles, and how to be a better human being. She found humor and the bright side in everything.

After every meal that we prepared, whether it was in our home or hers, she and I always did the dishes and cleaned up the kitchen. Even if there was a dishwasher, we always chose to wash everything by hand, as it gave us more time to talk. Her daughters would come into the kitchen and offer to help, and we always told them to go and relax, that we had it covered.

She passed away in 2009, and it has left a huge empty hole in our hearts. I will forever miss her, but when I smell Ivory dish soap and clean tea towels, I always smile tearfully inside. It takes me back to that Christmas of 1987, and that feeling in her kitchen, when an awkward teenager met her best friend and the most amazing mom ever, bonding over the kitchen sink.

Years later, when my husband and I were having some communication problems, our dishwasher mysteriously quit working. We didn't have the money to have it repaired, so we needed to wash dishes by hand. We would make sure that our daughter had something to keep her busy, and I'd fill the sink with Ivory dish soap and hot water. Never in a million years would his mother have believed it, but my husband dried dishes for me every evening. We actually enjoyed doing the chore together after a couple nights of having to work through it. In fact, we enjoyed our time together so much that we left the dishwasher broken for the next two months. We talked through some issues, had some laughs and shared memories. It made our marriage strong again.

My belief is that his mother was sending us her love and understanding, along with a reminder that something as small as washing dishes together can completely change a relationship.

— Christina Hausauer —

Money Well Spent

We keep moving forward, opening new doors,
and doing new things, because we're curious
and curiosity keeps leading us down new paths.
~Walt Disney

"Hey, Mom, I made it to the airport. Just waiting to board my flight." I hit Send and watch my phone in anticipation. I see the "dot-dot-dot" bubble pop up.

"We loved having you," she replies.

I want to pump my hand in the air. My eighty-four-year-old mom just texted me.

I was always proud of my mom's technical ability. She first embraced the Internet when she was in her sixties, using e-mail and comparing prices for big purchases. She even made a small killing selling Beanie Babies on eBay in the mid-1990s.

But as the world's online speed grew infinitely faster, hers slowed down. The remote area where my parents live only provided a dial-up connection, and the fifty dollars a month seemed like a huge part of their fixed income to pay for a frustrating, spotty experience, so she dropped her service.

Whenever we'd get together, she'd marvel at all the great photos of grand- and great-grandchildren on Facebook. It felt like my mom was completely missing out on special moments. "I need to get my computer sorted out," she'd lament.

This year, when I went to visit her for her birthday, I brought her a smartphone. My husband and I sprung for the extra-large iPhone 6 Plus, with its big screen only slightly smaller than a tablet.

"We have a phone, honey!" she protested, waving the ancient flip phone the two of them shared.

"Mom, you can do anything with an iPhone: get on the web, e-mail, Facebook. I'll even teach you how to text."

I spent much of that visit coaching her. At first, she was intimidated, afraid she was going to "mess things up." I tried to keep things simple, moving all but a few apps off the home screen, leaving only e-mail, phone, Facebook, text, Safari, and the camera. I threw in the weather app because I knew she would love it. I made her practice, and she caught on quickly. She even bought something on Amazon.

"Sorry, Clayson," my husband joked with my stepfather. "You're never going to see her face anymore. It'll be buried in her new phone."

The ability to shoot off a quick text has greatly increased the frequency of her interactions with our entire family. She checks Facebook daily, often sending cheery comments to her kids and grandkids.

The cost of the phone? I purchased it for $750 and added her to our monthly plan for an additional $15. I taught her to close down her apps; her sparse use barely makes a blip on our data.

I feel like getting her back on the Internet was like throwing her a lifeline. When I see her "like" something on Facebook or respond to a group text or e-mail, it warms my heart to know she's connected to the rest of the family. My octogenarian mother is now an avowed iPhone lover, and I couldn't be more thrilled.

— Barbara Brockway —

67

Baby Stuff

Becoming a grandmother is wonderful.
One moment you're just a mother.
The next you are all-wise and prehistoric.
~Pam Brown

My mother and I prepared for the birth of my first child at the dawn of the specialty baby store. We walked through floor displays of cribs, feeding tables and carriages; we explored "modern" paraphernalia like bouncers, swings and plastic baby carriers. In a time when no one knew babies shouldn't be unrestrained in flimsy car beds, these sometimes shoddy or dangerous items were considered state-of-the-art.

Mom was breathless with wonder at all the newly invented conveniences. She oohed and aahed over portable cribs, mobiles, umbrella strollers, swings, car seats and electric bottle warmers. Thanks to her encouragement, I started motherhood with a remarkable collection of baby "stuff" that grew as each new device hit the market. At first, the baby's paraphernalia was restricted to the nursery. Then it overflowed into the living room, kitchen, a corner of the dining room... even the bathroom. Before I knew it, time and work-saving devices snaked their insidious way into every room of the house. Unbelievably, I used all of it — at least once! What didn't break got passed down from my first daughter to my second daughter, and then on to assorted young mothers in the neighborhood.

When my own daughter announced she was pregnant with my

first grandchild, I couldn't wait to get back into the baby store and look at all the improved baby gear. Our first shopping foray was to a specialty store on steroids, a mega baby supermarket of warehouse proportions! Like my mother before me, I gasped audibly at the steep walls of colorful merchandise that reached majestically to the ceiling. I was wide-eyed and open-mouthed as my daughter guided us through the aisles. Determined to demonstrate cool sophistication, I nevertheless acted as naive as my mother had decades before.

A helpful employee appeared out of nowhere to answer questions, give product demonstrations and tout the advantages of buying everything. She showed us how to record selections for the gift registry. Gift registry? I was in disbelief. An infant and toddler wonderland of commercialism with a gift registry? I mumbled something about marketing genius, and my daughter gave me a gentle elbow to the ribs and that you-are-so-embarrassing look. She didn't appreciate what a monumental leap forward this was for womankind — a guarantee of perfect gifts. No need to return unwanted or duplicate items. No more groans at baby showers when the mother-to-be opened a third breast pump!

That first trip to the baby superstore lasted hours because I had to gawk at every new invention and swoon over each improvement. Just as my mother gasped when she discovered disposable diapers, I almost fainted when I saw… disposable bibs. Imagine!

"You won't have to carry dirty bibs home in your diaper bag," I exclaimed a bit loudly, exhausting my daughter's patience.

"Mom," she whispered, glancing around to see if anyone heard, "you're acting so weird… so… old. Like you've just stepped off the bus from the 16th century."

I laughed. Out loud.

"It wasn't that funny," she said.

I told her that I had thought the same thing about my own mother, emphasizing my point with a spontaneous, exaggerated imitation of her grandmother's long-ago, wide-eyed drool-fest. My daughter and I laughed together with the easy joy of two women who share the same sense of humor. Then a second wave of hysteria hit me.

"What?" she was barely able to say between giggles.

"It's finally happened," I gasped between fits of laughter. "I've become my mother!"

— Lynne Daroff Foosaner —

68

How to Raise an Adventurer

The purpose of life, after all, is to live it, to taste
experience to the utmost, to reach out eagerly and
without fear for newer and richer experience.
~Eleanor Roosevelt

When I was six years old, my mom let me walk all the way to the corner store by myself. It was an adventurous, independent move I'd been begging for, and when she handed me two dollars and let me take the leap from supervised activities to independence, it was exhilarating.

What I didn't know at the time was that she could see me from our kitchen window for nearly the entire length of the walk. It was a straight shot from our house to the corner store, three blocks down the sidewalk. There were no traffic lights anywhere in our small town in those days, and only a stop sign marked the crosswalk at the three-way intersection that I had to traverse. She must have been terrified. I can imagine her now, hugely pregnant with my brother, washing dishes as my little sister napped, watching from the kitchen window as her headstrong daughter left the safety of home. She must have wondered what was taking so long as I painstakingly chose a treat from the delicious options offered on the store shelves. She's told me the story many times of how she finally caught a glimpse of me walking home, and imagined me enjoying my newfound freedom, before I got close enough for her to see my tear-stained face. In my excitement, I'd forgotten my money at home.

My mom always says that she was "loving her kids away" from her. She hadn't let me wallow in disappointment that day or taken charge of things after my failed first attempt. She'd hugged me close and listened to my sad tale. Then she wiped my cheeks, tucked the coins tightly into my grubby little fist, and sent me back down the street again to get what I wanted.

It was candy that day, but it's been many different things in the years since: staying the week in a cabin at summer camp, weekends away with friends, driving three hours to the big city by myself for the first time. At fifteen, I traveled to Scotland with a team of people I'd only known for a week. This was before cell phones and the Internet; long distance calls were expensive, and I would only be able to call home once in the three weeks that we would be gone. I remember my dad speaking to the young team leaders about bringing me home safely as my mom tried her best not to let me see her cry. She never wanted her kids to give up doing something they wanted to do because it was hard for her.

Even now that the three of us are grown up, my mother does her best to hide her heartache as she watches us leave on planes and chase our dreams in different cities, knowing it will be months before she will see us again. Putting on an excited face and holding back her tears until we were off were always her gifts to us. Mom knew from her own experience how hard it was to leave a crying mother. My grandmother had struggled with agoraphobia for years after my grandfather passed away. Grandma would have happily kept Mom safely home with her always.

It was my grandpa's sister, my mom's aunt, who nudged Grandma into allowing Mom her independence. My great-aunt made sure my grandma knew how much my mom would enjoy attending community activities, having a visit with friends or family, going to swimming lessons, and riding the bus to school.

My great-aunt's actions ensured my mom never carried my grandma's heavy burden of fear with her. In the same way, my mom has never limited her children's freedom because of her own anxieties. Instead, she has helped us practice decision-making, coached us through consequences, and trusted us with small things so we could learn to trust ourselves. As life gets bigger, the risks increase, and the stakes become costlier. She didn't put herself between us and the fallout of our mistakes, not even the painful ones. She understood, as my great-aunt did, that she would not have been shielding us, but rather depriving us of experiences from which we needed to learn and grow. She understood the value of that difficult but necessary training.

Some parents never quite let their children leave home. They help too much to allow their kids to persevere and develop resiliency and grit. They limit life to a comfortable script, and counter possibility and imagination with doubt. It was hard for my mom to let us go, to "raise us away" and let us learn to rescue ourselves, but that is why we became self-sufficient adults. We've learned to follow our dreams and discover our destinies. She's the reason we've been able to grow into adventurous people.

Years ago, my mom explained that the umbilical cord doesn't ever go away. I was going backpacking on my own through Southeast Asia, and she said she would feel that connection "stretch all the way around the world." I'm sure the irony wasn't lost on her when my thirty-year-old self had to call home on that trip and ask her to book me a hotel room because I had lost my credit cards.

I may still be learning a few of the lessons that began at age six, but I've never been afraid to embark on the adventure of trying new things or tackling new challenges. My mother has given all of her children the gifts of confidence, perseverance, and self-sufficiency.

— Liz Harrison —

69

Chicken Soup for the Soul

Showing Up

It isn't what we say or think that defines us,
but what we do.
~Jane Austen

Mom quickly let go of my hand as we walked through the door, delivering a warm hug and a sweet hello to each resident in the living room. I didn't want to be there, but this was what my mother did. She loved visiting the elderly.

Many years before, when I was a kid, Mom often sent me across the street with a plate of supper for an elderly neighbor. I grew up watching her not only share delicious homemade suppers with these thankful neighbors, but also take the time to sit and visit with them — delivering not just food but friendship.

As I got older, I joined her as she visited elderly friends and family, even strangers — visits that were filled with laughter and fun stories. Mom wasted no time while she was there — sweeping the kitchen floor, checking the fridge for old food, washing any dishes left in the sink, and placing a warm, homemade apple cake on the countertop to be enjoyed later. She held hands and listened closely to stories, and it was as if an artist were repainting the portraits around us — adding a new sparkle to unhappy eyes, and smiles to sorrowful faces.

Mom laughed one day as she told me that someone in town had started calling her van the "widow wagon." In the small town where she and Dad lived, all the folks traveled seventy-five miles to the next town to see the doctor and shop for groceries. Mom regularly chauffeured older ladies for days filled with miscellaneous errands, appointments, and lunch at the Golden Corral. The space in the "widow wagon" was filled with laughter and chatter, along with bags of groceries and filled prescriptions, as this band of women completed their journey before Mom deposited them at their homes.

Of course, Mom gave me great care along the way as well. When the doctor told me that I would have to stay in bed for the last two months of my third pregnancy, Mom moved in with us—cooking, cleaning, doing the laundry, and caring for our two little boys. I vividly remember her walking into my bedroom with a plate of freshly cut pineapple, strawberries, blackberries and green apples on top of a serving of cottage cheese and a glass of iced water. I felt so loved. We didn't ask Mom to come; she didn't ask how she could help; she knew what to do and simply showed up—like Mary Poppins landing on the porch, bag and umbrella in tow.

Mom taught me a lot about making time for others—not with words necessarily, but with her actions. She was the very best at seeing a need and taking care of it—not just offering to help, but showing up.

So, I shouldn't have been surprised that day as she let go of my hand when we walked in. She loved this place. She was in her element and began immediately doing what she always had—warmly greeting each person. Mom didn't remember the days of feeding neighbors, driving ladies to town, or visiting lonely friends and family. The sweet memories of visiting folks at the nursing home, however, must have been hidden in a corner, safe for now from that unwelcome stalker: Alzheimer's. She had told me many years ago, "I love this place! When it's time, please just bring me here!" And so, here we were, about eight years after that dreadful diagnosis.

As we stumbled down the rough and rocky road to goodbye, I realized Mom had taught us long ago how to do this. It was okay to have no idea what to say at times. It was most important just to be there—to laugh even if I had no idea what was funny, and to hold her hand and tell her she was beautiful. She loved it when I visited, even if I was someone she had never met before.

At least once a week, I reminded her who I was. Sometimes, she believed me, and sometimes she didn't. Mostly, it didn't really matter to her, one way or the other.

"Did you know I'm your daughter?"

"Nope."

"Well, I am. My name is Tracie Marie."

"Hmmm."

"You're a good mom."

"Good."

Mom had taught me what to do — how to show up and repaint the portraits all around us, adding a new sparkle to unhappy eyes and smiles to sorrowful faces.

— Tracie Bevers —

70

My Mother the Model

*Over the years I have learned that what is important
in a dress is the woman who's wearing it.*
~Yves Saint Laurent

My mom's the very model of the modern modeling mother. And she could soon share a runway with Heidi Klum and other model moms because she (my mother, not Heidi) began her modeling career recently at a fashion show in Stamford, Connecticut.

Heidi, who's forty-one as of this writing, has gotten a lot more exposure, mainly because she's not shy about wearing lingerie in public. Besides, she began her career as a teenager.

My mom, Rosina Zezima, who's a bit more modest, just turned ninety.

Because ninety is the new sixty, which happens to be my age, my mother was asked to take part in a fashion show at Chico's, a women's clothing chain with a store in the Stamford Town Center mall.

"I must have good genes," my mother said.

"Did you wear jeans?" I asked.

"No," she replied. "I had on a pair of boysenberry slacks."

"What about a top?" I inquired.

"I was wearing one," my mother assured me. "In fact, I wore a couple of tops."

"At the same time?" I wondered.

My mother sighed because she knows I have a fashion plate in my head. She explained that first she wore a print blouse and then changed into another top with a coordinating jacket.

I was going to ask if she also wore the diamond-studded, $10-million bra that Heidi Klum famously sported on the cover of the Victoria's Secret catalog, but I thought better of it because Chico's doesn't sell stuff like that. And this was, after all, my mother.

"But you could," I suggested, "be in the Chico's catalog."

"Yes, she could," said store manager Terry Mrijaj.

"Do you know that my mother is ninety?" I asked when I called to talk about the new supermodel.

"She's amazing," Terry stated. "She's stylish, elegant and beautiful. Whenever she comes in, customers remark on how great she looks in our clothes. She's a walking advertisement for the store."

Not bad considering my mom couldn't walk a year and a half ago after she fell and broke her leg. But she has bounced back and is driving again. And now, she's modeling.

"She's a natural," said Terry, adding that the fashion show, a breast-cancer fundraiser, featured seven models, the youngest of whom was in her teens. My mom, not surprisingly, was the oldest.

"I'm forty-five now, so I'm half your mom's age," she said. "I hope I look that good when I'm ninety."

My mother said that when she was sixteen or seventeen, she was asked to model a sable coat at Levine & Smith, a fur shop in New York City.

"My father was so insulted — he didn't think modeling was very reputable — that he refused to let me do it, and we never went back," my mother remembered. "So I went into nursing."

"Those white uniforms weren't too stylish," I noted.

"No, they weren't," my mother agreed. "I wear better clothes now."

They include the fringe skirt and black top she wore to a family birthday bash.

"How does it feel to be ninety?" I asked.

"Pretty good," she said. "I don't feel like it, and I don't act like it."

"And," added my wife, Sue, who shares her birthday with my

mother but is, of course, considerably younger, "you don't look like it."
Sue should know because she could be a model herself.

My mother's next gig will be another fashion show at Chico's.

"I know your mom will be a hit again," said Terry. "She's a star."

Let's see if Heidi Klum can say that when she's ninety.

—Jerry Zezima—

Chapter
8

Always There for Us

71

Chicken Soup for the Soul

My Mother's Chicken Soup

Soup puts the heart at ease, calms down the violence
of hunger, eliminates the tension of the day,
and awakens and refines the appetite.
~Auguste Escoffier

I hit rock bottom last week. My children had been sick for a week and they were growing more and more irritable. Then, my husband returned from work; he was to take over bedtime so I could work on some writing projects. As he stepped through the door, however, my hope for a break crumbled. His shoulders drooped, and his eyes looked swollen. He shuffled directly to our bed just as a fit of chills crashed over him. His forehead burned against my open hand.

"I'm sorry," came a remorseful voice from under the covers. In minutes, he was asleep.

I could barely walk back down the stairs, so I slid to a seating position in the stairwell and sent a text to my mother. I thanked her for all the thankless jobs she did when we were kids. I thanked her for the countless times she'd cleaned up after us or kept us from strangling each other. She had dreams and ambitions of her own that took second place so often when we needed her. Finally, I understood how that felt.

Mom responded to my text within minutes by offering to watch my children so I could catch up on work. I let out a sigh and felt my shoulders relax.

Our disheveled crew arrived on her doorstep a few days later.

"Hi, Gwandmah," my younger child said, bouncing through the

doorway and wrapping his arms around my mother's knee.

"I'm so glad you came to see me," she said as she patted his stocking cap.

"Hey, Mom," I said with a tired smile. "You're the best for doing this."

In seconds, my children peeled off their coats, boots, and hats and flew toward Grandpa in the next room.

"Are you hungry?" my mother asked.

"Thanks, but I've got some snacks with me." A local library was just down the road. Once my laptop was open and I was pounding the keys, my appetite typically fell by the wayside.

"Okay," Mom said, heading toward the kitchen. "But if you don't think that'll be enough, I made that Thanksgiving soup I told you about." She opened the refrigerator and held up a dish full of broth and vegetables. "You know, the one with all the traditional ingredients from a Thanksgiving meal? Except this time I used chicken." She pried off the lid and placed it in the microwave.

"Looks awesome. I bet the kids will love it. I'll probably just head out and get started on my article."

"Oh, that reminds me." Mom hurried to her desk. She held out two *Chicken Soup for the Soul* books. I stood there, puzzled. "I know you're working on those submissions today," she said, "and wanted to help you with the research. They're older editions, but they might help."

This was my mother to her very core. My advocate. She could make an egg sandwich in less than two minutes as I flew around the house getting ready for softball practice. At first, I'd tell her, "Don't worry about it; I'll be fine." But sure enough, halfway through practice, that extra boost of energy from her sandwich would kick in, and I'd keep swinging, throwing and running with everything I had.

I took the books from my mother and began flipping through them. "These are great, Mom. Thanks." I looked up to see her studying me.

"Are you sure you don't want some soup? I can send some with you in a Thermos."

She saw something in me, I realized. The empty tank. The fatigue. The guilt in my voice when I accepted her offer to watch the kids. It was hard to accept help when I felt like such a failure — when many others faced bigger struggles than mine and didn't have help.

It didn't matter if I was in my thirties. I realized this was one of those sacred moments in life when a mother wants to tend to her child — when the house fills with the aroma of chicken soup, and she says with a smile, "It's going to be alright."

I'd just tended to my own sick children. Now she wanted to tend to hers. We don't get that mom forever. This moment together was suddenly about much more than meeting deadlines. It wasn't even about soup. This was my mother reaching out to say, "You don't have to do this all on your own. I'm here. It's going to be alright."

A lump grew in my throat.

"I think I will take some. Thanks."

Mom ladled spoonfuls of steaming broth with carrots, celery, herbs, spices, and bits of chicken into a small Thermos on the counter. I could almost taste the rich, warm broth already.

"There." Mom tightened the lid and handed the canister and a spoon to me. "Now you've got some chicken soup for your soul."

She met my eyes and smiled.

There it was. In a single sentence, Mom changed my day. If feeding the soul isn't a superpower, then I don't know what is. If I can become even half the woman she is, then I'll do my best to pass that legacy on to others. It's that quiet, selfless strength that sees through the surface and reaches out to say, "I'm here. I see you. It's going to be alright."

— Laura Harris —

72

She Kept My Room Ready

Home is where you feel loved, appreciated, and safe.
~Tracey Taylor

When I traveled across the United States to be with the one I loved,
She told me that I would be back,
So she kept my room ready.

When I moved out of state again because I thought the grass was
    greener on the other side,
She piled her clothes on my bed,
But she kept my room ready.

The first time I came back, she picked me up from the airport.
The second time, from the train station.
Both times, she couldn't help but tell me how she told me so.

Both times, I told her she was right.
Pride and disappointment wouldn't let me say it with my words.
My actions said it as I lay down.

She kept me ready to rebel,
To fail,
To live and learn and know that she kept my room ready.

— Carla Varner —

73

Mirror Image

A good dress can make you remember
what is beautiful about life.
~Rachael Ray

I shut the passenger's side door of the golden Buick and shuffled into a wedding boutique behind my mom. Though the Michigan air held hopeful warmth, we wore jackets to ward off the lingering chill. It was spring of 2010, and my wedding was a few months away.

I looked over at my mom, trying to read her thoughts as we walked slowly through aisles filled with white, white, and more white. I am the sixth of seven children, and as the only girl, I felt the pressure. But, as tomboys, we both loathed shopping. Back-to-school shopping trips had always left us frustrated. We didn't like searching for the perfect pair of jeans, shoes, or a new winter coat. I worried silently about what could happen as we hunted for a wedding dress together.

I didn't want a dress with a princess poof or a boring nightgown dress. I was looking for a fun, strapless dress with maybe some pulled tufts on the bottom. I picked out three gowns, and we carried them to the back.

The store was almost empty, and Mom sat alone on a bystander's simple plastic chair. I climbed up on the podium adorned in the first dress. I looked at myself in the mirror, my blond hair pulled into my usual casual ponytail. I slipped my hands across the silky gown and loved its softness. But when I looked in the mirror, I cringed at how the milky gown made my skin look even paler. I peered back at Mom while feeling underwhelmed.

Her head tilted sideways. "Do you like it?"

I swung to and fro, feeling the material beneath my fingers, but longing to rid myself of it.

"No, not really. I look like the ghost of Christmas past." I ducked back into the dressing room for dresses two and three.

While they looked elegant, the material felt flat, even though one was a beautiful mermaid shape. They didn't feel right. But my mother, who birthed one unique little girl in a sea of boys, reacted differently. Tears peeked out of the corners of her eyes. She looked at me curiously after the third one and then flitted her hand up in a quick motion. "Oh, Kim, I am no help at all. You are so beautiful in each one."

We left the store empty-handed, but I had slightly more knowledge about the styles that might interest me. It wouldn't take long for the work to pay off.

David's Bridal was bustling with dozens of people underneath its bright lights. The entire middle section was a dressing room arranged for queens. The platforms in front of giant mirrors were like stages for the stunning brides. A small crowd of women huddled around one bride, touching the fabric and commenting loudly while she spun around daintily. This intrigued me, but I wasn't dying to be on the podium. I had always been the one who ran away from these overly girlish situations.

We walked down the aisles on a mission, sifting through the discount racks and finding nothing. We flipped over price tags, promptly moving on or peering in for a closer look. *Is this too sparkly? Do I want a short or long train?* I was hoping the perfect dress would reach out and grab me. Somehow, my arms filled up with possibilities. At the dressing-room castle, I climbed into a dress and then stood under the lights for my audience. Nope. Not the one.

A spark lit within me as I saw myself in the next gown, and I slowly pushed open the door to climb onto the pedestal. I swished back and forth in what felt like a magic dress. My fingers touched the gorgeous beads sewn delicately onto the surface. I wrapped my hands around the middle sash, feeling its tight band splitting top and bottom. The tufts pulled up, scattered all over the skirt from waist to floor, and I delighted in every square inch.

I laughed, enchanted. This was the dress. Not for any logical reason, but because of the pure joy it brought. Looking in the mirror at the brightest smile I had seen all day, I turned around, and my smile was mirrored on my mom's face.

An attendant gently set a veil on my head, and it was then that the tears welled up. I was wearing the dress in which I would whisper the vows that would make me Mrs. Kimberly Patton.

Though it was obvious to me that this pursuit was complete, the task wasn't over yet. In plain clothes, I stood in the lobby away from the brightly lit dressing room. I held the heavy bagged dress in my hands. My mom has always been wise with money: clipping coupons, ordering water at restaurants, avoiding name-brand products. The dress wasn't exactly pulled from the $99 rack. It would be far more expensive than anything she had ever bought for me. I looked her in the eyes. "Mom, it's the one. I love it. Can we… please?"

We approached the counter slowly, and my frugal mother was hesitant. Whatever she felt, she swallowed it. In one quick movement, she did something so loving, so full of understanding and trust. She pulled out her credit card.

— Kimberly Patton —

74

Trusting Your Gut

Sometimes the strength of motherhood
is greater than natural laws.
~Barbara Kingsolver

My mother seems a bit unhinged to most people, including her children. But over the years, she has taught us that the best people are. My mom has a big personality. She's smart and nerdy, and she has five kids so she's a little crazy. She does what she feels is best without regard to anyone else's opinion. And, above all else, she listens to her gut and trusts her instincts.

It took me many years to realize how amazing my mother was, and it took me becoming a mother myself to realize not only how difficult it must've been, but how strong she had to become to get through it.

When I was about thirteen, I seemed like a typical teenager. I started rebelling, making really dumb choices, and acting out. I thought my mom was an idiot and I knew everything. It was also a really low time for me, and I started having serious depression and becoming suicidal. Thinking back now, I know that a lot of my behavior was to get attention. I felt that something was wrong, but I didn't know how to tell anyone. My mom, though, knew something was up, and she did the only thing she could think of at the time: She read my journal.

To most people, this would seem like the ultimate form of betrayal, and to teenage me, it was. But that day, my mom listened to her gut. And as she read all my thoughts, she found out that not only did I want to kill myself, but I had already started to self-harm. When I got home that day from school and found out, I was furious. But my mom kept her cool and took me to a hospital to get me the help I desperately needed.

While I was there, I was diagnosed with bipolar and anxiety disorder, and my mental-health journey began. Before I could accept that what she did had literally saved my life, I called her every name in the book. I fought back every step of the way, for a very long time, but my mom stood by me. She loved me and supported me. And, most importantly, she listened to me. It took me many years to realize that invading my privacy was the hardest thing for her. And that taking me to a hospital was even harder. But in doing all that, my mom saved me and got me started on a path of self-discovery and mental health. It gave me the tools not only to be able to understand what I was going through, and how to get through it, but also to help others on their own journeys.

Being a mom of four teenage girls couldn't have been easy, but she did it the best way she could by always keeping an open dialog, making it a point to honestly tell us about things, and teaching us how to take care of ourselves. She may not have been the most graceful, and she would be the first to tell you she made mistakes, but my mom's heart has always been focused on doing what she felt was right and best for her kids. As a teenager, I didn't quite understand this, and her methods not only angered me to my core but made me absolutely crazy. But as an adult, I am thankful because I honestly don't know where I would be today without her.

I love my mom. And now that I have children of my own, I can see the strength she needed to raise us — not just me, but all of us. We have been through many stages of our relationship through the years. We are now in the mother/daughter/friend stage, and it is by far my favorite.

I am thankful every single day for that woman. I am thankful for her craziness and her prying. I am thankful for her friendship and her love. But, most of all, I am thankful that she taught me how to listen to my gut instincts, too. Hopefully, when my kids are grown, they too will know that they are loved and important. That their mother would do anything in the world to protect and keep them safe — even if that means keeping them safe from themselves.

— Amburr Phillips —

75

I Didn't Know, but My Mom Did

Grown don't mean nothing to a mother.
A child is a child. They get bigger, older, but grown.
In my heart it don't mean a thing.
~Toni Morrison

With a newborn screaming in the Rock 'n Play, I hurriedly pulled my hair into a neater ponytail, slapped some bronzer on my face and stabbed studs into my ears. I was utterly exhausted, but my poor husband was desperate for a date night.

We dropped our girl off at my mom's and went to dinner at Chili's. I cried at dinner because that is what new moms do, so we decided to try bowling since that is one of my favorite activities. I was too weak to even pretend to bowl well. I apologized to my husband; he assured me it was okay. We headed back to my girl, who was probably hungry because she was used to eating constantly, and I had left only four pumped ounces with my mom.

When we walked in the door, I acted as normally as I could. My mom was at ease in her favorite white sweatshirt, and my girl was crying in her arms. "She sucked that down in the first hour. I really wanted to give her some formula, but I didn't," she said. I sat down and proceeded to breastfeed. I could feel the tears welling in my eyes. I didn't have time to blink them back or look up before my mom said,

"You can't keep doing this, Abb."

I explained that I didn't want to give up on breastfeeding, and that my husband helped a lot at night. "But he's exhausted, too, and he has to go to work. And all she wants to do is eat anyway, so she might as well be with me. And I'm just really tired, and my laundry is piled up." I said it all in one breath just like that.

Mom went into her kitchen, and I could hear her clanking dishes and pushing microwave buttons. In a few minutes, she told me to come over to the table. She had a huge plate of spaghetti ready for me. "You aren't eating enough. If you are going to keep breastfeeding and pumping this much, you need to eat more." I sat down (while my baby cried somewhere) and ate a massive plate of spaghetti despite the fact that I had just eaten an hour before. My mom told me to go shower, and she insisted that my husband, baby and I sleep at her house so we could get adequate sleep but still be together. She knew I wouldn't sleep at home without my girl, and she knew I wouldn't sleep there without my husband, so we all stayed. I breastfed one more time before I went to sleep and agreed to one bottle of formula for her at some point in the night.

At 3:00 a.m., I woke up needing to pump or feed her. I had slept four to five hours straight for the first time in weeks. I pumped and then walked across the house to find my daughter asleep in my mom's arms, while my mom watched the TV on mute. She smiled and said, "She just sucked down six ounces." I gave her the full bottle I had just pumped and went back to sleep without a second thought. Four hours later, I woke up to repeat this exact same process, and we did it again three hours after that.

I woke up for the day at 10:00 a.m. knowing my mom had taken perfect care of my girl at the expense of her own sleep. My sister delivered Sonic breakfast burritos and local doughnuts. It was a team effort letting me sleep and getting me full. My husband was able to sleep eight hours straight with no interruption. It was exactly what we both needed.

I knew I was tired and overwhelmed, but I didn't know I was hungry. But my mom did. In my new-mom fog, I wanted to breastfeed (and I am so glad I did), but I didn't realize in that moment that it would be okay to give my girl a bottle of formula if it meant taking care of myself for a second. But my mom did. I wasn't sure my mom would honor my wishes of not giving her formula while I was gone on my date, but she did.

In that season, I remember giving everything I could every single day to this new little person. I never even considered anything less than that because she was mine. It was my job to take care of her, and I wanted to more than anything. I didn't sleep so that she could get what she needed from me. She was my priority above all others because she simply needed to be. Despite me being twenty-seven years old, my mom took care of me. I did not ask her to; she just did it. She didn't sleep so that I could. My mom made me the priority that night above all others because she knew—even when I didn't—that I needed to be.

After the burritos and doughnuts were eaten, my mom and sister drove my girl and me home. I watched my sister follow the example of my mother as she started cleaning my house and folding my laundry. My mom got ready to leave, and for the first time in my life, I had to hold back tears because she was leaving. I didn't cry when my mom took me to kindergarten. I went to Texas for ten days in middle school, and jumped in the car and waved without a second thought. I have been to Africa and Argentina and moved out of her house, having never shed a tear over not being with that woman. But on this day, as she stood on my porch saying goodbye, I had to hold back the tears.

—Abbie Dunlap—

76

Blue Stitches

Don't ask what the world needs. Ask what makes you
come alive, and go do it. Because what the world needs
is people who have come alive.
~Howard Thurman

My mother winked as she asked her seemingly innocent question. "How 'bout a game of *Scrabble*?"

"You win all the time, Mama."

"Someday, you'll beat me. Today just might be your day."

I acquiesced and set up the board. In 1980, I was a junior in high school, and my siblings were long gone to college and beyond. Mama relied on me for her daily dose of conquering someone.

That *Scrabble* game in 1980 holds another special remembrance for me. No, I didn't win. But that night, as we waged war with words, I brought up another competition — one that would change the way I saw myself.

"Mama, student council elections are in two weeks."

"Uh-huh."

She spelled out Q-U-I-E-T on a red triple-word space and whistled.

"That's pretty good, if I do say so myself." She smiled at me and then started counting her gazillions of points.

"Mama, did you hear what I just said?"

"Uh-huh. Forty-two points for 'quiet.' Your turn."

I looked at my tiles and sighed. I plopped down M-A-K-E-R on a double-word space and counted: 22.

"I like the idea of being part of student council my senior year."

"Sounds good. Twenty-eight points."

"So, I have to go to the office tomorrow and pick up a form to fill out if I want to run."

"Do you want to run for student council?"

"I don't know. Sounds fun."

"Fun?" She finally looked up from the board and into my eyes.

"Mother, it will be my senior year. I want to have fun."

She looked back at her tiles. "Leadership is about serving. How do you want to serve?"

As Mama spelled out a Z word I'd never heard of, I thought about serving. She'd run for elected office in my small town three times, winning the office of District County Clerk.

"Maybe I won't run."

Again, Mama looked up at me.

"You aren't going to run because you have to serve?"

I felt flustered at the way this conversation, not to mention the score, was headed.

"Robbie, think about your talents. What do you have to offer others? Once you get a clear picture of that, I bet you that service will sound… well, it will sound fun."

Mama won the game. I went to bed undecided.

The next day, I came home with the application. After dinner, Mama called me into the living room.

"How about a game of spades?"

The wink accompanied the request.

"You're on, Mama. I've beaten you at spades. Do you remember?"

Mother grinned and started shuffling the deck. "I don't know what you're talking about."

"I am going to run for student council," I announced as we each drew our cards.

"Excellent."

"But I don't know what position. I don't really want to be treasurer, but maybe secretary or even the vice president."

Her eyes met mine.

"Why not president?"

I couldn't believe this woman. Mom knew my high school's enrollment was 250, grades 9 through 12. She also knew that we lived in a town of 3,000 people, 85 percent of whom were Hispanic, 15 percent white.

"You know why."

"No."

"Mother, I am a white girl."

"Really?"

"White girls don't win against Hispanic guys. Eddie Rodriguez has already told everyone he is running for president. No way will I win."

"Robbie, what talents do you have? How are you going to serve?"

"I think I could be a good leader."

"Leading? Sounds like a perfect talent for president."

"I told you, Eddie is running. Most of the time, the president is a guy, and Eddie is really popular."

"So, you are not running for president because you are a girl and your competition is popular?"

"Mother, you don't understand the politics of high school."

"Robbie, believe in yourself and who you are meant to be. Do this for the right reasons. Win or lose, play the game well."

With that, she won our first hand. And the second…

The next day, I drew in a deep breath as I wrote the word "president" on the application.

Mama happened to be an excellent seamstress, so I asked her to make me a dress for my Election Day speech. Immediately, she headed over to Mrs. Woods's fabric store and found a bolt of royal-blue rayon knit. It was my favorite color and so soft.

"You will look very presidential in this," she teased me. That night, I went to sleep to the hum of her Singer sewing machine.

The next day, as I sat in the library working on my speech, Susan Banks approached me.

"Robbie, is it true? You're running for student council president?"

I took a deep breath. "Yes."

"Wow, you got guts. But you do know that Eddie is running, right?"

"Yes."

"Um, no offense, but you aren't going to win. Eddie is really popular."

With that, Susan turned and left.

She wasn't the only classmate who offered the same encouragement. But I couldn't back down; everyone knew I was running. Besides, Mama was sewing my new blue dress.

Two days before the election, I tried on my mother's creation. I looked and felt beautiful.

"Mama, this is incredible. Thank you."

"Robbie, listen to what I am about to tell you. I prayed for you as I made this dress. It doesn't matter if you win. It matters that you are being who you are meant to be."

It was the only time I remember my mother saying she prayed for me.

On Election Day, all the students were herded into the auditorium. Eddie and I sat on the stage with Robert, Laura and Maria. They were running unopposed for vice president, treasurer and secretary. They would give their speeches, and then Eddie and I would go.

As I watched Eddie give his speech, my knees knocked. He was calm and easygoing, encouraging the students to do the best thing for our high school by voting for him. His speech was very short and ended with cheers from the student body.

What had possessed me to subject myself to this? Suddenly, I was hot and sweaty. No way was I going to win this.

My turn came, and I walked to the podium and looked out at my classmates. That's when something powerful happened. I launched into my speech confidently, even making my classmates laugh.

When I reflect on that day, I like to think that my blue dress was my Superman outfit. As Mama sewed, she infused each blue stitch with her confidence and strength. After that day, my belief in myself quadrupled. No longer was I mild-mannered Robbie, scared of revealing my true identity. I was Robbie Floyd, a young lady meant to be exactly who she was.

When I came home that day, my mother was frying chicken on

the stove.

"Mama, you will never believe it!"

"You think you can beat me at *Scrabble*?"

She grinned, but kept focused on the chicken.

"Mama, I won!"

Mama looked up at me. No wink.

"Of course, you did."

— Robbie Iobst —

77

Truth and Consequences

Forget Superman, Batman, Spiderman and all the
other comic book heroes. They should make a movie
about you — Supermom.
~Author Unknown

My mother grew up in a generation that venerated teachers, and her children were raised to believe that these paragons were above reproach. Consequently, I handed her my eighth-grade report card tearfully. As a conscientious student who was accustomed to receiving good marks, I could not bear the injustice this report card contained. My mark in Spanish, one of my strongest subjects, was the lowest grade I had ever received — a skimpy 75 percent that looked all the more forlorn among its neighboring 85s, 90s and 95s.

Considering her high regard of educators, I was beyond astonished when my mother asked me, "Maybe this is a mistake?"

"Well," I replied, feeling miserable, "I approached Mrs. Whitman" — an incredible feat for fearful me — "but she told me she doesn't discuss grades with students."

"Then I will speak to her."

My immigrant mother, with her imperfect, accented and emotional English, was willing to speak to my self-assured, unflappable, no-nonsense teacher? I couldn't picture it, but I felt desperate enough to want it to happen.

Conflicting emotions prompted my strange outburst. "Ma, please don't!" In response, she patted my back reassuringly. Somehow, she intuitively understood my wish that she could do precisely what I was dreading she would.

The appointment was granted the following day after school hours. It was not a day I had Spanish, so I couldn't gauge the teacher's mood. Instead, I worried about her reaction when she'd meet my parent. Would she even understand what my mother was trying to say? Would it matter? What if my mother didn't understand her and answered questions inappropriately? Worse, perhaps Mother would incorrectly use a new word or expression that had caught her attention because she liked the way it sounded! This had happened more times than I cared to recall, the most memorable being when she had thanked my friend's mother for her "sensual" rather than sensible advice.

Precisely when I imagined Mrs. Whitman dismissing my mother's justified but ill-expressed complaint on my behalf with a wave of her daunting hand, my spokeswoman walked through our door. "You got the 95 you deserve," she announced matter-of-factly.

I couldn't process this right away, then finally blurted, "How?"

"She changed the seven to a nine. Here, look." I saw the initialed change and shook my head.

"No, Ma, I mean, how did it happen? What did she say?"

"I just convinced her that you do not remember Spanish from your first five years in Chile."

This was important because Mrs. Whitman had evidently used the information about my birthplace against me, even though I had voluntarily conveyed it in a composition! Apparently, she decided I had an unfair advantage over the other students in the class, and this could somehow be "equalized" by giving me a grade that was considerably lower than my achievements in class. Being a great believer in extending credit for hard work, she must have justified deducting twenty points by reasoning that I had committed the unforgivable sin of exerting zero effort.

But the truth was precisely the opposite. I expended great energy in learning the language I had spoken with some degree of fluency in my early childhood, but then had promptly forgotten upon arrival in New York and enrollment in kindergarten, where I learned English very quickly. It was the third language I learned to speak, so I seemingly did have an ear for languages. But my speedy grasp of English just as speedily eradicated any trace of Spanish, my second language, which was not even a dim memory for me anymore. Whenever I recalled incidents from Chile, I thought about them in English!

My attention turned back to the report that was unfolding before me now. "How did you manage to convince her?"

Mother waved her hand again. "Easy. I started to speak to her in my *pobrecito* [poor] Spanish," she smiled. "I told her Spanish is language number six for me, and we don't speak it at home. Even in Chile, we conversed little in Spanish." I would let her know about her consonant reversal and the resultant confused meanings later; just then, I was too intent on hearing the rest of the drama leading to the happy ending.

"And that was enough for her to agree my mark was a mistake?"

"Maybe it helped that I gave her a piece of my mine."

It must have been a gold mine.

"I told her I feel it is not fair to punish before we know the facts for sure. And one thing is sure. I see my daughter studying her Spanish. She is not faking. She is really working, and she succeeds on tests without help from anyone. We came to America because it is the land of opportunity. If you work hard, you can do well. Then I asked her if she agreed. She did not answer, just took out her pen and changed the mark."

"Goodness, you said that to my teacher?"

"Why not? I showed respect and said the truth. And the truth speaks for itself."

I embraced my mother, grateful for her help. She never said the experience was difficult. She just went to do what had to be done, sure that the truth would speak for her.

The long-range benefit I gained from this incident is the inspiration I still draw from it. Whenever I need a dose of courage to deal with an imposing person, I remember that sincerity, not a glib tongue, yields results.

— Barbara Bank —

78

Chicken Soup for the Soul

The First "I Love You"

*The heart of a mother is a deep abyss at the bottom of
which you will always find forgiveness.*
~Honoré de Balzac

I could describe in detail almost all the times when I've told my mother that I hate her. I would run out of fingers to count on before I would run out of stories. "She's insane," I would tell my friends, moving through the halls of my middle school.

"She just doesn't understand me," I complained to my high-school classmates.

"I can't wait to move out," I spat to her as I searched for cheap apartments after graduation. Anything to get away from her.

"Don't expect me to visit," I said, as I lugged my last overstuffed duffle bag to my car.

Oh, yes, I could tell you dozens of stories about my mother: the wicked witch who wanted nothing more than to control me. I could tell you about the dozens of times I screamed that I hated her. Every time I said those words, I truly believed that I did. I can also tell you about when I realized that wasn't true.

The genes were strong in my family; all of us women could have been carbon copies of each other. My mother gave me thick brown hair, thicker eyebrows and an attitude even fiercer than hers.

I remember her face when I drove away to my first apartment. She was watching me wearily, and I watched her watching me in my rearview mirror. Her arms were wrapped around her torso, pulling her sweater close around her body as if to warm her, although it was in the middle of July. She had her head tilted just enough to let me know she was watching, and I knew her well enough to know she wanted to say something. But I also knew her well enough to know that whatever she wanted to say would remain unsaid. I pulled out of the driveway of the home I had lived in for eighteen years and drove to my new apartment.

"You'll regret this, you know," my mother snapped at me when I informed her of my upcoming move. "This is way too expensive. You don't make enough money, and you're not ready."

"I don't care." I rolled my eyes. "I'd rather go broke in an empty apartment than live under your roof one moment longer."

Of course, she was right. One night, when my stomach was grumbling so loud I couldn't concentrate, when I was running off the last of my laptop battery, trying hard to figure out my online taxes before my laptop died, I found myself reaching for my cell phone, my fingers automatically dialing my home phone number. Through burning eyes, I completed the call and placed the phone to my ear. I choked back tears until I heard my mother's sleepy voice over my hoarse sobs.

"Miranda?" I heard her clear her throat and click on the light next to her bed. "Is that you? What's wrong? It's almost 11:00."

"Oh, Mom, I'm so sorry to bother you, but…" I gasped through my tears. "My computer is about to die, and I can't figure out this stupid tax website, and I'm so stressed out and confused and…"

"I'll be right there," she interrupted.

She disconnected our phone call, and she was at my door within a half-hour, clutching a bag of McDonald's in one hand and a steaming cup of coffee in the other. "I know you don't normally like McDonald's," she started, "but that's all that was open."

I gathered her in my arms, my beautiful sleepy mother, her short hair rumpled, a pillow mark still on her cheek.

"Thank you, Mom," I heard myself whisper. "I love you." Her body stiffened in my embrace, but soon relaxed before she pulled away.

"Let's get these taxes under control," she said. My mother raised an eyebrow at my living room, devoid of furniture, and cleared her throat again.

We sat cross-legged on my living-room floor for three hours that night, eating double cheeseburgers and drinking far too much coffee for the middle of the night. My taxes were done in twenty minutes, but she stayed for hours. Our faces became streaked with tears of laughter until she finally left to go home, promising to be back with an old couch for me.

"Thanks again, Mom," I said at the door. "I love you."

"I know." She smiled at me with the same smile she gave me — with lips just slightly too big and teeth too far apart — a smile I'm proud to have.

— Miranda Lamb —

79

And the Good News Is...

I cannot tell you how much I owe to the solemn word of
my good mother.
~Charles Haddon Spurgeon

My Cajun mom, Ginger, a beekeeper by day and a ballroom dancer by night, is the most positive and jovial person I have ever known. Her bubbly personality draws praise from everyone she meets. Ginger believes that humor is essential in our daily lives because it brings balance and a sense of humility whenever we are confronting challenging situations or demanding people. According to her, "With humor, we can always look and find the lighter side of things to be positive, regardless of whatever we encounter." She always leads off any consoling advice with her signature phrase "And the good news is..." followed by the biggest smile of confidence!

Somehow, Ginger could see the silver linings in all the difficult and arduous experiences I shared with her. One of those treasured moments was when she nudged me to re-invent myself when I moved to Dallas, Texas to establish a start-up business. In 2001, after spending eighteen successful years in the restaurant industry, I had the opportunity to pursue my dream of owning my own company. The grand idea of selling beautiful Malaysian batik sarongs and tribal art from Borneo consumed every breath I took. Projecting a quick sprint to success that summer, I invested $80,000 in inventory and signed a one-year lease with the Dallas Market Center to display my products in one of their shared showrooms. I also staffed temporary booths at several fashion markets in Las Vegas and Los Angeles.

The one thing I did not take into account in my business plan was the ripple effect of a terrorist attack in America. The tragedy created a national mood shift that affected everyone's spending habits. My sales came to a screeching halt after fulfilling a large order with the women's handbag manufacturer, Isabella Fiore, in January 2002. The aftermath also affected my antique tribal art sales as well. My portfolio also took a huge hit, first due to the overall financial market turmoil, and later because of my indecision to act accordingly. By summer, I had lost 60 percent of my net worth. I was also maintaining two residences — my house in Baton Rouge, Louisiana, and an apartment in Dallas. Although my house was on the market, no one was interested in buying it. During these agonizing months when I started to feel that my dream of owning a business was in jeopardy, I found myself quickly running out of liquidity. All of these factors compounded the stress.

To make matters worse, I had recently broken up with my fiancée. The year-and-a-half engagement finally ended when I learned that her mother had changed her mind about being supportive of our plan to marry. Although she had given me permission when I had asked for her daughter's hand in marriage eighteen months earlier, she decided that an inter-faith marriage for her daughter was not in the best interest for her family. When the truth came out, my fiancée suggested we run off to Vegas and get married. She felt that once we had children, the dynamic would be different from her mother. However, I felt the remedy was not prudent. I thought I should not be the cause of any animosity between a mother and her daughter. So, with a heavy heart, we decided to call off the engagement.

I was in need of an encouraging pep talk, and also perhaps a hard kick in the butt to get me out of the downward spiral. So I called Ginger one evening and started to share the events in my life. Some forty-five minutes later, when I finally finished expressing myself, she began by saying three words, "God heard you." She went on to say, "I heard you as well, and the good news is that… you realized where you are. Now, it is your time to do what you have always done so well:

organizing and planning."

She continued, "Johnny, have faith! Look at all that you have accomplished out of life's other challenges. The current situation is no different. Let the history of past successes comfort you as you regroup and refocus. Allow hope to present a clean sheet of paper for you to write your new chapter in re-inventing yourself. Always remember, God loves you, and I love you, dear!"

With that, I felt her genuine, warm and loving smile come through my cell phone. Ginger's consoling and encouraging words had alleviated the psychological weight that was paralyzing me. Feeling drained but inspired, I slept well for the first time in months.

In the ensuing months, filled with energy and a can-do attitude, I revamped Batik World, my original company. Within a year, it morphed into The Reyna Collection, a premier multi-line wholesale showroom resource group, located in the Dallas Market Center, representing nine major international and American companies. The collection includes certified green furniture from Brazil, Chinese painted porcelain vases, architectural antiques from India, handmade decorative lamps from Indonesia, architectural bronze statues from Thailand, and custom-made water features from the U.S. My house eventually sold during the process, and I completed transforming myself into a Texan.

My Cajun mom, Ginger, taught me something new: Faith comforts, hope inspires, and love empowers! With faith, I was able to look back to the past constructively. There, I drew the energy I needed to create the hope that helped me plan a new future. Her unconditional motherly love fueled the lamp that lit the path to a new beginning for me.

— Johnny Tan —

80

Hope in an Envelope

The meaning of life is to find your gift.
The purpose of life is to give it away.
~Pablo Picasso

While I battled breast cancer, my husband died of a heart attack. My mother flew from Oregon to Nebraska to stay with me. Physically a mess, lost in grief, I wondered what I'd do with my eighty-six-year-old mother. I didn't feel well enough to sit in a chair and keep her company. I certainly couldn't plop her in front of the TV and say, "Have fun, Mom."

A week after she arrived, I asked, "Mom, why don't you crochet anymore?"

"Don't know what I'd make."

"I need those crocheted coat hangers you made in years past." I found yarn and brought Mom a couple dozen coat hangers.

A few days later, Mom said, "This is boring. Don't you have any other ideas?"

"How about bookmarks? We'll share them with family and friends."

Mom couldn't read a pattern, but in a few hours she'd perfected a length of squares. In the evenings, I laced ribbon through the holes. The following day, we sent out a note with the bookmark to another woman struggling with breast cancer. We also sent bookmarks to several relatives.

One day, Mom's youngest sister called from Oregon. "I love the bookmarks," Aunt Millie said. She asked if Mom might consider donating a bunch for her Tops fundraiser. My aunt said she'd buy the crochet thread and ribbon, and pay for the postage.

The project did more than help my aunt; it gave my mother purpose. While Mom kept her fingers busy crocheting, I threaded ribbons through those bookmarks and listened to Mom reminisce. Every day, I sent out at least one of Mom's bookmarks or took one with me to the oncology department for a nurse to share with someone.

Several thank-you notes arrived in our mailbox over the next few weeks, but once Mom finished my aunt's project, she wanted a change. "I'd like to make a pansy."

I Googled "crocheted pansies," enlarged the photo and gave it to Mom. In one evening, she had crocheted several flowers. But what to do with piles of pansies?

"Mom, I think we could glue the pansies on a wire, wind the wire with green floral tape, and send them out with our cards." Once more, we sent a pile of beautiful, variegated encouragement flowers and notes.

Bored with pansies, Mom wanted a butterfly pattern. I Googled, and again Mom created. I wired the butterflies on stems.

We sent a lavender, variegated butterfly to my friend Yvonne. In a few days, a thank-you note arrived. Yvonne explained how she had cut the butterfly off the stem and glued it onto a hairclip.

"Our church was sending a mission group to Haiti to help with the disaster there," Yvonne said. "I asked a man if he would clip the butterfly into a child's hair to offer her hope." At the bottom of her note, she added, "I love the butterfly, June. Do you think you could send me another one just for me?"

Of course, Mom crocheted her another one.

Two months later, the phone rang. "Kat, I called to tell your mom she's awesome."

"Mom, Yvonne thinks you are awesome. She's on the phone and wants to talk with you." Mom set her never-ending crochet project in her lap and reached for the phone next to her.

"Okay, Yvonne, we're both on the line," I said.

"June, do you remember I gave one of your crocheted butterflies to a man going to Haiti?" Yvonne said. "After the group returned from Haiti, the man never said anything about the butterfly. I thought maybe he forgot to take it, and I didn't know him well enough to ask. Guess what? Today, he gave a PowerPoint presentation showing the devastation in Haiti, the tent cities, and the work they accomplished. Then a picture of a sad-faced child holding the butterfly hair clip in her hands came up on the screen."

"Wow, Mom, I told you your creativity is touching lives around the world," I said.

"But there's more," Yvonne said. "The next photo showed the same girl with the butterfly in her hair and a smile on her face. Because our mission men worked with males, the fellow had handed the butterfly clip to a female worker. She later told him the girl had been raped and hadn't spoken in four days. The woman told him, 'When I handed the butterfly to the girl, I told her it represented hope, and you can see her smile.'"

Yvonne said many of the people in the worship service who watched the presentation cried, but Mom and I celebrated. How exciting to know Mom's hope in an envelope not only encouraged breast-cancer patients and our relatives, but also touched the life of a young girl in Haiti.

A few days later, on a drive to the grocery store, I said, "Mom, do you realize how special you are? You said no one wanted or needed anything you crocheted, but look at how many people you have blessed."

My sweet mom reached her right hand to her left shoulder and patted herself. "You are a good girl, June."

We both laughed at her nonsense, but we knew how true her statement was. She truly did bless many with her "crocheted hope in an envelope."

— Kat Crawford —

Chapter
9

Special
Fun

81

The Great Escape

A smile is a curve that sets everything straight.
~Phyllis Diller

Mom thought it seemed like a good idea at the time, going for a little drive with our family friend, Helen. What fun it would be to get out of the house for a coffee klatsch and gossip with Aunt Margaret in the next town. Little did my mother know the chain of events she would set off with this simple action.

My mother had been living on the farm alone since my father's death years earlier. She walked with a cane and had stopped driving a few years earlier. With twelve children (nine boys and three girls), we divided up jobs to keep her safe, mostly healthy and living at home. One of the compromises she made was to agree to the "Help, I've Fallen and Can't Get Up" button. This made us feel better about her being alone on the farm — that, and one of my brothers lived only a mile away so he was first on the call list.

One lovely summer day, the phone went out at the farm. This was actually not that unusual in our area, but Mom worried about not having contact and decided it would be a good idea to press her "button" to inform them her phone was not working. Mom's lack of knowledge about anything technical made her unaware that the "button" actually needed a working telephone to communicate with the "button people." After several minutes of no answers from the "button people," she gave up and started on Plan B.

This was before cell phones were common, and most of us would probably just have waited a few hours to see if the phone company got it fixed. Well, not my mother. She decided she really needed the phone repaired ASAP, and since driving wasn't an option, she was determined to come up with a plan.

Her plan was simple. Cane and all, she would drag a folding chair to the end of the driveway, almost a football field in length. Then she would sit alongside the road and wave her cane at cars driving by to get someone to stop. Once she got them to stop, she would talk them into driving into town, going to the phone company and informing them her phone wasn't working.

I can't imagine how she pulled off dragging that chair to the road. And I can't shake off the image of her shaking her cane at strangers driving by. They must have thought she was a crazy, old woman yelling at them for driving on her road!

According to her, it took a few cars before someone stopped, and she was able to convince them to do this task. However, not really trusting the first driver, she decided she would wait for another one to stop — just to be safe. Only a short time later, she snagged her second driver, who agreed to her request. She was in business.

Just as she was getting ready to drag her chair back to the house, Helen drove up on an impromptu trip to visit Mom. Mom was itching to get out and about, so she convinced Helen to drive into the next town where they would visit my mom's sister, Margaret.

Remember that "button" she pushed? Yup, you guessed it — the phone came back on, and the people on the other end of the "button" were notified that Marie needed some help. But she wasn't answering. And then the phone calls began. My brother who lived the closest couldn't be reached, so the next one on the list was my attorney brother living about thirty miles away. His response? "Call the sheriff's department."

Within thirty minutes, the farm was swarming with sheriff's deputies, EMTs, and several of my brothers looking in ditches, cornfields, barns, and the house. When they had arrived at the farm, all they found was an empty folding chair at the end of the driveway. Had she been kidnapped? Was she dead in the ditch? She couldn't walk that far, so had someone taken her? The search was on, and my brothers were frantic — but apparently not frantic enough to call me. I sat at work not having a clue.

After nearly an hour of combing the ditches, my mom and Helen drove slowly up the gravel road, totally oblivious to the chaos they had created. I can hear them now, screaming "Oh, crap!" as they came over the hill and saw sheriff's cars, an ambulance and even a fire truck at the farm. Right then and there, they knew they were in a sticky predicament.

How were they going to get out of this one? Helen was particularly concerned since she had worked at the courthouse for years and was on a first-name basis with most of the deputies. She would never live this one down. So she did the only thing she could figure out: She drove down the back side of the driveway behind the garage, had my mom do a tuck-and-roll out of the car and then ditched her. Well, she probably stopped the car and helped her out, but she skedaddled as fast as she could, hoping she wasn't seen by all the hubbub.

Oddly enough, I really never heard what my brothers said to my mom — probably a bad nursing-home threat and something about leaving a note when she left the farm. She probably said, "Okay" and then said something sassy under her breath. I thought it was hysterical when I finally heard the story later that night. Go, Mom, go! My brothers — not so much!

Thereafter, whenever Mom left the house, she always left a note written on a paper plate that she tucked in a kitchen cabinet door. It read only, "Here is the note."

— Mary Lovstad —

Christmas Mysteries

*Love is what's in the room with you at Christmas if you
stop opening presents and listen.*
~Author Unknown

Christmas morning always starts off with a little bit of chaos,
especially in a house full of seven kids. The first child to wake
up runs to the nearest sibling's room. First, he knocks quietly,
but the knocks generally get louder and louder until the target
wakes up. Then, the group builds until all seven kids are awake and
knocking at my parents' door, begging to be allowed into the living
room to see if Santa has visited. Once the okay is given, all seven kids
rush out to see what Santa has left them. But what is unusual about
my house is that we have to wait for my mother to tell us our names
before opening presents.

Now, I promise we aren't all insane. We do actually know our
names. But my mother discovered at an early age that we could not
be trusted with our presents before Christmas morning. Patience is a
virtue not abundant in my family. So, she developed a plan. Instead of
letting my ruffian siblings tear through her beautiful display of presents
and complain that someone received more presents or anything of
the sort, she decided to change the names on our gifts. Each year,
after picking a theme, she comes up with code names. The themes
have included *Harry Potter* characters, candy bars, sodas, TV show
characters, planets, and many more.

However, kids will be kids; my siblings and I developed our own tradition. We would take stock of all of the names. Then, from there, we would attempt to use our powers of deduction to figure out which code name matched up to each child. If there were two presents that felt alike, we would assume they were for my twin brothers. If there were a few that were identical we would conclude that they were either for the boys or the girls. Really, we developed a lot of tricks. We would all end up sitting on the living-room floor and sprawled under the Christmas tree, announcing our theories and sharing ideas.

My mother would sit and watch us climbing all around the tree, giggling to herself. When we would try to confirm our suspicions, she would merely smirk. Honestly, the month before Christmas was the time when my siblings really learned how to work as a team. Weirdly, we also all score very high in our logic and deduction skills; it is almost like we have been developing them for years. On Christmas morning, she would announce our names or give us the item that we were named after, like a specific candy bar or soda, and laugh as we all teased each other about who was right or wrong.

My siblings are all pretty much grown now. My older sisters live in another state, and my older brothers no longer live at home. But even after twenty-plus years, if you show up at the right time, you can see a couple of grown children snooping under the tree. Even this year, on Christmas morning, you can find lists of names tucked into pajama pockets and my mom smirking behind her coffee cup.

— Rose Hofer —

The Ever Blooming Hibiscus

The best way of keeping a secret
is to pretend there isn't one.
~Margaret Atwood

The family had gathered to celebrate my father's sixty-fifth birthday, but we were planning his funeral instead. He'd collapsed on the tennis court from a heart attack.

The next day, my brother, my mother and I were in the florist shop, selecting arrangements to be displayed at the funeral home. With that task complete, we were leaving the shop, Mom walking a few steps ahead of me.

She stopped so suddenly that I almost walked into her. I saw her artist's eye had been drawn to an arrangement on the floor, a beautiful hibiscus in full bloom. The vibrant red flower with deep green leaves sat in a basket near the door.

I let Mom go ahead and hurried back to the sales desk. Quickly selecting a card, I wrote a message and left instructions for the flowers to be delivered to my mom at home, not as part of the funeral arrangements.

Later, I had to smile when I saw the surprise on Mom's face as the plant was delivered, with the card saying, "To Mom, with love…" from her three children.

That was June, and Mom kept that plant through the summer

months and into the fall. When she decided to go to Florida for a couple of months over the winter, as she and my dad had done for years, I was given the responsibility of caring for the plant in her absence.

I have absolutely no green thumb and have stayed away from any "real" houseplants. I always blamed the cat — the cat digs in the pot, the leaves are poisonous, and so on.

I tried, I really tried, to keep that hibiscus alive and blooming, but I failed. So, just before Mom was to return home, I went back to the florist and bought another plant, replacing the old one with the new in the same decorative basket.

When Mom returned, I gave her back the plant and never said a word about the replacement. Mom did have a green thumb, and the plant thrived, as had the one before. When the trip to Florida came due, the plant was once again given into my trust. I thought Mom might have reconsidered if she had known I had killed the first one.

I took the plant with the best of intentions, but when spring came, I made what was becoming an annual trip to the florist. I bought a new hibiscus and settled it into the basket.

I wanted to keep this tradition going because every time I gave Mom the plant, we had a special yet unspoken shared memory of where the plant came from and the occasion. That beautiful flower represented love — the love of children for their mother, and the love a family felt for a father no longer with us.

I should have known that was not the only thing unspoken between us. My mother was fully aware that I replaced her hibiscus with a new one every spring, and, I think, needed that ongoing connection as part of her grieving process.

When she left me the flowers that third year, she gave me a hug and told me to enjoy the plant, but when it was gone, to let it go. I was not to replace it, as it had served its purpose.

I should have known I couldn't fool my mom, but I wanted to keep that plant, that memory, alive for her. I learned we didn't need the plant to understand and feel the love and caring in our relationship.

My mom is gone now, too. I can never see a hibiscus without

thinking of her and the first plant we shared. It makes me happy and sad at the same time, but it's a nice memory, one I cherish always.

— Deborah Lean —

84

Chicken Soup
for the Soul

Mom's Last Rites

A well-balanced person is one who finds
both sides of an issue laughable.
~Herbert Prockno

wo weeks before Thanksgiving, my dad called. This was an "event," since he doesn't like phones and has not called me more than four times in my life. He said my eighty-five-year-old mother had asked if I could fly home that weekend because she was dying, and the priest was coming the next day to give her the Last Sacrament.

I was shocked. I had talked to her just a few days before, and she had only complained of a stomachache. Then again, this was a woman who had had a mastectomy before she told anyone she'd been diagnosed with cancer. Earlier in the current year, she fell while going up the stairs to attend an investment seminar. She got up, climbed the remaining six steps and attended the two-hour program. It wasn't until it was over and she discovered she couldn't stand up that she mentioned her fall to the seminar staff. They rushed her to the hospital where she learned that she had broken her hip.

Financially, Mom's request was also a shock. I was leaving in ninety minutes to catch a plane to Spokane, Washington, where I would give a half-day workshop the next morning. I would return home to Seattle for two days, and then fly to Myrtle Beach, South Carolina, for four days of work. That was all of my speaking (and my income) for the rest of the year.

I asked if she was in the hospital. Dad said no, but she had been bedridden for two weeks. He was waiting for the doctor to call with some test results. Dad concluded that I should give my workshop and check back the next afternoon.

When I called the next day, Mom answered the phone.

"I thought you were dying!" I blurted out.

"No, it's hardly worth it," she sighed.

She complained that the priest was twenty-five minutes late. "I mean, you just don't come late to give someone the last rites! And then he only spent five minutes performing what should have been a much more impressive ceremony.

"After all," she said, "it is the Last Sacrament. I thought there would be a lot more to it. Not only that, the Host was stale. When it's your last Holy Communion, the least a priest could provide would be a fresh Host!"

She went on to concede, "He's actually a really nice man, but he's very young. He probably just needs a little feedback. I'll talk to him the next time I see him at Mass."

"You're right," I agreed. "He probably doesn't get much feedback from the parishioners he performs the last rites for. May I please talk to Dad?"

Long story short, the doctor reported that Mom's blood-pressure medication had lowered her salt levels too much, causing a form of dementia. Since she already had some disorientation, this made it much worse, generating her call for the priest. With a medication adjustment, she was quickly back to her old self.

I gave my presentations and arrived at my folks' home in Napa, California a week later. Mom was on her feet and, although frail, she was once more the "salt of the earth." We celebrated by going to Mass.

And, yes, after Mass, she did graciously give a rather surprised young priest some feedback!

— Patt Schwab —

85

Puzzle Me This

Not every puzzle is intended to be solved.
Some are in place to test your limits.
Others are, in fact, not puzzles at all.
~Vera Nazarian

My mother is complaining. "I can't believe you don't know the answer."

I scooch around in the recliner that sits next to my mother's chair, feeling like I've just been caught sneaking in after curfew. "Mom, I haven't seen every movie ever made. Therefore, I don't know the name of the character who was the best friend of the main character in a movie that came out twenty years ago."

She sighs. "All right. Let's try another one. Okay, this answer has six letters. Name of an island in the Pacific."

"Hawaii."

She shakes her head, her permed curls bouncing as she does. "No, it has to have a P in it."

"I have no idea."

Another head shake. "What did they teach you at school all those years? Let's try another puzzle."

I groan. I know better. Visiting my mother in the afternoon when her daily newspaper has arrived is akin to going on a Navy SEAL mission. No way I'm getting out of the house until I help her with today's crossword puzzle. I should be used to this routine by now. I'm always asked, either in person or on the phone when I call, if I know some random fact that could fit into little boxes going across or down.

I've never been a fan of crossword puzzles. Their air of superiority. Their way of tricking you. You rack your brain for the name of a mole species only to discover they were referring to a government spy, not a creature that lives underground.

But Mom is convinced crossword puzzles are the fountain of youth. "They keep your mind sharp, and no one wants a dull mind," she often said.

I know she's right because every time I do a puzzle with her, I get a sharp pain in my head.

"How do you spell Chihuahua?" she asks.

"D-O-G."

Another sigh. She picks up the dictionary she keeps beside her chair and reaches for her magnifying glass.

While she hunts for the word, I pick up another puzzle from the growing pile of unfinished puzzles that will taunt her until recycling day. The dark clouds of inferiority part in my mind. "Hey, I know the answer to this one."

She hands me a pen. "Good, write it in."

"Okay, but it changes the answer you had going across."

"What answer was that?"

"The name of the King of England during the Hundred Years' War."

"Whatever answer you want to use isn't correct because Edward is right."

I stare at her. "How do you know the name of the third King of England?"

Mom has no computer or smartphone or set of encyclopedias.

"I watch BBC."

I give up my answer. How do you argue with the BBC? I pounce like a lion, though, on the next one. "Your answer to thirteen across isn't right. *Dear Eleanor* is a movie."

"A movie? I thought they were referring to someone writing to Eleanor Roosevelt. That's why I put 'letter.'"

"Letter? There are only five boxes here, Mom."

"It fit."

"Because you left out one of the Ts."

She shakes her head. "Well, that's what I get for working a puzzle and watching *Judge Judy* at the same time. Go ahead and change it."

"This would be easier if you did this in pencil," I say, trying to squeeze the right letters in over the wrong ones.

"Using a pencil is admitting defeat before you even begin. Some things in life have to be done in pen, with confidence. What color was used most often in the painting of the Mona Lisa?"

And so I spend time with my mother this way. If my brain cells align just right, I'm blessed with a couple of right answers. Sometimes I cheat and ask Google for help. Other times, I tell her about the merits of Circle-a-Word puzzles.

I don't know if these crossword puzzles are keeping my mother's mind sharp. I don't know if maybe they're giving me an ulcer. But I do know these little squares running across and down keep my mother and me connected. They give us something to talk about besides the state of the world and my lousy day at work. They give us something to laugh about.

She nudges my foot. "What's a four-letter word for heart?"

"Love."

She looks up at me and smiles. "I love you, too, honey. Now figure out the answer, which, by the way, starts with a Z."

— Martha Willey —

86

The Easter Bunny Strikes Again

There is no way to be a perfect mother,
and a million ways to be a good one.
~Jill Churchill

One Easter, my older brother brought some friends home from university for the long weekend. They all lived far from home, and he knew my parents would make them feel welcome.

The boys arrived late Thursday night. Our home was suddenly full of more activity and laughter than usual, and Mom was in her glory. She loved organizing all the meals for our extended family. She saw to it that each guest had a sleeping bag, ample blankets, pillows and fresh towels for his stay.

Saturday night, after another of Mom`s home-cooked meals, the boys told us they were getting ready to go to a party. As they thanked Mom for another great meal, she mentioned casually, "Tomorrow is Easter Sunday. We'll be leaving for church at 8:30 if you care to join us. If you prefer to sleep in, help yourself to breakfast. Our Easter dinner will be at 1:00 p.m."

The boys thanked her politely for the offer, but figured they might be back a little late, plus they did not think to pack a jacket or tie. Mom smiled back and said, "Okay, have a good night — but don't be too late, or the Easter Bunny won't come!" The boys all laughed and wished her a good night.

Easter morning, my younger brother and I joined my parents in the car.

"I guess it's just the four of us," Mom said.

"I'm not surprised," Dad said. "I think it was after midnight when they got in."

"More like 2:30," Mom whispered under her breath.

We sat in our usual seats at church. Occasionally, Mom glanced back at the doors, ever hopeful.

"Mom, I don't think they're coming," my younger brother whispered.

The organist set up his music and began to play. The ushers quietly closed the back doors as the congregation turned their attention to the pulpit. Suddenly, we heard the sound of several feet pounding up the stairs. The back doors flew open. A congregation of heads turned as five boys were quickly ushered up the aisle to our pew. As we stood up to let them all in, Mom shook her head with a grin. For, over their sneakers and blue jeans, each one was wearing an assortment of poorly fitted jackets, shirts and ties — courtesy of my dad's and brothers' closets. Once they were seated, all five boys leaned over and gave a warm smile and good-morning nod to my mom.

After church, we helped Mom and Dad get dinner on the table. We were eating early so the boys could get back to school in good time. There was lots of laughter at the table. Still dressed in their ill-fitted duds, they told us how they had all tried on different clothes to make the Easter Sunday service.

During the meal, one of the boys said he had had a revelation the night before. Taking the bait, we all turned to hear what this revelation was.

"Well," he said, "all these years I thought the Easter bunny was a boy. But last night, I discovered he's a she!"

"A girl!" we said.

"Yes, it's true. Just as I was falling asleep last night, I saw her. She was wearing a fluffy pink housecoat and slippers. I saw her quietly tiptoe around each of our sleeping bags and place a beautiful Easter basket by our heads." Then he paused for effect and looked down the table to my mom with a wink.

"MOM!" we all shouted, laughing.

Smiling smugly, Mom said, "And I have it on very good authority that the Easter Bunny almost didn't make that final delivery... I think it was well after 2:00 a.m., wasn't it?"

With that, one of the boys stood up with a raised glass in hand, and said, "To the Easter Bunny — for her graciousness, generosity and making each one of us, far from our families, feel very much at home this weekend."

"To the Easter Bunny!" we all echoed, raising our glasses toward Mom.

Our family enjoyed many more Easters together. Our friends were always welcome, and each year Mom reprised her role for all who joined us. Though she did say, due to advancing years, the Easter Bunny might not get there until morning.

— Cheryl E. Uhrig —

87

The Queen of Yes

Happiness is not in money, but in shopping.
~Marilyn Monroe

We were at the store. "Mom, can I get a box of Frosted Flakes?" my eight-year-old self asked.

Mom shook her head. "It's your brother's turn to choose the cereal."

I scowled. "But he always chooses Rice Krispies, and I hate those."

"It's your turn to choose the chips."

I brightened a bit, already knowing that I would grab a bag of the sour-cream-and-onion variety — not because they were my favorite, but because my siblings didn't like them, leaving more chips for me. It seemed only fair since I wouldn't be eating any cereal that week.

Such was life growing up in a big family.

Our weekly shopping trips included the word "no" far more often than "yes."

"That's not in the budget this week," Mom would say. "Put that back. It's not on sale."

That's just the way it was — until Mom started entering sweepstakes. She'd read about a lady from Ohio who had won a brand-new car and enough money to pay off her mortgage. Mom wanted to be just like her.

This was in the days before the Internet, when all correspondence actually went through the post office. Mom subscribed to a monthly publication that told her about upcoming sweepstakes, the prizes they offered, and the deadlines to enter. Mom read all the tricks and tips for winning. She purchased colored envelopes of various sizes and bought the fanciest stamps she could find. "The judges are supposed to close their eyes when they pull out the winning entry, but I've heard that sometimes they peek," Mom said. "Having a brightly colored envelope or an interesting stamp can increase your chances of winning."

And Mom's efforts paid off. Just a few weeks later, she won her very first prize: a year's supply of Alka-Seltzer tablets.

My dad fell off his chair laughing.

Mom's second prize was a bit more exciting. She won a Budweiser T-shirt. It became my dad's new lawn-mowing shirt.

Over the years, Mom's prizes have gotten better. She's won all kinds of things, many of them quite valuable. She's won a car, multiple trips, and even a pair of jet skis.

But to this day, the prize I remember the best was a gift certificate to the biggest grocery store in our area. This grocery store was huge, but Mom never shopped there. "They have so many products that I've found I spend more money when I go there," Mom explained. "It's bad for our budget."

I don't recall the exact amount of the gift certificate, but it was generous, like double our monthly grocery budget. My dad encouraged Mom to spend the certificate a little bit at a time, but Mom wasn't having it. "We're going all out," she said.

She took my siblings and me with her. When we got inside the giant store, Mom smiled. "Grab a cart," she said. My oldest brother grabbed one, but Mom shook her head. "No, you can each grab a cart," she said. "And you can put whatever you want in it."

Our mouths dropped open. "We don't have to ask first?"

Mom's smile was enormous. "Not this time, guys."

My siblings and I walked through that grocery store, grabbing every type of food we'd always wanted, but was never in our budget. For kids who'd always had to take turns choosing a box of cereal or a bag of chips, this was an amazing experience.

Fruit Roll-Ups were a new product, but we hadn't tried them yet.

My friends would bring them to school in their lunches, and I was so envious. "My mom thinks they're a waste of money," I would tell my friends. "She thinks we should eat actual fruit, instead of rolled-up fruit."

On our shopping day, I threw a dozen boxes into my cart. Later that day, I would discover that I don't like Fruit Roll-Ups. But that was okay. I just traded them for snacks I did like.

I'll never forget the look on Mom's face in the grocery store that day. As happy as my siblings and I were, Mom looked positively elated.

Each time we would forget and ask her if we could get something, she'd say, "I told you, today the answer is 'yes' to everything!"

Mom loved us with all her heart, but on normal days, she couldn't say "yes" to very much. There were just too many of us, and not enough money in the budget. But that day, Mom didn't have to say "no" — not even one time.

At the checkout, Mom smiled when the clerk told her our total. It was more than we'd ever spent on groceries, and the gift certificate just covered it.

"Boy, you guys are some lucky kids," the clerk told us.

We grinned. "Our mom won this shopping trip, and she let us get everything we wanted."

"Your mom is awesome," the clerk said. "She's like a queen."

"She didn't say 'no' today, not even once," I said. "She was the Queen of Yes!"

Mom's smile grew even bigger. She definitely liked the nickname.

Today, one of Mom's favorite things is to be the Queen of Yes to her grandchildren. She prepares their favorite meals, takes them shopping and to amusement parks, spoiling them as only a grandma can.

And as I walk next to her on these trips, I can still see that young, frazzled mom who got to be the Queen of Yes in that grocery store so many years ago. That day, the thing that made her the happiest was making her children happy.

Even all these years later, making others happy is still Mom's greatest joy.

People always tell Mom how lucky she is to have won so many

prizes from the sweepstakes she enters.

But my siblings and I know that we're the lucky ones. After all, the Queen of Yes is our mom.

—Diane Stark—

Mom's Unexpected Birthday Guest

*I want to take all our best moments, put them in a jar,
and take them out like cookies and
savor each one of them forever.*
~Crystal Woods

Turning ninety was never something Mom expected to do. As she approached seventy, she instructed us, her children, to throw her a big party, and we did, gathering all her loved ones together one afternoon for a wonderful luncheon in a nice restaurant.

When eighty came on the horizon, she didn't think she'd make it. After all, she had outlived her first husband, all of her siblings, and her siblings-in-law. She'd also outlived many friends. But that day came, and again we gathered family and friends to celebrate the occasion.

As ninety approached, many things had changed for Mom, but one thing remained the same: She wanted a birthday party, a big one. So, we had a party, but this time it was a small gathering held in the dining room of the nursing facility where she was recovering from a fractured hip, sustained just three weeks before.

Before her injury, we had planned to give Mom a big bash in a restaurant. She'd talked about it for months and invited everyone she knew. But because of the fractured hip, we had to cancel that party, and arranged the smaller one at the rehab at the last minute. It wasn't what she'd hoped for, but the change in venue allowed an unexpected guest to join us, which made her day.

You see, Mom's husband, Fred, was also in the facility, admitted to the dementia unit a little more than a year prior to her admission. Mom visited him a few times each week, but these visits distressed her because he was usually asleep and did not respond to her voice or her touch. She often left their visits in tears and was melancholy for days. Sometimes, we thought it would be better if she didn't visit him.

On the day of the party, we decorated the dining room with forty-eight-inch-tall gold Mylar balloons that screamed "90," a beautiful arrangement of summer flowers, and a sheet cake decorated in her favorite colors: red and orange. Twenty-five of Mom's family and closest friends came to wish her a happy birthday. Surrounded by her loved ones, Mom was overwhelmed with happiness. Only one other person could have made this day happier: Fred, her husband of thirty years.

And because the party was held in the nursing facility, and not in a restaurant miles away, we had arranged for him to join us, at least for a few minutes, to be part of the celebration. When an attendant brought him into the room, Mom shouted with joy. Her circle was complete. Her beloved Fred was there to share her special day. We positioned them side-by-side in their wheelchairs. He sat there with his eyes closed, unresponsive, and the party went on.

A short time later, there was a buzz in the room: "Fred's awake!" And he was! His handsome blue eyes were wide open. Mom spoke to him, and he responded. He said, "I love you." He ate birthday cake and ice cream. We took family pictures. He stayed for the rest of the party.

When I brought him back to his nursing unit, I said, "Bye, Fred." And he said, "Bye." It was the first word he had spoken to me in months. I returned to the party with tears in my eyes. The remaining guests were still talking about Fred and his miraculous awakening, just in time to share his wife's ninetieth birthday. Mom was ecstatic, crying that his presence was the best gift of all.

God works in strange ways. We were able to give Mom a lovely celebration after all, and with her husband at her side.

A happy birthday indeed.

—Marianne Sciucco—

89

Who Knew?

*A memory is a photograph taken by the heart to make
a special moment last forever.*
~Author Unknown

I grew up in rural southern Ohio, the oldest of seven boys. With seven of us, there were always games to play. We even constructed a baseball diamond in our front yard — albeit of a very crude design. First base was a maple tree, second base was the corner of the "old garden," and third base was a bare spot between two apple trees. A total of six apple trees ran down the left field line to a gradual uphill slope leading to Dad's grapevines and our pets' cemetery. Lastly, looming in the distance was a white fence in front of our barn, but none of us boys could hit the ball that far.

Well, as luck would have it one summer afternoon, none of the neighbor boys could play a game. So we had to resort to one last option.

We trudged back into the house, interrupted my mother doing her chores, and asked, "Mom, could you come out and just hit us some high-flies?"

To our surprise, she said, "Yes."

Five minutes later, Mom was standing over home plate, with a baseball in her left hand and a bat in her right.

Not expecting much, my four oldest brothers and I only stood at second base.

Mom yelled, "Are you ready?"

"Yeah… whatever," we replied.

Mom tossed the ball up over home plate with her left hand.

WHACK!

We watched a towering high-fly sail over our heads and land back near Dad's grapes.

Five brothers just stood there and looked at each other. "What was that?"

Meanwhile, Mom bent over at home plate and picked up another ball.

"Are you ready?"

"Wait a second, Mom."

Five brothers moved back — walking up the slope toward the pet cemetery — and turned around.

"Okay, Mom. We're ready!"

Mom tossed the ball up over home plate with her left hand.

WHACK!

Once again, we watched a monstrous high-fly coming down with moon dust on it.

"I got it!" Jerry called. He snagged the ball right next to King's grave.

Meanwhile, Mom bent over at home plate and picked up another ball.

"Are you ready?"

"Wait a second, Mom."

Five brothers moved back again — walking beyond the pet cemetery toward the white fence — and turned around.

"Okay, Mom. We're ready now!"

WHACK!

And that's the way the afternoon went. We had more fun chasing Mom's high-flies in front of the white fence than we ever did playing a normal baseball game.

Who knew that Mom possessed such talent?

— John M. Scanlan —

90

My Mother's Matron of Honor

Bridesmaid for a day, best friend for life.
~Author Unknown

A s the doors in the back of the church opened and light flooded in behind her, my mother began to walk down the aisle, holding the arm of her eleven-year-old grandson. She wore a cream-colored dress and had a matching flower in her hair. Colorful stained-glass windows lined the brick walls of the sanctuary. The afternoon light streamed through them as she made her way to the front of the church, her face beaming.

I stood there along with her lifelong friends and bridesmaids. The granddaughters were junior bridesmaids, and the youngest was the flower girl, happily tossing flower petals as she passed each pew in her white patent-leather shoes. As the classical music soared from the piano, I took in the beauty of the moment. My mom was my greatest friend in the world, and here I was, her Matron of Honor, watching her walk down the aisle on her wedding day.

The ceremony was well underway, and it was time for the bride's daughter and the groom's son to each light a candle from which the bride and groom would later light a unity candle. I handed my bouquet to one of the bridesmaids and stepped forward to perform my task. I remembered my own wedding, and how my mother lit a candle for me. I never imagined I would someday be at her wedding, doing the same for her.

I thought about all the valuable things I had learned from her through the years — about faith, creativity and perseverance. She had endured losses, injuries and heartbreak, but she had never given up on living. She kept her heart open and held onto her faith no matter the circumstances. And she was always creating something.

I had seen her creative abilities shine through the years — everything from making her famous Oreo balls to teaching a calligraphy class at a local art store. As a little girl, I often saw her leaning over a table with a calligraphy pen in hand, creating beautiful words and artwork. I guess I thought everybody's mother could write like a medieval scribe from the twelfth century. And there were lessons I learned just by watching her work. If a spot of ink dropped in the wrong place, she would transform it into a flower petal or an angel's wing. Without even saying it, her message was clear: No mistake is beyond fixing, and beauty can emerge where you least expect it.

The service was almost over now, and the minister pronounced them husband and wife. I watched my mother — a woman seasoned by life, deepened by the wisdom of her experience, joyfully embrace this new beginning. Of all the things I had learned from her through the years, maybe this was the most important: Although life never turns out exactly like we expect, we don't give up when things are difficult. We learn to see the angel's wing instead of the drop of ink in the wrong place. Hope is always around the corner, and it's never too late to live happily ever after.

— Suzannah Kiper —

91

My Mother and the Dress

Youth fades; love droops; the leaves of friendship fall;
A mother's secret hope outlives them all.
~Oliver Wendell Holmes

My mother is ninety. She resides in a nursing home and has few physical capabilities. She is often confused, irritable and cantankerous. There are times, however, when she is very rational, sharing stories of the past and remembering people who were important to her when she was young.

Because my mother has not been healthy for many years, it is hard for me to remember the woman who raised me. I will always credit her with taking me to the library and letting me read whatever I wanted. Yet I was having difficulty recalling any other strengths she had.

Then we found the dress. It was made in 1949. My mother sewed it. She was expecting her first child, and she crafted the dress for the christening. She included two hats — one for a boy and one for a girl. No ultrasounds then. Babies were always a surprise. My brothers, sister and I all wore that dress. Then, somehow, it got packed away, forgotten in a cedar chest.

After the dress was discovered, my granddaughter wore it at her christening. We all watched as her parents and family promised to teach her about God and the importance of faith in our lives. Of course, she looked beautiful and perfect while six other children cheered from the pews as she joined them in their journey of faith. She shares my name, and she wore my dress.

As I watched, I wondered if my mother knew how many lives she would affect as she stitched those little flower appliqués. Did she wonder, as she ironed that dress, about the gift of life? Did she somehow hear the laughter of these children and all the joy they would bring?

I brought that dress to the nursing home. I showed it to the nurses and aides so they could see a part of my mother that they most certainly did not know. They oohed and aahed over the tiny buttons and handmade stitches. They held the tiny bonnet and had a chance to see my mother in a totally different light.

When I presented the dress to my mother, she smiled and patted the fabric almost reverently, quietly remembering. She shared a little about how that dress was made and how carefully it was stitched together. She even recalled that she was afraid my younger brother might be a little too chubby for it. And she smiled. I remembered that smile and how many times I had seen it in the past.

The dress is not just a few pieces of cloth. It is much more than that. It is memories and a prayer for the future all rolled into one.

— Diane St. Laurent —

Chapter
10

A Mother's Strength

92

The Way I Love My Babies

*We have a secret in our culture, and it's not that birth
is painful. It's that women are strong.*
~Laura Stavoe Harm

I stand in my kitchen, resting my head on the wall. I'm holding my premature son in my arms, watching my mother give his identical twin brother the first bath since coming home from the NICU. I watch as she sinks his four-pound body into the baby tub we put on the counter. She turns to me and asks, "Are you sure you want me to do this?"

I remember giving their older sister, Haley, her first bath; my husband took pictures, and the experience filled me with such joy. This seems different.

"Yes, please," I say. That first bath is one of the memories parents treasure, and I'm handing it over to my mother. I just can't muster the energy to do it myself, and they're so small and fragile. She methodically washes little Holden, and then passes him to me and changes the water before gently placing his brother, Hayden, in the tub.

Again, she asks, "Do you want me to keep going?"

I respond with a simple nod of my head. She doesn't push. A silence looms in the house as I watch her dip a cloth into the water and ever so gently wash his little face. I glance at her, and the sadness I feel is there with her, too, at the corners of her mouth. When she washes his tiny hand, trying to clean between the slender fingers, I see her smile as he instinctively balls his fist around her finger. Then, slowly, her smile recedes. And I know why — she's wondering if I will regret this moment, me not giving them their first baths. To be honest, I'm wondering, too. Will I regret giving away such a cherished milestone?

Ever since my pregnancy went awry, my mother had been by my side as much as I allowed. When I asked everyone to refrain from visiting me in the hospital, she showed up. I wanted to be alone, but it wasn't intrusive having her there. Instinctively, she knew when to speak, when to hold my hand, and when to stay ten feet away and sit silently. I spent six days in labor, or more accurately trying to stop labor, to no avail. I paced my hospital room in excruciating pain, while she fidgeted on the small couch, twisting her wedding band in a never-ending circle. We stayed mostly quiet as we understood the magnitude of the inevitable delivery when the doctors said we were out of options. The babies would be ten weeks early.

Finally, I crawled onto all fours in the bed and asked her to call the nurse. "I can't take anymore." She stood to leave and promised to check in on me later. I turned myself back over in the bed to receive her kiss on my forehead, and then watched her leave the room as the nurse walked in. That was the last of the quiet for me, the last of the calm for a long time.

Now, she pulls Hayden out of the warm water and wraps him in a towel, carrying him to the changing table to dress him. She smiles, kissing his forehead. We sit together on the couch, each holding a baby. After a long silence, I speak up, "I can't do this, Mom. It's too hard. They need so much. They're frail and sick. I haven't slept. I can't keep going. It's too difficult."

She lets the silence hang there before responding slowly. "You don't have a choice — you are their mother." I expected her to tell me life isn't fair, that I am strong, that I can do anything I put my mind to — all the inspiring words of wisdom she usually declares. Her curt response makes me pause. Not long after, she places Hayden in the swing and says goodbye. I hear the front door close, yet it's quite a while before I hear her drive off down the street.

Later that evening, our toddler Haley comes home with Daddy and, gathering my strength, I meet them at the door. I swing her into the air. "Wheee!" she shouts. We play together until bedtime. I laugh when she tickles me and scream at all the expected moments during peek-a-boo. At bedtime, I snuggle her into my chest, rocking her in the chair, smelling her freshly washed hair. In the dark quiet of her nursery, the weight of life bears down on me. Tears begin to well up inside me like a rising tide. But as I glance down at her precious face, I see her big eyes peeping out at me between those dark eyelashes, so I quickly compose myself and kiss her one more time.

Abruptly, the rising tide of tears grows like a tsunami as I am hit with the realization that my mother hadn't been talking to me at all — she had been talking to herself. Every ounce of hardship in my life was hers to feel, as well, because she doesn't have a choice — she is my mother. And mothers are so bound to their babies that a child's pain multiplies in the heart of its mother. I quickly place my little girl in her crib, just managing to shut her door before I collapse.

Crumpling onto the floor in the hall, I bawl, thinking about how Mom must have sat in the car crying before she drove off. Oh, the love and strength of mothers! I think about all the energy it must take for her to support me in silence because that's what mothers do — they silently carry as much of the burden as the world allows, and they'd gratefully carry more if they could, even when the weight feels like it will bury them. A warmth, beginning in my cheeks, radiates within me. I force myself to stand, wiping away my tears. My breathing slows, and I begin to smile.

With strength returning to my body, I feel determined once more to keep fighting for my boys. And with a mother's strength, I know we will make it through any obstacle. A thought fills me with pleasure: I will never regret relinquishing that first bath because I will always cherish that memory of her, the woman who loves me the way I love my babies, the depth and power of which knows no equal.

— Kristin Baldwin Homsi —

Row Strong

*Anyone can give up, it's the easiest thing in the world
to do. But to hold it together when everyone else would
understand if you fell apart, that's true strength.*
~Author Unknown

On her eightieth birthday, I watched my mother row almost two miles during our indoor rowing class. It wasn't the first time she'd sat on the Concept2 erg, for she had been rowing for over six years, two to three times a week. But this day was special because a party had been planned in her honor after class, with cake, flowers, gifts and many well wishes for one of the oldest rowers in the rowing club.

It's been said that once an athlete, always an athlete, and it may be true in some cases, but my mom was never the athlete of our family. She was the one who sat in the stands cheering for my dad as he played a variety of sports. She also spent hours in the car taking my brothers and me to practice for the different sports we played.

Even though she wasn't the athlete of the family, at five feet, one inch tall and a little over 100 pounds, she has now rowed over four million meters. Who knew she had this in her?

When cancer took my dad's physical strength, I watched my mother become the stronger one of the two. He was the portrait of an athlete as he tried to use his grit to fight the effects of the disease and many treatments.

I found out cancer can strip a lot from people and their families. As the layers are ripped off, labels, experiences, and preconceived notions are often pulled away, too. As I watched my sixty-four-year-old dad's strong six-foot-three-inch frame become weak and frail, I also noticed a new strength in my mother.

As the hospital bed replaced my parents' bed, and the walker collected dust in the corner, the carpet began showing a path made by family and friends who came to visit Daddy. It wasn't long before a startling realization came to the forefront of this daughter's heart.

The irony was not lost on me as my dad, the strong one, became the sweet one, and my mom, the sweet one, became the strong one.

As time passed, my dad needed more assistance as we tried to keep him as comfortable as possible at home. Whether we were administering meds, bringing his meals, reading to him, or sitting with him, he always thanked us, even if it was only a nod or a whisper. His boisterous and bigger-than-life personality became more subdued, but his sense of humor, love for his family and friends, and genuine gratitude never grew weak.

In her quiet way, my mother was by his side. From telling him the devastating news that he had lung cancer after his biopsy, to accompanying him to every treatment, she grew in strength. And that sweet, gentle woman grew ever stronger as she leaned in to tell him goodbye at the end.

Nineteen years later, my petite mother is a picture of health, our dynamo of a rower. Underneath all the sweetness is a strength that has carried her and our entire family through all the years since my father's passing.

It's a hushed strength that can go unnoticed because of her gentle demeanor — the opposite of my dad. But to those of us who are close to her and witnessed her transformation as she cared for the love of her life, we know it's there.

Tomorrow, I'll meet her early in the morning at the rowing studio and strap my feet into the machine beside her. (Yes, she will be there first, waiting for me.) She will row as hard as anyone else in the room, and for just as long.

— Beth Fortune —

Breaking Down Walls

Sometimes the poorest woman leaves her children
the richest inheritance.
~Ruth E. Renkel

My mom found her own way no matter what life threw at her. It was not an easy life. Growing up, she felt unwanted, got pregnant at seventeen, lost a child to SIDS, got divorced after seventeen years of marriage, and lost her hearing and then her life to scleroderma. Yet, it is easy to look back on her life and smile at all she did. I do it every day. She gave to so many people and lived a truly full life in her short forty-nine years.

My dad had left us in the winter of 1986, and it was that summer when my mom finally found her voice. She spent some time grieving the divorce, and because I was fifteen, I went into automatic pilot as new parent to my sisters, who were eight and nine. Everyone was upset except me. I seemed to come alive. I was mothering my sisters, cleaning house, doing laundry, making dinners and helping run the house. My mom was working full-time and spending her evenings with us, but she was depressed. She seemed to go through the motions of life and barely made it to the end of each day. But she never forgot to thank me for helping.

Dad had left us with old appliances and an older car. Everything was always breaking. We spent more time trying to fix things or finding a way to live without them than anything else. We never really had a car that worked, but my dad was a mechanic who could fix them, so it had never been a real problem. Mom was lucky enough to find a friendly and reasonable mechanic shop run by a woman who ended up being a blessing—especially since the car we had was six years older than I was.

When the washer and dryer started giving us problems, it seemed like the last straw. With three kids, any mom knows there is a ton of laundry. The dryer was the first to go, and hanging clothes became necessary. The ten thousand socks were a problem, but we kept going. Mom started to worry about what we would do if the washer went. She began to save money for a new set. It took several months, but she did it, and just in time. She picked them out and set up a time to have them delivered. It was the first time since my dad left that she was really happy about something. Proud of herself.

The deliverymen came with the brand-new washer and dryer and went down to the basement to get the old ones out. They wouldn't fit through the door and couldn't be removed. They told her they couldn't do anything about it. The men took her washer-and-dryer set back to the store.

It seems that when my dad built a room in the basement, a few years before, he had blocked in the laundry area, leaving it with a small doorway. No one thought much about it until that day.

My mom just sat on the stairs to the basement crying. Praying. She sat there for a long time. I left her there, not knowing what to do or how to help. After a long while, I heard banging. Then yelling. I ran to find her attacking the wall with a sledgehammer. She pounded and tore open that wall. It was like she was breaking through all her grief and helplessness. She was not going to let that wall keep her from her goal!

With the wall down, she called those men to bring back the washer-and-dryer set. They tried to reason with her. "Lady, we can't fit them through that door."

"Oh, they will fit now," she said calmly. It had only been a couple of hours since they had left. They said they would come check. With the wall down and a sledgehammer propped up against the entrance, they could still see a faint dust in the air. The men just gave my mom a frightened look and swapped out the old washer and dryer for the new.

Knocking down that wall marked a turning point for her, and she seemed to find her life again. She went back for her GED and on to college. She helped her kids find their walls and break them down, too.

I learned a valuable lesson from her: No wall built by another should ever stand in the way of moving forward.

— Kathleen Monroe —

95

All-American Mom

*My mother is my root, my foundation. She planted the
seed that I base my life on, and that is the belief that
the ability to achieve starts in your mind.*
~Michael Jordan

The paramedics had my mother strapped to a stretcher, balanced precariously on the railing. "Lower her slowly. We don't want to drop her," the paramedic cautioned his partner.

I gasped — my heart racing. They were going to lower her right over the edge of the staircase — a fifteen-foot drop.

It was harrowing.

At forty-five years old, Mom had herniated two discs in her back and couldn't get out of bed. Taken by ambulance to the hospital, she consulted with a neurosurgeon and underwent back surgery. Two weeks later, she transferred to a hospital bed in our living room — basically bedbound for the next forty days.

Although unable to walk, Mom stayed busy. She crocheted about three million scrubbies for scouring pans. That was scary. My sister and I worried she might expect us to *use* all those scrubbies! She read books. And she notched a piece of wood each day — each notch marking one day closer to being medically cleared to walk outside. I thought that obsessive wood notching was pretty morbid until, years later, she told me it had been her inspiration — a daily reminder that she was getting closer to that magic number of forty. And if she grew frustrated, she never showed it. There was no wayward cursing or even a slipped "Hell's Bells" — Mom's version of cussing when she's really, really angry, which I only heard probably twice in my life.

Three weeks passed. Mom was hanging out in the living room, whittling wood and stockpiling scrubbies. My sister, Becky, had become the master chef. I had become the queen of laundry. We were doing okay.

Then Mom dropped the bomb.

"Can you shave my legs? They feel so gross," Mom asked me.

"Really? Um, okay," I stammered, my mind screaming, "Eww!" At sixteen years old, this just seemed like the worst thing ever. But I agreed reluctantly — totally unprepared for the shock of how weak and fragile my mom had become. I was stunned. There was no muscle left in her calves! I didn't even know how hard to press the razor because her skin just rolled under the blade. I probably hurt her feelings with my reaction, but she never said anything.

"Thank you so much. I feel so much better!" Mom thanked me profusely, her words and spirit taking on whatever strength her body had lost.

This had to have been a difficult time for my mom — confined to bed, unable to teach her students, unable to take care of her kids or dog, unable even to walk outside — and yet she never complained. She never criticized our efforts. Not ever. She just praised our hard work over and over again, sincerely grateful and appreciative of our attempts to help out.

Many years later, Becky and I confessed how scared we were that something might go wrong with her back surgery. Mom was shocked.

"Why would it?" she asked. "I had a great doctor and medical team. What was there to worry about?"

Seriously? I could think of many reasons why something could have gone wrong: Sometimes, bad things happen to good people. Sometimes, doctors make mistakes. Sometimes, things just happen. But that's not the way Mom's brain is wired. She's an eternally optimistic person, and that positive spirit radiates throughout all aspects of her life, flowing through her as naturally as her blood.

Two months later, Mom was up and moving around, slowly getting "back to normal." But her recovery caused her to miss a large part of my high-school running career. There was no way she could sit long periods of time on bleachers or stand in the cold for the hours that track and cross-country meets demanded. I understood. But when I got home from practice, she always had a healthy, home-cooked meal ready for me to eat. Immediately.

"I will puke if I eat right now," my sixteen-year-old self would explain bluntly.

Mom wanted to keep me strong and injury-free.

I wanted to cool down and not vomit.

It became a source of tension, but she never gave up. She was determined to keep me healthy. She must have felt I didn't appreciate her extra effort to cook nutritious meals and have them waiting when I got home after late practices. I know I felt like she just didn't get it. She wasn't a runner — she didn't understand. And it's true — she didn't get it — until she became a runner-eighteen months after her back surgery.

My dad and brother were on a fishing trip. Mom was feeling out of shape and unhealthy, so Becky and I suggested she try running. We were both running competitively, and our dad had always been a runner, so running was the natural choice. So the three of us headed to Center Road — the country road that Becky and I ran for cross-country and track practices. Painted lines marked the first few quarter-mile increments, and then landmarks filled in the longer miles.

We stretched.

We talked.

We were ready.

Mom started a slow jog. Becky and I cheered wildly. About an eighth of a mile later, Mom stopped abruptly. She started walking — totally winded and huffing.

Becky and I were horrified — and a little scared.

"Does your back hurt? Are you okay?" we shouted, trying not to freak out.

"Dad will kill us if Mom gets hurt," Becky breathed.

"I know," I acknowledged, swallowing hard and trying not to panic.

"No, I'm okay." Mom said, honestly.

"Then why'd you stop?" we demanded, confused.

"I don't know," Mom said, bewildered.

"Then run!" we shouted.

"Okay," she said and started running again — finishing her first quarter-mile.

And she didn't stop running until she became a Masters All-American in the 400-meter-run at fifty-five years old. She and my dad spent sixteen years competing in road races all over the state of Wisconsin, earning numerous medals, ribbons, trophies, awards and, ultimately, her Masters All-American status.

Amazing? You bet!

However, despite all her accomplishments, her unwavering positive attitude inspires me the most. When faced with a challenge, I just have to think of my mom, notching away on her little piece of wood. If she could endure all that and still become a Masters champion, I should be able to bake a pie. Or give a speech. Or parallel park. Or drive my son from Small Town, Wisconsin, to Washington, D.C. — alone.

Shouldn't I?

She's been called amazing, kind, funny and smart. She's been called a talented athlete, a remarkable teacher, and a devoted dog lover. She's even been called "Super-Grandma!" The list goes on and on. And it's all true — she is all those things and more.

But I'm the lucky one.

I call her Mom.

— Elizabeth A. Pickart —

96

The Bell

To live in hearts we leave behind is not to die.
~Thomas Campbell

My mom's morning check-in was like clockwork ever since I moved six thousand miles away to work in London. It became a running joke amongst my colleagues. Without fail, she would get up at 1:30 a.m. Philadelphia time so we could have our morning chat at 7:30 before I started my busy day. It was so predictable that on the odd day she may have missed calling in, I had my co-workers demanding that I call to make sure she was still alive. The sound of that bell was my assurance that she was okay.

My mom and I were always bonded. Perhaps it was because I was the baby of the family, or because my father had died when I was nine and she was really the only parent I ever knew. Mom and I were connected in a way that was so much more than mother and daughter, best friends or soul mates.

When I was offered the opportunity to move to Europe for work, my mom told me to reach for that brass ring. She encouraged me to live my life while I could, when I had no commitments or nothing holding me back. So, yes, those early-morning calls may seem obsessive in nature to others, but to me they were the sustenance I needed to keep moving forward.

Ever since I was a little girl, Lucia (Lucy) Flowers was the model of everything I wanted to be in life. Standing only 4' 9", this power-house had more resilience and courage than three hundred Spartans.

I do not need to go into detail about her upbringing except to say she had loving parents and grew up in very humble settings. She and my father married when they were in their early twenties and had five children — a daughter, three sons and then myself. We were the typical 1970s suburban family, with a brown station wagon and polyester clothes. Mom was the storybook stay-at-home mother, baking for bake sales, sewing costumes, and being a Cub Scout den leader.

Like most fairy tales, there is an end, and in the process of adversity a heroine is born. Disney could never have dreamed up anything as amazing as Lucy, though. She faced her first of many challenges when my father was diagnosed with terminal lung cancer at the age of forty. He died a year later, leaving her to raise five children alone. Like everything else, she accepted the challenge head-on and made sure we never felt a true void. She was her children's biggest cheerleader and instilled a sense of living life to the fullest in all of us.

Her next battle was with medical issues. Again, she powered through with Herculean strength in a body the size of Mighty Mouse. But it was the suicide of her middle son that would be her truest test. That one left some permanent chinks in her armor. Yet again, her inner fortitude compelled her to carry the heaviest weight of the pain on her own shoulders in order that her other children could continue to fly.

My years abroad were made possible because, despite the obstacles we faced as a family, I had a role model like no other. In fact, this model of resilience helped me to persevere when faced with my own greatest personal struggle. Would I be able to raise my infant son alone after my husband abandoned us to start a new family? On those days when I just wanted to stay in bed, Mom once again pulled down those proverbial covers and forced me to get up and get going. She gave me the confidence to move back home and set the same example for my son that she had for me.

I guess that is why it became inconceivable to me that this force of nature could be felled by what began as a common cold. When doctors informed me that my best friend would not recover, due to unforeseen complications that combined themselves into a medical perfect storm, I refused to believe it. Neither did Lucy. We did everything we could to prove the professionals wrong. Mom would not retreat so easily.

Despite remaining hospitalized for months and losing fifty pounds, her mental fortitude only strengthened. Even the doctors marveled at her will to live. She empowered them, too. Treatment after treatment, specialist after specialist, she battled on. For a brief moment, it appeared she had done the impossible and made science-based doctors believe in the presence of miracles. However, it was merely the magnificent sparkle of Lucy that created this trompe l'oeil. She wasn't winning; she was dying in the only way she knew how... as a fighter.

Therefore, when faced with the ultimate decision to either allow her to continue this endless existence in a hospital bed, attached to tubes and cared for by kindhearted but virtual strangers, or to come home to be surrounded by those who would cherish her like she deserved, the answer was clear.

The most important facet of this choice was to never let her know that she was indeed coming home to die. Lucy would never have wanted to put that upon her family. She knew all too well what it was like to hold someone until his or her last breath, and I know in her heart she would not want that to be the final narrative of our love story.

Of course, I would have had it no other way. The final two months we shared at home were happy but bittersweet. In a nod to her early-morning calls to me in London, I gave her an old-fashioned brass bell to ring for me if she needed something. It was meant to be a point of humor. But, oddly enough, that bell, like the calls abroad, were what kept me going.

Although completely bed-bound and reliant upon others for even the most mundane acts, Mom and I shared the laughs, dreams and hopes we always had. We made plans for the holidays, watched Hallmark movies, and made lists of everything we would do "when" she got better. In her mind, it was never "if" she got better. Once again, despite having no physical strength of her own, she was the source of strength for the entire family. She willed us to continue moving forward as always.

The impish side of her enjoyed making that bell clang for no reason at all. I would run up three flights of stairs only to find her laughing alongside my six-year-old son. Yet I never once resented the ringing, whether it was 3:00 in the afternoon or 2:00 in the morning. As long as I heard its sound, I still had the Lucy I loved and adored, and its echoes sustained me.

Therefore, when I was met with silence early one Monday in August 2014, I knew something had changed. I ran up to her room and was momentarily relieved to see that she was alert, and her eyes were open. But that ever-present twinkle had gone. She no longer knew who I was. Instead of our lifelong connection, she looked directly through me. Mom died peacefully a few days later in my arms.

About ten days after we buried her, I was down in the kitchen. I heard the ringing of the bell and sprinted up those stairs with hope in my heart. I guess I thought the past week had been a dream, and Mom was up there waiting to tell me what Paula Deen had just cooked. Instead, I found my beautiful little boy with what had been my "lifeline" in his hand.

He smiled at me and giggled, full of innocence and the promise of the future. At that moment, it dawned on me that my strength was sitting there on the bed, reflected in the eyes of my son. My mom would never be gone. She would exist in my dreams, my heart, and my memories. Nothing ever truly dies as long as we have something worth remembering.

— Tara Flowers —

Potato Salad School

A good cook is like a sorceress
who dispenses happiness.
~Elsa Schiaparelli

We have friends and family coming over tomorrow, so I've just finished making a giant batch of potato salad. It's my mother-in-law's recipe, and it's the only one I ever make anymore. It wasn't always my favorite, though.

It was love at first sight when my husband and I met. I fell in love with his family as well. Their taste in food, however, was another story. The goulash was good. The nachos were great, but I just couldn't understand why this family insisted on putting green olives in everything. I've often heard that they are an acquired taste. At that point, I still didn't care for them much. Imagine my surprise, then, when they even showed up in the potato salad! I was beginning to worry I might starve at family functions.

Fast-forward many years. My husband and I had been married for almost a decade. We had three beautiful children, and I had learned to love green olives — especially in Cathy's potato salad. She was called upon to make it for all the picnics, potlucks, and gatherings. The last few get-togethers had been difficult, however. My mother-in-law had cancer, and it had begun to manifest itself in interesting ways, including some we did not expect. There was, of course, the fatigue and nausea. But there were other things, too — more campout weekends together; the re-telling of childhood stories; the increasingly frequent exchanges

A Mother's Strength | 289

of wan, knowing smiles.

She arrived at my house one afternoon with three huge bags of supplies — potatoes, bowls, special kitchen equipment, and (of course) green olives. Apparently, Potato-Salad School was in session, and I was ready to be a diligent pupil. It wasn't a recipe she had ever written down, but rather a labor of love with each and every batch. We mixed, chopped, and tasted together. I took copious notes. By the end of the afternoon, we had a big bowl of what was unquestionably her special potato salad. I had a recipe in hand, and she wore a tired but triumphant expression.

Then I really stopped to take a good look at her. Her hair had been short, wavy, and black before the chemo. The wig she had chosen that day was a chin-length, blond bob. (Even in the face of such loss, she chose to find the bright side, experimenting with hairstyles she never would have been able to achieve otherwise.) She was thin and didn't have the stamina she used to. In that moment, I suddenly realized Potato-Salad School was about far more than just passing along a recipe. It was one part rite of passage for a daughter-in-law, one part passing-of-the-torch for a mother-in-law. It was, in short, the assurance that her potato salad — and all that it entailed — would continue, even if she did not.

Cathy passed away about a year later. It had been a long, hard process, and we were blessed to be by her side during the weeks she was in the hospital and hospice. The whole family gathered with my father-in-law back at their house the morning after she died, numb and unsure of what to do. I found myself drawn to the kitchen and began dragging out her giant bowl, methodically peeling potatoes and hunting around in the cupboard for the jars of green olives that I knew I would find there. After all, the family was together, and that meant someone had to make the potato salad. I'm not sure it tasted as good as hers, but it was a comfort to have it there anyway.

Since then, I've been the one expected to make it for all the picnics, potlucks, and gatherings, and I couldn't be more pleased. Every second helping and satisfied "mmmmm" are reminders of my beloved mother-in-law, all the love she had for her family, and our special afternoon together when I learned so much more than just how to make potato salad.

—Andrea K. Farrier—

98

A Foundation Built on Love

I realized when you look at your mother, you are
looking at the purest love you will ever know.
~Mitch Albom

For years, I thought my father was the strongest person I had ever met. He worked construction most of his life, he was physically fit, and he was tough. He had a deep, strong voice, and people listened when he spoke.

Then he became terminally ill at age fifty. He battled the disease for twelve years. I watched him beat the odds and survive two liver transplants and countless traumatic procedures. Each time there was a "close call" he came out on top and lived to see another day.

I never stopped to notice how hard my mother was fighting alongside him. She bore the brunt of the illness as his caretaker. It was her strength that kept him alive, but I didn't realize that until his passing.

My mother managed to hold a full-time job in a management position and raise three children, all while helping my father with his health battles. She never wavered in each emergent situation and never lost faith that my father would be standing next to her again, and the pair would be gardening together in the spring. Her strength kept everyone going.

Each morning, she would smile at him, say "hi," and keep moving forward with her day. She pushed through it, and she taught us to, as well. I'm sure she was crying behind closed doors. I'm sure she feared the inevitable, but she never let us see her fear. She stayed strong and held back tears when we cried.

She kept her babies from having to face a very real fear for as long as she could.

Now, at thirty-two, with two babies of my own, I understand her strength. I see her mourning her loss while still showing love to her children and grandchildren — and putting her best foot forward in her career.

Her strength is our family's pillar. It's our foundation.

— Kori Sciandra —

99

The Photographs

Choices are the hinges of destiny.
~Edwin Markham

I was scooting into the front seat after we dropped off my brother, Michael, at his high school. My elementary school was on the other side of town, and I usually napped the whole way there. But my mom had something to say.

"Now, I know you've been asking questions," she started, "about the photos you saw at Grandma's house."

Oh, that. I'd nearly forgotten about that. That had happened the previous weekend when Michael and I had slept over at my grandparents' house with our sixteen-year-old cousin, Francy. Francy was the one who had actually been asking questions. She'd asked me about a box of old photographs she'd found while snooping through my grandparents' bookcase. When she showed them to me, I was equally shocked. They were photographs I had never seen before. Photographs I didn't quite understand.

A costume party was the first thing that sprang to my ten-year-old mind to explain them. It was a seemingly plausible reason that my mom, looking really young at the time, was dressed in a big white dress and veil. It almost explained the longhaired, blond man with blue eyes, who so obviously wasn't my father, standing beside her. I examined the pictures closely until I got to the ones at the church. And the one of them kissing... a movie shoot?

Not until my grandmother caught us red-handed did I realize that my guesses were way off track. If my mom had acted in some movie, my grandmother wouldn't have reacted the way she had. She wouldn't have snatched the photos out of our hands with that horrified look upon her face. She wouldn't have hidden the box in her bedroom. She wouldn't have pretended the whole thing never happened and not mentioned it again for the rest of the evening. Her reaction made it clear that this was something much deeper. That's why I hadn't asked any questions. Maybe I didn't want to know.

"When I was in my early twenties, I met a man, and I got married," my mom revealed slowly, whether I wanted to know or not. We got on the on-ramp to the highway. "He was much older than me, and he was American, from Mobile, Alabama. His parents were very wealthy. After we got married, I moved there with him for a few years."

I was utterly shocked. It was hard enough for me to accept that my mom even had a life before I was born, let alone this unexpected alternate life! My Latina mom had lived in Alabama? It seemed so unlike her to move so far away from my grandparents. To move out of Canada. Gradually, I began to accept that I didn't know my own mother as well as I thought I did. To be sure, I confirmed incredulously, "You lived in Alabama?"

"Yes," my mom replied, a little defensively. We exited the highway now. "For the first few months of our marriage, we camped on the Gulf of Mexico."

My mom camping? Did she bring her vintage Burberry suitcase with her? Did she apply her nightly routine of skincare products in a tent? It felt like we were talking about a different person.

That's when I remembered her face in those old photographs. It was definitely her. A more exciting version of herself. Her hair was long, and her face was bright. She was so happy. So free. I realized this story made sense. After all, the beach was my mom's favourite place in the world. She always did say if she could live on the beach, she would. And, apparently, she had. In fact, I realized, living on the Gulf of Mexico with her hunky new husband sounded like her ideal life. Incredibly romantic, too. Why would she give that up? Why would anyone give that up? Now I had more questions. "So what happened?"

"We got divorced," she declared matter-of-factly. "Grandma doesn't like to talk about it, but it's no big deal."

Something still didn't make sense to me. "But why did you get divorced?"

"He didn't want kids."

Realization and guilt dawned on me instantaneously. My mom had given up her carefree ocean life for me. And Michael.

"Does Michael know?"

"I don't think so," my mom shrugged, as if there were any other way to access this information without her telling him directly. "But it's not a secret or anything. We even used to keep in touch. We wrote letters to each other until Michael was born. Then I never heard from him again."

That made me sad for her. And for him, too, this mysterious American man. He wanted her, but she wanted us instead. She traded camping on the beach for shoveling snow in the driveway. If she hadn't done that, I wouldn't have existed.

My mother had given up her dream life for ungrateful kids who didn't bother to put away their toys at the end of the night. Who didn't come to dinner when called. Who wouldn't soak their dishes in the sink after they ate. It didn't seem like a fair exchange. I couldn't help but wonder if she ever regretted her decision.

In that moment, I gained a deeper appreciation for my mother. I had never felt so wanted. I decided from then on that I would be the kind of daughter she'd left her first life for. Well, most of the time, anyway.

— Daniela Trivino —

More than Life

All the forces on this planet,
will never beat that of a mother's love.
~Elle Smith, The Way Back Home

W hen my mother was a girl, she went to a fortuneteller during a night out with friends. The fortuneteller told her that she would experience an event of catastrophic proportion in midlife.

Who believes in fortunetellers anyway? she thought.

And yet it happened.

My mother has known the ultimate happiness and lived the ultimate tragedy.

In 1963, she lost her mother in a plane crash. She never fully healed from that loss. Yet through her strength and faith, she continued her life and inspired a legacy of family through which my sisters and I built our lives.

When I would have sleepover parties during my childhood, I would find my friends gathered around the kitchen table late at night listening to my mother tell stories about her life. Every girl would sit there mesmerized. My mother was a housewife, actress, and born oral historian. Even today, my now sixty-five-year-old friends quote from my mother's stories.

Eleven years after her mother died, we had another catastrophe. My father and my youngest sister, Ivy, were killed in another plane crash. My parents had been married thirty years at that point. My two remaining sisters and I persevered, led by our courageous mother.

Thirty years later, when my mother turned eighty, my sisters and I had a birthday party for her. We compiled the wisdom and quotes that she had passed on to family members over the years and put them into a book that was distributed to every guest. We had family and friends come to the microphone and read a quote or thought from the book after introducing themselves and stating their relationship to my mother.

As she watched and listened, my mother had a faraway look in her eyes. She was with us, listening and enjoying this tribute to her. Yet the full tapestry of her life had holes that could not be filled by toasts and testimonials. She started to cry. She felt the presence of her missing mother, husband, and daughter as she sat listening to family members reading quotes from her birthday celebration book.

When we finished the program, we all took our seats. It was now my mother's turn to go to the lectern and take the microphone.

As she began to speak, I looked at her face. My mother and I are twenty years apart. I could remember most of her birthdays. With each year, I watched her beauty mature. Physically, she was a truly stunning woman, but it was her ability to empathize and persevere that was awe-inspiring.

I thought of my mother's words about the pride she felt as she looked at her own mother. At that moment, I understood. My mother's face glowed. Reflected in her eyes were the loved ones of her present and her past.

I remembered a trip my mother and I had taken to New Orleans when I was single. It was very special to me because it was just the two of us. We walked blocks together, enjoying the city's unique sights and atmosphere. Every street had signs inviting us to come in to stores to have our fortunes told. New Orleans' seduction was irresistible. We opened a door and entered.

A man asked me to follow him into a room for a tarot-card reading, and my mother accompanied a woman to her reading area.

The fortuneteller asked me if I was married. I answered "no." Then he looked at my cards and announced that I would never marry. After a few more inane predictions, we were finished.

I returned to the front of the store and sat down to wait for my mother. I waited and waited. I kept looking at my watch and wondering what her fortuneteller was saying. Finally, my mother emerged from her reading. We left the shop and began walking down the street hand in hand.

"You tell me first," she said. "What did the fortuneteller tell you?"

"He told me I would never marry," I replied calmly.

My mother stopped and looked at me. Her eldest daughter, who was single and involved in building a career, had just been told the curse of all curses.

"Oh, please," she answered in disgust. "He did not know what he was talking about."

"What took you so long?" I asked. "What did she tell you?"

"Well," my mother began, "she asked me if I was a widow. I told her I was, and she told me that she was, too. Then she told me her life story."

This time it was I who stopped and looked at my mother. "What?" I asked in disbelief. "She told you *her* life story?"

"She needed an ear," my mother answered softly.

"Did you pay her?" I asked incredulously.

"Of course," my mother answered.

Growing up, wherever I went, I would be stopped by strangers and asked if I was Miriam Chaplik's daughter. Nothing made me prouder than to look in the mirror and see a face very much like my mother's looking back at me.

My mother has faced the devastation of her life with an uncanny grace and strength. There is no bitterness in her. She does not curse fate. She focuses on the blessings she has in her life, not the deficits.

The catastrophe the fortuneteller predicted happened twice in my mother's life, but she survived, allowing love to guide her way. Her life is an example of how to live through tragedy, and to love through

Her Final Mountain

It's not the mountain we conquer, but ourselves.
~Sir Edmund Hillary

I was twenty years old when my mom succumbed to breast cancer. I try not to focus only on the chemo treatments, stem-cell transplants and other procedures she endured for five years. I need to remember all the fun times we had, too.

The most amazing memory I have of her was when we took a day trip out to Natural Bridge in the beautiful mountains of Virginia. It was only four months before her passing. By this time, her cancer had spread to her lungs, so she was constantly trying to catch her breath. Yet, it was my twentieth birthday, and she wanted to do something special. That was just the way mom was, always putting her family ahead of herself.

Dad drove the couple of hours out to the mountains where my sister, my mom, my dad and I would spend the day hiking down to the mountain to see Natural Bridge. Mom had a challenging time traversing the many stairs to get to the bridge. We would walk a little and then have to stop for a bit so she could catch her breath. Being as young and exuberant as I was, I was frustrated not only for my mom, but for myself. I was concerned that people were staring. Eventually, with much patience and great pride in herself, we made it to the bridge area. There, on flatter terrain, she was able to stop and take in the majestic view.

I look fondly at the photos that I took of her and my dad as

Natural Bridge towered over them in the background. Having watched her literally climb her last mountain, I realize the powerful lesson she taught me. Mom's major obstacle wasn't just her cancer, but also accepting the prospect of death with dignity and grace.

Even as her battle was ending, she pushed through each experience. The interesting part was she never once complained or felt sorry for herself. She worked at her job until she absolutely couldn't work anymore. She continued her creative pursuits — cross-stitching, crocheting, sewing, arranging flowers, working in the garden — until the month before she died. She left behind many crafts and crocheted afghans. She didn't like her hands to remain idle even when getting her chemo treatments.

I've stumbled and fallen and at times forgotten how to get back up again. I try to remember my mother climbing back up those steps at Natural Bridge that day. Now it is my duty as a grown woman to follow my mother's example.

— Carrie Bennett Bland —

Meet Our Contributors

Barbara Bank, MA, is a freelance writer, editor, and English instructor who derives satisfaction from each of these occupations. She enjoys the simple pleasures of life, especially watching the third generation of her family grow to adulthood — not a simple feat since they are spread out over two continents.

Jana Bernal grew up in rural Nebraska then relocated to Washington for several years. Jana now resides in Missouri with her son. Jana enjoys game nights, vacationing in Branson, camping, reading and keeping in touch with extended family through letters. Jana loves to garden even though she does not have a green thumb!

Jill Berni is excited to be a contributor to the *Chicken Soup for the Soul* series for the third time. She is a history buff, animal lover and avid reader. She lives in Mississauga, Ontario with her loving husband, Fred and her two dogs, Max and Maggie. Learn more at www.jillberni.com.

Tracie Bevers, author of *Dancing Around the Chaos*, spent well over a decade journeying through the world of Alzheimer's after her parents were diagnosed. She learned much about real, true love and became passionate about encouraging others just beginning their own long journey to goodbye. Read her blog at traciebevers.com.

Carrie Bennett Bland received her Bachelor of Arts in English from Christopher Newport University in 2002. She has been happily married for six years and works in Smithfield, VA. When she's not writing,

Carrie enjoys reading, quilting, photography and scrapbooking.

Heidi Griminger Blanke, Ph.D., was raised in Peoria, IL. She is the author of two books: *Redesigning Love* and *The Flashiest Time of My Life*. Her work has appeared in many anthologies and magazines and she is a founding member of Women Writers Ink. Heidi is married and the mother of three grown children.

Jan Bono writes a cozy mystery series set on the SW Washington coast. She's also published five collections of humorous personal experience, two poetry chapbooks, nine one-act plays, a dinner theater play, and has written for magazines ranging from *Guideposts* to *Woman's World*. Learn more at www.JanBonoBooks.com.

Barbara Brockway's work has appeared in several publications including *Brain, Child* magazine, *Seven Hills Review*, *The Binnacle*, *Torrid Literature Journal*, *The Southern Tablet*, and *Grand Central Review*. Barbara has received awards from WOW! Women On Writing, the Chattahoochee Valley Writers, the Tallahassee Writers Association, and the Atlanta Writers Club.

Michelle Bruce received her degree, with honors, in Nursing in 1993. She and her husband have four children and enjoy their quiet life in rural Nebraska. Michelle spends her days antiquing and refinishing furniture. She plans to continue writing about the beauty in life.

Barbara A. Bruner is an aspiring writer who lives in Southern California. As a former sales representative she now savors her roles as parent to an adult son and grandmother to a precocious granddaughter. Explorations of family, relationships and events past and present fuel her writing and inspire her travels.

Daughter of a published author, **Kim Carney**, has writing in her blood. Kim writes for several online publications, including *Music Mafia Radio*, *Artistic Echoes*, BeyondSkinDeep.net and others. She currently splits her time between Colorado, caring for her mother, and Western New York, where her three sons and grandchildren live.

S. Chamberlain works as a library assistant in her hometown and has been writing both fiction and nonfiction since a very early age. She plans to write a novel, but short stories are her favourite weakness.

Sara Siddiqui Chansarkar is an Indian American. She was born to a middle-class family in India and will forever be indebted to her parents for educating her beyond their means. Her essays, stories, and poems have appeared in print and online. She is also a Pushcart Prize and Best of Net nominee.

Elynne Chaplik-Aleskow, Pushcart Prize-nominated, is founding general manager of WYCC-TV/PBS and distinguished professor emeritus of Wright College. Her stories have been performed throughout the U.S. and Canada and are published in anthologies and her book, *My Gift of Now*. Her husband Richard is her muse.

In-Young Choi is currently attending Hankuk University of Foreign Studies, majoring in English Literature and Culture. She has been an avid reader since she was little, and has read many books that have fueled her love for English Literature. She hopes to study English Literature further, and write more stories as well.

Weston L. Collins, originally from Houston, TX, is a sci-fi and fiction author. His family valued education and he grew up under the watchful eye of his grandfather, Reverend Dr. William H. Como and his granduncle, Dr. Timothy Cotton, who was a biology, botany, and agricultural professor.

Kat Crawford, known as Lionhearted Kat, is the author of *Dew Drops of Hope: Help for Those Going Through Grief and Loss*. Widowed, she is a mother and grandmother with a passion to encourage others. Kat is one of four on the Leadership Team for the Wordsowers Christian

Writers Conference in Omaha, NE.

Tracy Kirk Crump has published two dozen anthology stories and numerous articles and devotionals. She co-directs Write Life Workshops, speaks at conferences, and edits a popular writers newsletter, "The Write Life." But her most important job is Grandma for two completely unspoiled grandchildren. Visit her at TracyCrump.com.

Brian Danforth received a bachelor's in mechanical engineering, runs a metal fabrication shop with his brother, draws nightly, writes uncontrollably, and watches a healthy dose of soccer and anime in between. With this desire to pursue every possible path in his journey he jumps between writing sci-fi to fantasy to romance.

Abbie Dunlap writes about her personal experiences in hopes that others may be able to draw encouragement through reading about them. She is a mother, writer, and former teacher. Learn more at abbiedunlap. wixsite.com/blog and herviewfromhome.com/author/abbie-dunlap/.

Wendy Newell Dyer graduated magna cum laude from the University of Maine at Machias in 2003. She found her biological parents at twenty-five and learned she was from the Passamaquoddy Tribe. They welcomed her with open arms. She has three sons and three grandsons. She enjoys hiking and other adventures with her Lab, Jack.

A teacher's unexpected whisper, "You've got writing talent," ignited **Sara Etgen-Baker's** writing desire. But Sara ignored that whisper and pursued a different career; she later re-discovered her inner writer and began writing. Her stories have been published in *Guideposts*, *Wisdom Has a Voice*, *The Santa Claus Project*, and the *Chicken Soup for the Soul* series.

Andrea K. Farrier is a very happy wife and homeschooling mother. She and her family spent four years as missionaries in Guatemala and hope to return to international missions again soon. Until then, Andrea can be found teaching, writing, walking in the Iowa woods, and trying in vain to get her stubborn Basset Hound to behave.

Kati Felix is a full-time mom who writes poetry and speculative fiction. As a young woman, she interned as a trainee librarian and edited for a university publication. With a strong literary background, she also has experience writing for international media platforms. She plans to publish her first novel next year.

Tara Flowers is a former European fashion director. When not sitting in the car line, she runs lepapillonmarketing.com, a consultancy for those in need of a reinvention. And despite the fact that shopping in the ethnic food aisle at Whole Foods is as exotic as it gets these days, she has never doubted that Mom indeed knew best.

Lynne Daroff Foosaner is a political activist, freelance writer and grandmother... not necessarily in that order!

Beth Fortune is co-founder of Extreme Joy Ministries. She's a speaker and writer and has been published in magazines, anthologies and devotionals. She enjoys gardening, indoor rowing and spending time with family. She lives in Greenville, SC with her husband and their rescue, Gracie. Learn more at www.bethfortune.net.

Kim Freeman worked as a newspaper reporter and magazine editor before receiving her law degree. She now uses her legal experience in human resources. Kim loves spending time with her husband, Clayton, and their six children. She is committed to social justice causes and mentoring women.

Jessica Gray received both her Bachelor of Science and Master of Science in Nursing from Virginia Commonwealth University. She lives outside of Richmond, VA with her husband and two boys. Jessica enjoys traveling, attending VCU men's basketball games, and spending time with her family.

Michelle H. received her Bachelor of Arts from the University of South Florida and enjoys a career in communication and marketing. She spends much of her free time attending sports games, going to theme parks, and getting together with friends.

Nancy Learned Haines worked for seventeen years as an engineer, and then ran an antiquarian bookstore. After twenty-five years, she retired and fulfilled a lifelong dream of becoming an author. She wrote a book about Quakers in France during WWI based on the love letters of two pacifists, and a picture book for Quaker children. She lives in North Carolina.

Laura Harris is a wife, mother, and Christ follower. She is the author of *The Stay-at-Home Mom Blueprint* and has been featured on *The Huffington Post*, *Motherly*, and *LifeHack*. She uses her faith, her passion for writing, and her background in personal finance to encourage, educate, and inspire young families.

Liz Harrison teaches high school English in Grande Prairie, Alberta. She loves sharing great literature with wonderful students, and is pursuing her MFA in creative writing. She loves travel, yoga, art, and spending time with friends and family. Liz is currently working on her first novel.

Christina Hausauer is a Child Care Licensing Officer in Calgary, Alberta. She loves spending time with her twenty-five-year-old daughter, Amanda. She resides with her partner Dave in Airdrie, Alberta. Christina loves to travel, read, write and spend time with children. She aspires to publish her first book within the next year.

Linda J. Hawkins is the award-winning author of the dietitian endorsed and curriculum approved *Alexander* children book series. *Southern Seasons*, her adult books, have garnered multiple awards. She travels, speaks and makes the most of her memories in Kentucky with the love of her life for forty-plus years, Ray. Learn more at www.lindajhawkins. com.

Kathleen Healy-Schmieder teaches Workforce Development classes at a local college. She enjoys writing, and previously published a book of essays, *Seasons of Bittersweet*, and a memoir, *Serenity, Courage, Wisdom*. Kathleen is currently working on a second book of essays titled *Silver Linings*.

Christy Heitger-Ewing is an award-winning writer who has written more than 900 human-interest stories for national, regional, and local magazines. She's also contributed to twenty-two anthologies and is the author of *Cabin Glory: Amusing Tales of Time Spent at the Family Retreat*. Learn more at christyheitger-ewing.com.

Rose Hofer studies nursing, business, and literature at Front Range Community College. She grew up with her six siblings in Oregon and Colorado. She loves reading, writing, and helping others. She plans to continue writing and hopes to complete her first novel in the coming years.

Kristin Baldwin Homsi lives in Houston, TX with her husband and three small children. She is a Strategy Manager in the oil and gas industry and an avid runner. Kristin chronicles her continual attempts at managing life with a career and three babies in her blog, RaisingTrinity.com.

Cheyenne H. Huffman is a journalism student at King's College, from which she will graduate in 2019. She enjoys writing, crafting, and volunteering in her community. She would love to continue writing inspirational and feel-good stories documenting her life and its many lessons.

Robbie Iobst is an author and speaker from Centennial, CO. She is Mom to Noah and Step Mama to Marriah, Sarah and Hannah. This is the tenth *Chicken Soup for the Soul* book in which Robbie's stories have appeared. Need a speaker? Learn more at www.robbieiobst.com.

Anju Jain is an engineer by education and profession but a creative person at heart. She loves to read, write and research Indian spirituality and culture in her free time. She is also a certified yoga teacher and lives in India with her family.

Kim Kelly Johnson is a Southern girl at heart, a loving wife and a mother to three kids. Writing became her prime outlet while studying at Valdosta State University. Her beloved mother, Linda, passed away from pancreatic cancer in 2015 but continues to be Kim's inspiration each and every day — both in writing and in life.

Suzannah Kiper is a University of Louisville grad and seventh generation Kentuckian. She has been married to her high school sweetheart, Tim, for more than twenty years. She is the mother of two amazing kids (Daniel and Lydia) and two Maltese dogs (Bella and Chloe). She was previously published in *Chicken Soup for the Soul: The Joy of Less*.

Shelby Kisgen is happiest when writing, reading, or adventuring outside. She lives in the mountains with her hilarious husband and adorable rescue dog. Follow her musings at www.shelbykisgen.com.

Vicki Kitchner recently retired after teaching Exceptional Student Education for thirty years. She and her husband divide their time between North Carolina and Florida. She loves to travel, garden and hike. E-mail her at vicki@hikersrest.com.

Kathleen Kohler writes about the ups and downs of family life for numerous magazines and anthologies. She and her husband live in the Pacific Northwest and have three children and seven grandchildren. Learn more at www.kathleenkohler.com.

Miranda Lamb is addicted to coffee, reading and using far too many commas in her writing. Her story definitely contains a spelling error. She is working on her second novel. Feel free to connect on Instagram @mirandadianalamb or via e-mail at mirandadlamb@gmail.com.

Traci E. Langston enjoys telling stories of all kinds from children's books to romance novels. From the time she was a little girl, she has dreamed of being a writer. Her mom was her biggest fan. After her mom passed, Traci took the plunge and began sharing her stories with the world.

Deborah Lean is a mixed media artist and writer. She is a retired nurse living in Ontario and she enjoys painting, writing, crocheting and spending time with her family.

Victoria Marie Lees graduated, with honors, from University of Pennsylvania while mothering her five children. She's published fiction, nonfiction, poetry and personal essays and leads writing workshops at libraries and nursing homes. Victoria camps with the family and shares adventures at campingwithfivekids.blogspot.com.

After twenty years of teaching college level Information Technology, **Mary Lovstad**, an Iowa farm girl, now runs a farm wedding venue and writes a cooking blog. She aspires to write a cookbook featuring vintage recipes. Erma Bombeck is her writing hero and she regularly participates in the Erma Bombeck Writer's Workshop.

Julia Lucas is a retired Construction Estimator and Draftsperson, who has two stepsons and two step-grandsons. She lives in Aurora, Ontario. Julia has also designed and sold over 500 needlework patterns and projects to various magazines and fabric companies all around the world.

Christine Many Luff is a writer/editor and fitness trainer in northern New Jersey. She has been running competitively for more than thirty years and coaching runners of all ages for fifteen years. A contributor to numerous books, magazines, and websites, Christine writes about running and other topics at run-for-good.com.

Susan G. Mathis is a multi-published author of stories set in the beautiful Thousand Islands in upstate New York. She has six published books including *Christmas Charity*, *The Fabric of Hope* and *Katelyn's Choice*. Learn more at www.SusanGMathis.com.

Marie Loper Maxwell is the mom of many, lover of learning and devourer of books. She spends most of her time with her husband and seven children reading, writing and making memories.

Randi Mazzella is a freelance writer. She is a regular contributor to *The Fine Line*, *Parent Map*, *Your Teen* and *Next Avenue*. She loves to write about parenting, family life and issues facing women in midlife. Randi loves spending time with her husband and three children. Learn more at www.randimazzella.com.

Nicole Ann Rook McAlister has studied journalism and pursues an avid interest in world religion and mythology. Nicole enjoys adventures in camping, sunrises on the beach, painting, crafting and all manner of such things. Several of her pieces have been on exhibit at the Whitesbog Historic Village in Browns Mills, NJ.

Eugene Mead served in the U.S. Navy Reserves for eight years. While in college he worked on the Apollo Moon Program and helped to put a man on the moon. He and his wife now live in New Braunfels, TX, and spend time visiting their four children and twelve grandchildren.

Dennis Mitton is an obsessed writer, an avid reader, a scientist, and a dedicated coffee drinker. He is married and has seven children. Originally from Seattle, he now lives in the South and misses the snow. When not working or writing, he enjoys family time, woodworking, and living the good life.

Kathleen Monroe graduated from Akron University with a degree in American Sign Language in 1996. She lives with her daughter and husband in Michigan. She has written short stories her entire life. She loves to read, bake, craft and write. She hopes to one day write a novel.

Angelique Morvant is a graduate student at Texas A&M University. When she is not studying mathematics, she likes to spend time reading and riding her bicycle.

Nicole L.V. Mullis is the author of *A Teacher Named Faith*. Her work has appeared in newspapers, magazines, and anthologies, including the *Chicken Soup for the Soul* series. Her plays have been produced across the United States. She lives in Michigan with her family and understands her mother a little more every day.

Alice Muschany enjoys the outdoors, especially early morning walks where she witnesses magnificent sunrises. Her hobbies include photography and writing, and her inspirations come from her grandchildren who help keep her young at heart.

Gavan Norton is a twelve-year-old active boy. He was born in Minnesota and lives in North Dakota. He enjoys sports such as hockey, running and lacrosse. Gavan loves being a leader and spending time with his younger brother, Austin.

Linda O'Connell is an accomplished writer and teacher from St. Louis, MO. She is a frequent contributor to *Chicken Soup for the Soul* books. Linda holds her life together with humor, dark chocolate, and duct tape. A positive thinker, Linda writes from the heart at lindaoconnell. blogspot.com.

Shannon Pannell received her Bachelor of Arts from Virginia's Old Dominion University in 2009. She is a freelance writer and stay-at-home mom to three boys. She enjoys reading, baking, doing the crossword in blue pen, and exploring the outdoors with her husband and kids. E-mail her at shannonlpannell@yahoo.com.

Kimberly Patton lives an adventurous life in Florida with her favorite human, her husband, Kevin. If she's not teaching English or Spanish, she can be found running, biking, reading creative nonfiction, or working on her manuscript. She is the author of the memoir, *A Cub Among Bears: How Love and Toughness Raised Me*.

Cherise Payne has spent eight years overseas teaching English as a Second Language to children in grades 4 through 7. She enjoys reading mystery novels, writing, and camping with her very large family. She plans to continue writing short stories for children while working on her first adult novel.

Lisa Solorzano Petit received her Bachelor of Science in Rehabilitation Services from the University of Maine at Farmington in 2005. She loves her family and loves being a stay-at-home mom to her two boys. Lisa is excited to realize a dream in seeing her work published! She enjoys living life to its fullest.

Amburr Phillips is a stay-at-home military wife working toward her Bachelor of Science degree in history at Liberty University.

Elizabeth A. Pickart lives in Wisconsin with her husband, three children, four cats and two guinea pigs. She's had twenty-one stories in *Guide* magazine and this is her second published in the *Chicken Soup for the Soul* series. She enjoys reading, running, and copywriting and is working on a middle grade novel series. E-mail her at pickart.liz@gmail.com.

Donna L. Roberts is a native of upstate New York who lives and works in Europe. She is an Associate Professor and holds a Ph.D. in Psychology. Donna is an animal and human rights advocate. When she is researching or writing, she can be found at her computer buried in rescue animals. E-mail her at donna_roberts13@yahoo.com.

Brenda Keller Robertson has a B.S. in nursing and is a CCRN, a certified critical care nurse (retired). Brenda enjoys classic movies with an appreciation of film noir, cooking, and reading. Her faith and family are most important to her. She lives with her husband and daughter in Pendleton, IN.

Stephen Rusiniak is a former police detective who specialized in juvenile/family matters. Today he shares his thoughts through his writings including stories in several *Chicken Soup for the Soul* books. Contact him via Facebook, Twitter: @StephenRusiniak, e-mail at stephenrusiniak@yahoo.com or visit stephenrusiniak.com to learn more.

Melanie Saxton is an author, book editor, ghostwriter, scriptwriter, and award-winning journalist located near Houston, TX. She credits her parents for instilling in her a love of books and she is pursuing a master's degree in digital media to better assist her clients. E-mail her at melanie@melaniesaxtonmedia.com.

John M. Scanlan is a 1983 graduate of the United States Naval Academy, and retired from the Marine Corps as a Lieutenant Colonel aviator. He currently resides on Hilton Head Island, SC, and is pursuing a second career as a writer. E-mail John at ping1@hargray.com.

Candy Schulman is an award-winning writer whose essays, articles, and humor have appeared in *The New York Times*, *The Washington Post*, *Chicago Tribune*, *Brain*, *Child* magazine, and elsewhere. She is a creative writing professor at the New School in New York City.

Patt Schwab, Ph.D. had careers as a college administrator and an international speaker on the topic of humor as a leadership skill. The author of four books on humor, including *Leave a Mark, Not a Stain*, Patt insists the fresh perspective humor provides helps identify what really matters and puts the rest into perspective.

Kori Sciandra received her Bachelor of Arts in Journalism from Buffalo State College in 2010. She is a freelance writer living in New York with her fiancé and their two children. She values her time with her family and plans to continue writing for various publications.

Marianne Sciucco is the author of *Blue Hydrangeas*, an Alzheimer's love story. She is a co-founder and administrator of AlzAuthors, the international organization of authors writing about Alzheimer's and the dementias. A registered nurse, she has worked with hundreds of families struggling with dementia care.

Diane St. Laurent is a wife, mother of three daughters and grand-mother to seven perfect children. She enjoys writing, swimming and even practicing the piano. She plans on continuing her adventures with words.

Diane Stark is a mother of five and a freelance writer. She is a frequent contributor to the *Chicken Soup for the Soul* series. She writes about the important things in life: her family and her faith.

Mary Vigliante Szydlowski writes across several genres, using this and other pseudonyms. She's the author of ten adult novels and eight children's books. Her short stories, articles, essays, and poems have been published in anthologies, books, magazines, newspapers, and on the Internet.

Johnny Tan is a talk show host, inspirational speaker, award-winning and bestselling author, and founder of "From My Mama's Kitchen." His radio show has amassed over one million downloads. His Inspirations for Better Living signs enrich humanity with the engaging power of words. He welcomes comments at FromMyMamasKitchen.com.

Julia M. Toto shares stories of hope, forgiveness, and second chances. She's a published author of inspirational fiction and a previous con-tributor to the *Chicken Soup for the Soul* series. Learn more at www.juliamtoto.com.

Daniela Trivino has been writing for as long as she can remember. Last year, she turned her hobby into a small blog to further explore her experiences and share them with a larger audience, under a pen name. Her blog now has over 100 posts and 1,500 followers. She's currently teaching English in Toronto, Ontario.

Cheryl E. Uhrig is a writer, illustrator, cartoonist and painter. Her work appears in children's books, magazines and in local galleries. Cheryl lives in Newmarket, Ontario with her family.

Carla Varner attended Kean University, studying English to become an English teacher. However, circumstances required her to study, in depth, her own life. Through her writing, she is on a mission to help people heal and tackle difficult issues. She plans to use many different avenues to reach people where they are.

Martha Willey has been published in seven anthologies, enjoys writing YA and has just started blogging. She works as a library paraprofessional in a public school. She is married with three grown children. When she isn't writing, she enjoys reading.

Patricia Wood is a former English teacher turned stay-at-home mom, pursuing her dreams of writing while raising her amazing daughters. When not on mom-duty, Patricia enjoys painting and creating stories for children and moms in hopes of one day achieving the ultimate goal of getting those published as well.

Katie Wright received her Bachelor of Arts in English and Education from Wilmington College (2006) and her Masters in Education from Northern Kentucky University (2013). Katie teaches high school English in Ohio where she resides with her husband and two daughters. Her story is dedicated to her mother, Dinah Isaacs.

Audrey RL Wyatt bases her novels, short stories and even a television sitcom on her experiences and culture. Her stories often feature strong-willed, quirky women. Audrey's novel, *Poles Apart*, has been honored with five awards and her essays and short fiction have been published in various forums, both in print and online.

Sheri Zeck enjoys writing nonfiction stories that encourage, inspire and entertain others. Her freelance works include stories for *Guideposts*, *Angels on Earth* and numerous *Chicken Soup for the Soul* books. Visit her blog, "Writing for the Heart," at www.sherizeck.com.

Jerry Zezima writes a humor column for Hearst Connecticut Media Group and is the author of four books: *Leave It to Boomer*, *The Empty Nest Chronicles*, *Grandfather Knows Best* and *Nini and Poppie's Excellent Adventures*. E-mail him at JerryZ111@optonline.net. And read his blog at www.jerryzezima.blogspot.com.

Dyan Zuber is a former guidance counselor who felt a high school wasn't a big enough audience to spread her message of living life to the fullest. She is now a freelance writer who chronicles her adventures of travel and parenting joys on www.toshowhertheworld.com.

Meet Amy Newmark

Amy Newmark is the bestselling author, editor-in-chief, and publisher of the *Chicken Soup for the Soul* book series. Since 2008, she has published more than 150 new books, most of them national bestsellers in the U.S. and Canada, more than doubling the number of Chicken Soup for the Soul titles in print today. She is also the author of *Simply Happy*, a crash course in Chicken Soup for the Soul advice and wisdom that is filled with easy-to-implement, practical tips for enjoying a better life.

Amy is credited with revitalizing the Chicken Soup for the Soul brand, which has been a publishing industry phenomenon since the first book came out in 1993. By compiling inspirational and aspirational true stories curated from ordinary people who have had extraordinary experiences, Amy has kept the twenty-six-year-old Chicken Soup for the Soul brand fresh and relevant.

Amy graduated *magna cum laude* from Harvard University where she majored in Portuguese and minored in French. She then embarked on a three-decade career as a Wall Street analyst, a hedge fund manager, and a corporate executive in the technology field. She is a Chartered Financial Analyst.

Her return to literary pursuits was inevitable, as her honors thesis in college involved traveling throughout Brazil's impoverished northeast region, collecting stories from regular people. She is delighted to have come full circle in her writing career — from collecting stories "from the people" in Brazil as a twenty-year-old to, decades later, collecting stories "from the people" for Chicken Soup for the Soul.

When Amy and her husband Bill, the CEO of Chicken Soup for the Soul, are not working, they are visiting their four grown children and their first grandchild.

Follow Amy on Twitter @amynewmark. Listen to her free podcast — "Chicken Soup for the Soul with Amy Newmark" — on Apple Podcasts, Google Play, the Podcasts app on iPhone, or by using your favorite podcast app on other devices.

Thank You

We owe huge thanks to all of our contributors and fans. We were overwhelmed by the thousands of stories and poems you submitted about your mothers, grandmothers, mothers-in-law, and honorary mothers. Our Associate Publisher D'ette Corona, and our editors Laura Dean and Elaine Kimbler made sure they read every single one.

Susan Heim did the first round of editing, D'ette Corona chose the perfect quotations to put at the beginning of each story, and editor-in-chief Amy Newmark edited and shaped the final manuscript.

As we finished our work, D'ette Corona continued to be Amy's right-hand woman in creating the final manuscript and working with all our wonderful writers. Barbara LoMonaco and Kristiana Pastir, along with Elaine Kimbler, jumped in at the end to proof, proof, proof. And, yes, there will always be typos anyway, so feel free to let us know about them at webmaster@chickensoupforthesoul.com, and we will correct them in future printings.

The whole publishing team deserves a hand, including Executive Assistant Mary Fisher, Senior Director of Marketing Maureen Peltier, Senior Director of Production Victor Cataldo, and our graphic designer Daniel Zaccari, who turned our manuscript into this beautiful book.

Sharing Happiness, Inspiration, and Hope

Real people sharing real stories, every day, all over the world. In 2007, *USA Today* named *Chicken Soup for the Soul* one of the five most memorable books in the last quarter-century. With over 100 million books sold to date in the U.S. and Canada alone, more than 250 titles in print, and translations into nearly fifty languages, "chicken soup for the soul®" is one of the world's best-known phrases.

Today, twenty-five years after we first began sharing happiness, inspiration and hope through our books, we continue to delight our readers with new titles, but have also evolved beyond the bookstore with super premium pet food, television shows, podcasts, positive journalism from aplus.com, movies and TV shows on the Popcornflix app, and licensed products, all revolving around true stories, as we continue "changing the world one story at a time®." Thanks for reading!

Share with Us

We all have had Chicken Soup for the Soul moments in our lives. If you would like to share your story or poem with millions of people around the world, go to chickensoup. com and click on "Submit Your Story." You may be able to help another reader and become a published author at the same time. Some of our past contributors have launched writing and speaking careers from the publication of their stories in our books!

We only accept story submissions via our website. They are no longer accepted via mail or fax. Visit our website, www.chickensoup. com, and click on Submit Your Story for our writing guidelines and a list of topics we are working on.

To contact us regarding other matters, please send us an e-mail through webmaster@chickensoupforthesoul.com, or fax or write us at:

Chicken Soup for the Soul
P.O. Box 700
Cos Cob, CT 06807-0700
Fax: 203-861-7194

One more note from your friends at Chicken Soup for the Soul: Occasionally, we receive an unsolicited book manuscript from one of our readers, and we would like to respectfully inform you that we do not accept unsolicited manuscripts, and we must discard the ones that appear.

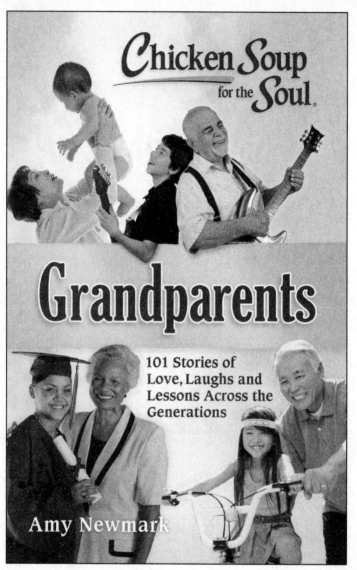

Chicken Soup for the Soul®

Grandparents

101 Stories of Love, Laughs and Lessons Across the Generations

Amy Newmark

Paperback: 978-1-61159-986-2
eBook: 978-1-61159-286-3

More family fun

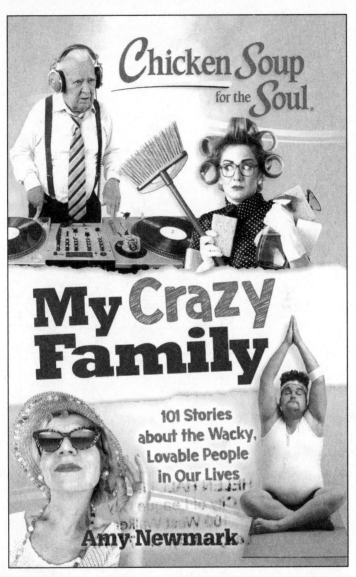

Chicken Soup for the Soul.

My Crazy Family

101 Stories about the Wacky, Lovable People in Our Lives

Amy Newmark

Paperback: 978-1-61159-977-0
eBook: 978-1-61159-277-1

and heartwarming tales

Changing the world one story at a time ®
www.chickensoup.com